Tom Godwin's memoir is readable, informativ[e]
There is realism and candor in his descriptions [of]
joy, failure, success — and invariably an expla[nation of]
its treatment that is understandable by the avera[ge ------]

> — RAMSAY W. GUNTON, CM, MD, FRCP(C)
> Member of the Order of Canada, Pioneer in cardiac catheterization
> Former head, Dept of Medicine, University of Western Ontario
> Former president, Royal College of Physicians & Surgeons of Canada

There is absolutely no doubt that "what you see is what you get" with Tom. He is sincere, genuine, and honest as the day is long, and was always highly respected by colleagues and idolized by patients and staff. His anecdotes will draw big pictures because the stories are fascinating reflections on the challenges that confronted a conscientious physician as the practice of medicine was rapidly evolving. As I read what he refers to as "my little book," I could hear his voice echoing each word. His experience and insight enable him to simply tell it as it is — warm and human, as well as a delightful read!

> — JAMES FAIR
> Former President and CEO
> Royal Columbian Hospital

This book, first and foremost is a remarkable memoir. The reader gets a real flesh-and-blood taste—quite literally at some points—of what medicine is really all about. It is also a personal testament. Medicine is a very demanding trade, if seriously, indeed passionately pursued and practiced, as Tom has done. It makes a very important point: the serious practice of medicine is not for the faint-hearted.

Finally, the issues raised throughout the book are legitimate and important; they provide a summary and powerful focus and they leave the reader with some simple, clear and strong messages, and with a rallying call to thought and action.

> — MICHAEL VICKERS, PhD (BIRM)
> Author and historian

There are not many people who get to start something from scratch as you did and now you have the ultimate with heart catheterization, angioplasty, and bypass surgery in your own hospital. That is a tremendous accomplishment and all very much due to your own pioneering efforts.

> — E. DOUGLAS WIGLE, OC, MD, FRCP(C), FACC
> Officer of the Order of Canada
> Professor of Medicine, Chief of Cardiology
> Toronto General Hospital (Retired)

It was a treat to read, and I enjoyed every word. It is one of the finest books I have read for a long time — good comments, not rude, honest. His conclusions are valid.

> — DON HUTCHINS, MD
> General practitioner, Royal Columbian Hospital (retired)

Tom has done more to develop cardiac services at the Royal Columbian over the past 30+ years than anyone else. Indeed, our cardiac catheterization laboratories bear his name. His book gave me interesting and much-appreciated insight into how our program developed.

But the ties between us go back even further. Tom worked as a resident in the first coronary unit in the world, which opened in March 1962 at the Toronto General Hospital. The coronary unit had been the brainchild of my father, Dr. Ken Brown, and his good friend and colleague, Dr. Bob MacMillan.

This book is a good read for anyone with an interest in the development of modern day cardiology, delivered with an abundance of "Godwinesque" humour and wisdom. I thoroughly enjoyed it!

— ROBERT I.G. BROWN, MD, FRCP(C)
Director, Dr. Thomas F. Godwin Cardiac Catheterization Laboratories
Royal Columbian Hospital

Tom Godwin has written a very personal and entertaining account of his life. The stories range from hilarious to heartbreaking, and are told in Tom's own endearing, "folksy" style. Medical terminology is demystified, and he has explained things I haven't understood in 35 years of practice!

Lest anyone think that Dr. Godwin's accounts are exaggerated or embellished, I can vouch for the authenticity and accuracy of his tales of the bad old days of medical training (or indentured servitude).

He has divided his memoir into bite-sized portions — perfect for somebody like me who cannot read a book in one sitting. This is a book I loved to read and will re-read. I can recommend it without reservation.

— BERNIE TOEWS, MD
Former clinical chief, Dept. of General Practice
Royal Columbian Hospital

The easy style allows a layperson to understand the fascinating, and occasionally humorous, medical stories. I first met the author in 1972 and we have remained close friends. We shared many escapades on the Godwin farm often just for the bedevilment of it. I was well aware of his hair-raising and life-threatening incidents.

— TOM SMITH
Heavy-duty mechanic and businessman

With Tom, patients always came first, even if it bucked the administration. His liveliness and humour were legendary. Any person interested in medicine, both the professional and the layperson, would find this book very interesting. It brought back a lot of memories.

— FRAN KUHN, RN
Former manager, Coronary Care Unit
Royal Columbian Hospital

For Romaro, remembering many years of friendship!

A Doctor's Notes

Taken from Both Sides of the Bedsheets

Tom Godwin M.D.

T.F. Godwin, MD, FRCP(C)

hancock
house

ISBN 978-0-88839-654-9

Cataloguing in Publication Data

Godwin, T. F., 1937–
  A doctor's notes : taken from both sides of the bedsheets
  / T.F. Godwin.

  ISBN 978-0-88839-654-9

  1. Godwin, T. F., 1937–. 2. Physicians—Canada—Biography.
I. Title.

R464.G58 A3 2009   610.92   C2009-901370-3

Printed in Canada — Island Blue/Printorium Bookworks

Editor: Theresa Laviolette
Production: Ingrid Luters
Cover Design: Ingrid Luters
Illustrations: Florence Carlsen

We acknowledge the financial support of the Government of Canada through the Book Publishing Industry Development Program (BPIDP) for our publishing activities.

Published simultaneously in Canada and the United States by

HANCOCK HOUSE PUBLISHERS LTD.
19313 Zero Avenue, Surrey, BC Canada V3S 9R9
(604) 538-1114 Fax (604) 538-2262

HANCOCK HOUSE PUBLISHERS
1431 Harrison Avenue, Blaine, WA, USA 98230-5005
(604) 538-1114 Fax (604) 538-2262

Website: **www.hancockhouse.com**
Email: **sales@hancockhouse.com**

Contents

This book is dedicated to the staff at the Royal Columbian Hospital.

Foreword

The author became acquainted with our family in 1968 when I was a young chartered accountancy student. My mother had been hired by the Royal Columbian Hospital to be the head cardiology technician. Subsequently, my wife worked briefly as a nurse on the cardiology floor of the hospital. Over the ensuing four decades, Tom's exploits, adventures, and near escapes from "whatever" became legendary.

One might refer to him as Dr. Tom Godwin, FRCP, internal medicine, a.k.a. Tom Godwin, farmer, veterinarian, arborist, conservationist, aviator, innovator, chain saw carpenter, sailor, diver, explorer, adventurer, philosopher, status-quo #*?!-disturber, and now author. His pursuits have been sufficiently diverse that I am unable to certify that this list is complete!

Some of Tom's endearing qualities include a degree of irreverence, unconventionality, and eccentricity. He belongs to that rare breed that possesses the uncanny ability to shoot from the hip and almost unerringly hit a bull's eye. Tom does not suffer fools easily. Sometimes these traits got him into more than a little hot water. Certain aspects of his life could inspire sitcoms or movies.

At the Columbian, Dr. Tom Godwin was Chief of Cardiology from 1968 to 1987, and Chief of Medical Staff in 1988 and 1989. During his tenure he was considered the person most responsible for bringing modern cardiology to the hospital. He was awarded the Dr. Cam Coady Medal for "his outstanding contributions to cardiology"; however, fame, fortune, and titles are not his style. Knowing Tom, he would much prefer to be remembered for his good humour, humble and compassionate nature, and professional commitment.

On the home front, this caring husband and father was also extremely busy. The family acquired a small Surrey "stump" farm in 1969. Over the years they expanded it into a viable, well-run beef farm, planted thousands of trees, and rehabilitated a salmon-spawning stream on the property. They used very little outside labour to achieve these results.

For those of us outside medical circles, this book portrays an "up close and personal" perspective of the world of medicine. Many of the stories herein are hilarious, some are very sad, and all are interesting and thought provoking.

— Barry D. McKnight, FCA

Preface

Most people have interesting lives. I am always amazed that all those who have seen and done so much, simply pass on. After they're gone, nobody really knows the myriad things in which they played an integral and very personal part.

During my medical training, I worked at Toronto's Sunnybrook Hospital for very brief periods, and then for a full year at Shaughnessy Hospital in Vancouver (1962–63) as a senior resident. Both were basically military hospitals at the time. Many veterans I saw had war stories worth telling. It seemed wrong and a waste that these stories should just fade, over time, into oblivion.

I noticed the same thing with people I met on the west coast after starting practice in cardiology here in 1968. All these pioneers, fisherman, and loggers were full of such interesting stories. But their stories, too, would pass with them. It seemed a great shame. These were real people, with real, often remarkable stories. It was for me fascinating stuff — a special perk and privilege of the job. It opened my eyes to what real history is all about.

From a medical standpoint, I lived through a golden age of cardiology. I saw this particular branch of medicine go from a relatively primitive discipline to a high tech specialty. Surely, I felt, some of this should be documented, and in layman's terms, before this story, in turn, faded into oblivion. By a fluke, I trained with some of these great pioneers of cardiology. I just happened to be at the right place, at the right time.

Certainly, the Toronto General Hospital, where I started my medical career, was, from the 1950s to the 1970s and beyond, considered the "Mecca" of adult cardiology in Canada. It was also prominent in this field among the leading medical institutions in the USA.

I always preferred reading true stories, and conscientiously avoided reading fiction. In my later years I started to enjoy reading history, a subject that I had found boring as a youngster. Films, based on facts, were for me becoming preferable to the customary Hollywood fictitious fantasies. I was never a language person. Hence, sitting down and writing a piece of fiction just would not be something that I would want to do.

In this book I have strived to write the truth as I have experienced it. I have not embellished anything, and have firmly resisted any change any editor might suggest to make my book more dramatic. I have tried to be ruthlessly honest throughout. Only where it might break patient confidentiality have I altered the story slightly, in order not to break this trust. It has been said that truth is stranger than fiction. I am not sure about this, but sometimes it comes pretty close!

This book was actually more than thirty years in the planning and I am only submitting a small sample of what has impressed me. I kept seeing interesting people with their problems and was always amazed at the human desire not only to survive, but also to prosper despite terrible adversity. I saw so much raw courage and thought it was a shame to let all this, likewise, fade into oblivion. I periodically took notes, and kept some complete records for this undertaking. (Unfortunately, I did not take notes until I was well into my practice at the Royal Columbian and, hence, I cannot remember a few of the names of my earlier colleagues at the hospital in Orillia and the hospitals in Toronto.) When I was on heavy chemotherapy twelve years ago, I was in no condition to take up this task. But as I started to recover — and also to age further — I felt I had better get started! Otherwise it would be an unfinished task.

The character called "Harry" in this book is a composite, and represents the views of a number of doctors who, over the years, told me their ideas in the doctors' lounge or elsewhere, sometimes endlessly. Harry is, however, based on a true individual, and many of the comments cited are his. The late Dr. Harry Lewis, who is described in chapter nine, was above all a brilliant and original "ideas person." Were he alive today, I am sure he would have endorsed most, if not all, of these comments. I have let Harry express them, because it was just too complicated to attribute all these ideas — in some cases strange and even radical — to the various doctors who had introduced them into the discussion over the years. In many cases I didn't even know who had first thought of some of them. In the interests of simplicity, I have therefore attributed a number of these ideas to my friend, "Harry."

Fortunately, most of my exposure to medicine has been with admirable persons; and they have been described as such. Each incident that I have related, I have been personally involved in, or I have clearly stated the source of my information. There are, in fact, only three stories that are secondhand, and these have been clearly stated as such in the text. I can vouch for the veracity of the authors in each incident. These are: the story of the canary by Dr. Hughes; the big crabs by Dr. Harder; and nitrogen narcosis by our son Stephen.

I have chosen to mention the doctors' names in many of these stories, but where it might be embarrassing to the individual or the doctor's family, I have usually, but not always, omitted names or replaced them with initials. The people intimately involved with these incidents who are still alive now will know whom I am talking about.

Of course, medical personnel working in the various departments of any medium-sized or large hospital will have seen many similar incidents. The old "battle-axe" type of head nurse who worked herself up through the nursing ranks and wasn't just parachuted into her head position by having a newly acquired MA in nursing, would be familiar with histories similar to the ones described in this book. Such persons truly have seen it all. This also would apply to those veteran casualty officers (Emerg docs) and so many others who have worked a long time in these critical care areas facing the public. Unfortunately, the general population seldom gets to hear about these happenings in their raw state. Perhaps the only difference between my experiences and those of others is that I have undertaken the task of writing about it.

The reader may think that some of these histories are crude. It is not my intention to give offence. I am merely trying to tell it as it is, and how it happens. Real life is not always as clean as we might wish or suppose. The stories are all true and the language is "doctor talk." My wife always said that at MD functions she at-

11

tended, the doctors always tried to surpass themselves in trying to "out-gross" each other. I don't think this is always true, but, no doubt, black or gallows humour always plays a role. It tends to mitigate some of the horrors that we all see, particularly in the emergency department, the intensive care areas, in the operating rooms, in the heart catheterization laboratories, and special procedures areas.

In recent times, with more than half of the medical students being female, this boisterous attitude of my generation may be somewhat moderated, perhaps for the better. In my particular graduating class at the University of Toronto in 1961, of 161 students only twelve were women. They pretty much stuck to themselves and, perhaps sensibly, never showed up at our very disorderly and heavy beer-drinking parties.

Every doctor quickly discovers there is much more to medicine and treatment than what may be discovered in the consulting room. Many conditions we are called on to deal with have their origins in broader issues that extend far beyond the medical, but in fact constitute the environment in which we must work and try to heal.

In the chapters that follow, concerns such as drugs, homelessness, and the serious problems that plague a large proportion of the Native population, among many others, inevitably arise. These issues all too often determine the general health of many patients. Again, it doesn't take long for any doctor — or, no doubt, teacher, social worker, police officer, or indeed any other person in front-line occupations dealing with individual members of the public — to recognize that it is also these problems that need urgently to be attacked and resolved.

Why is it so difficult for our politicians to grasp and act upon what the rest of us see as self-evident commonsense? When you see, time and time again, the medical problems deriving from these issues, it is difficult not to form an opinion. I suspect that doctors, who see them so frequently, have a considerably better-informed opinion of what should be done than politicians who only know of these problems secondhand.

Here in Canada, we, with our often-protected employment, generous pay settlements, and of course comfy pensions, have frequently done nothing but follow the course of least resistance. Certainly the politicians and bureaucrats with their own very ample pensions have not done enough to help in the last fifty years. In fact, the problems of Native affairs, drug addiction, and homelessness have become worse. The *status quo* does absolutely nothing to help. Radical surgery is not just necessary, but mandatory.

In medical school I found the work to be hard, but fortunately my marks were always good; my biggest problems were the emotional ones that arise from living with all the death and destruction seen in medical practice. That was why for me medicine was always a struggle; however, it was usually (but not always) a worthwhile struggle.

Tribute to the Staff at the Royal Columbian Hospital

In the 1960s, The Royal Columbian Hospital in the metro Vancouver area of British Columbia, like so many medium and large hospitals across North America, had a reputation for giving good care and reliable service to its citizens, within the usual budgetary restraints. However, because of the geographical location of the Royal Columbian — near the new Trans Canada highway and between the two large bridges connecting greater Vancouver with the large territory south of the Fraser River — this hospital received an inordinate number of severe accident cases and also critical medical problems. It had a very good orthopedic department under Dr. Ralph Outerbridge and subsequently Dr. Dave Harder, and a growing neurosurgery unit. The hospital, however, lacked good angiographic services and a heart catheterization laboratory, which was thought to be essential for "tertiary" emergency care.

In 1967, Dr. Wally Brewster, a well-connected family doctor in the local area persuaded a very well-known philanthropist, "Chunky" Woodward, to donate a large sum of money from the Woodward Foundation to build a heart catheterization service at the Royal Columbian. This was contingent upon the provincial government matching the donation. The money was eventually secured, and then the hospital administration had to fish around to find someone to run this service.

Dr. Gerry Richards persuaded me to apply, and I accepted the position in July 1968. I believe that I was likely the only serious candidate for the job, as there were so few "invasive" cardiologists in Canada at the time. Not only were they scraping the barrel when they hired me, I was likely the only one in the barrel. At

14

that time, most jobs of this type — and there were several offered in the greater Toronto area — were university positions and considered to be "geographic full time." This meant a salaried position, and being under the thumb of the university. There were advantages, of course, to this type of university appointment, but it meant no independence.

The job at the Royal Columbian particularly appealed to me because I could be my own boss, the hospital community was enthusiastic, it was on the west coast of Canada, and it looked like a real challenge.

There was some residual opposition to setting up this service in the Royal Columbian, both from the downtown Vancouver people who perhaps feared the competition, and even from some local people who possibly feared a loss of prestige and even a hit to their pocket book. However, the vast majority of the medical staff welcomed the new service and worked very hard to bring it about. Our first heart catheterization took place in November 1969.

Although there is much controversy about the definitions of levels of care, and the lines are blurred and change as new techniques come along, medical care has been loosely divided into four levels.

Primary care is generally considered "first aid."

Secondary care is more advanced and would include admission to hospital, treatment for more common maladies such as casting, minor surgery, IV therapy, x-ray, ECG, and in some centres CAT services. This service would be expanded, such as in the case of an acute appendicitis and the weather doesn't allow evacuation of the patient.

Tertiary care would include all of the above, but also include all routine types of surgery, usually neurosurgery surgery, a full angiographic service and cardiac surgery, and in modern times, angioplasty, CAT scan and MRI, and many forms of cancer therapy.

Quaternary care would add transplant services, specialized isolation services, perhaps a spinal unit, a burn unit, and very specialized cancer therapies, including a PET (positron emission tomography) scan. And, hopefully, a lot of very sophisticated research facilities.

Our department expanded rapidly with the influx of well-trained cardiologists and support staff, and then in 1981 the "human dynamo," Dr. Dave Hilton, arrived and we had an increase in not only our volume, but also the complexity of our work. Dave also started training in angioplasty in anticipation of opening an angioplasty service at the Royal Columbian. Then, in August 1990, another dynamo in the form of Dr. Mark Henderson appeared. He was already well trained in the relatively new technique of angioplasty. Both of these high-energy doctors had trained under my former boss, Dr. Doug Wigle, in Toronto, and were very well recommended.

Up until this time, we had been sending a large number of our cases for open-heart surgery to Dr. Bob Hayden at the Vancouver General Hospital. When we finally got funding to start an open-heart unit at the Royal Columbian, we were able to persuade Bob to come and work at our hospital. Almost simultaneously, the open-heart unit and the angioplasty service were opened in February 1991.

Since then, the service has continued to expand and as of 2009 the hospital does 2500 angioplasties (the busiest service in Western Canada) and 750 open-heart cases a year. The hospital could do more surgery, but has to refer a number of open-heart cases to other hospitals because of a lack of beds and funding. The entire staff and the administration have provided excellent care to the wider community and, despite the continuing lack of adequate funding, have always risen to the challenge of looking after their patients.

I spent the greater part of my professional career working at the Royal Columbian. I always found it to be a very friendly place to work and it always provided excellent care to our community. Looking back, I can honestly say I never regretted a single day that I worked there.

This book is dedicated to the staff at the Royal Columbian Hospital. Any of my profits from the book will be donated to the cardiology department to buy the latest cardiac equipment so they can better serve their patients.

Personal Chronology

I graduated from high school, and started premed at the University of Toronto in 1955, and simultaneously joined the University Navy program (a naval officer-training program spread out over three years at the end of which the successful candidate received his commission in the Canadian Navy Reserve Force), which helped to pay my tuition fees. I enrolled in medical school at the University of Toronto in 1958 and did a summer "externship" at Soldiers' Memorial Hospital, Ontario in 1960, graduating from medical school in 1961.

I then was a "junior" at the Toronto General for my first year of residency, and did my second year as a "senior" at Shaughnessy Hospital in Vancouver. My third year was at the Wellesley Hospital (technically, at the time, part of the Toronto General) again as a "senior." My fourth year was at the Toronto General as a "fellow" under Ramsay Gunton. My fifth year was once more as a "senior" at the Toronto General, but by then a "senior" finally had a "junior," basically a slave who was supposed to be working under us.

At the end of this time (1966) I got my fellowship in internal medicine, which made me a specialist in medicine or a diagnostician. Basically I was learning more and more about less and less.

I then did another 18 months working in cardiology at the Toronto General Hospital under Doug Wigle, becoming an "invasive" cardiologist, before setting up a practice in cardiology in 1968 at the Royal Columbian Hospital on the West Coast of Canada.

I started out as chief of cardiology in 1968. I was the only doctor in the department at that time, and remained chief of the department until I became chief of the medical staff for the two-year term 1988–89.

I retired from active medical practice in 1996.

CHAPTER 1

Two Medics Named "Bill"

L ife is tough. A lot of what happens seems to be arbitrary and we are supposed to carry on. But, above all we need to have a good sense of humour and be optimistic, because some clouds indeed have a silver lining.

I was in grade thirteen, my last year in high school. At seventeen, I was six feet tall, all of one hundred and sixty pounds and not much of a football player. My coordination was probably average or perhaps slightly below. I had noticed that Butch Powell, a student in our school who was definitely coordinated, would run like mad for the ball when he went for a pass, and at the last possible moment would stretch out his hands and collect the ball with aplomb. That just wasn't my style. I too would run like mad for the ball, but with my arms outstretched during most of the run, hoping to hold onto the awkwardly shaped article and run with it until somebody ploughed into me.

I much preferred to play defence. There I got to tackle the poor player if he came over to my side of the line. The target was much bigger and it didn't seem to matter where you grabbed him — though preferably below the waist — as long as you just held on until the inevitable crash took place. On my side, I had lots of energy and enthusiasm, wasn't particularly worried about cuts and bruises, and I seemed to be making our high school football team. However, during one of those exhibition games early in the season, our coach made me play wingback; that is to say I might have to try to catch that infernal ball!

Sure enough, I was soon running like mad with, no doubt, my arms prematurely stretched out. The stupid ball was about five feet over my longest fingers and I remember it descending gracefully into the hands of a player on the opposite team, about fifteen feet in front of me. Apparently I just kept running straight into this player, presumably with my arms still partially outstretched. Because of retrograde amnesia, I don't remember any of that last second or so.

I "came to" on my back and looking up. I saw a strange circle of helmeted heads looking down on me. I was vaguely aware of some mild pain at the back of my lower neck. It truly was a very mild pain and certainly nothing to write home about, as my mother would have said. It was embarrassing lying there with everyone making a fuss over me, and besides, I wanted to get up and find what had happened to that ball. I struggled to get up, and predictably these helmeted players rushed in to assist me — to the sidelines! With an arm over the shoulder and neck of a player on each side of me I was hustled off to the bench.

I was still a little groggy and undoubtedly my head was swinging side to side as I was transported off the playing field. Everything, however, seemed to work, although I still had that mild pain at the back of my neck. But the coach was watching me and I wanted to go back out on the field and show him that a little accident wasn't going to slow me down. Mr. Gilham was one of these conservative men, and he let me just sit there until the fourth quarter.

Having nothing better to do, I began testing my neck and found it was sore if I put it through a full range of motion, and I noticed if I clasped my fingers together and pulled forward on the back of my head, I would feel a peculiar burning sensation right inside my rectum. If I made a couple of fists under my chin and pushed up, I would get the same burning in the middle of my sternum. Odd, but again, nothing to write home about. Besides, I felt fine.

I slid along the bench and began to bug Mr. Gilham. He let me go back in towards the end of the game. As the other team had the ball and the play went around the opposite side of the field, I didn't get to show my stuff; I had wanted to do some spectacular tackle to make up for not having caught the ball in the early part of the game.

The next day, my neck didn't seem to be getting any better and I saw the school nurse, Miss B. She told me the school doctor would see me the following day. That would mean I would miss one class, and if he was late I might be fortunate enough to miss two. That didn't seem so bad.

The next morning, Dr. McTavish gave me a good going over and pronounced that I had a "strained muscle." Good news! But I would have to stay away from football and any other contact sport until all symptoms had gone. Bad news! My mother even suggested I would have more time to study English, always my weakest subject. I didn't need to hear that.

Three days after the injury, I told my father about the peculiar feeling of heat in my rectum and in my sternum when I stressed my neck. He thought that was really weird and phoned an old school friend of his, Dr. Stew Thompson, who had become a pediatric orthopedic surgeon. He asked my dad to send me to the Toronto Hospital for Sick Children emergency department for x-rays early the next morning.

The Sick Children's Hospital! Why couldn't my father have gone to school with a friend who looked after *adults*? Was it really necessary? I would be the biggest kid in the emergency. I knew because I had, like most kids in Toronto, been there before for stitches or broken bones.

In any event, I had no choice, as my mother drove me there the next morning. Most of my fears were swiftly realized. I was indeed the biggest kid in the department. But hopefully, everyone would think I was here to pick up my little brother. The nursing staff spoiled my cover because I was soon wearing a green gown like all the other good little boys and girls! I don't think these gowns — if they were ever designed to fit anyone — were ever meant to fit anyone over the age of twelve. I kept my fists pushed well down between my thighs to try to maintain some respectability. I was glad none of the guys on the football team would see me. At least I was allowed to keep my underwear on. The only plus was that I was missing English and French. And if nobody asked me specifically, I would just tell my friends I had some x-rays of my neck, and not say where I had them.

After what seemed a long time, x-rays were taken. And then, almost immediately afterwards, two young doctors dressed completely in white appeared in the waiting room, asking for me by name. The older of the two men asked, in a thick Irish accent, "Which one then, is Tommy Goodwin"? I felt I was big enough now to be called "Tom." And why couldn't he get my last name right? Also, I thought I was obvious, being at least six inches taller than the next tallest patient sitting in the waiting room. They seemed pretty serious though, so, somewhat reluctantly, I volunteered that I was the guy they were looking for.

The Irishman said, "Don't move your head!" Then he told me to "get very slowly out of the chair." And with the younger man behind me, and the Irishman in front clearing the way, we made our way into the plaster room.

On arrival I was told that, "Ye've got a *broken neck* lad! And you're to have a 'Minerva jacket' put on!" I told him I couldn't have a broken neck as it didn't hurt much, and what was a Minerva jacket?

"Indeed you have a broken neck, we saw it on the x-ray, and Minerva is the god of beauty. And you're going to be some beauty wearing that! A young lad like you should know all about that! Before we put it on, though, Dr. Thompson wants to examine you."

I started to protest again and began to show him that it couldn't be broken, "because, look how I can move it all around." He yelled at me to stay absolutely still. And I was just lucky, he said, "because in Ireland they would put you in tongs, instead of a Minerva jacket!" Thereupon my Irish bearer of bad news spoke briefly to the younger doctor and left abruptly.

The younger doctor, a first-year orthopedic resident who had not even opened his mouth up to this point, started to talk to me in a kindly fashion. He told me he was to sit with me until Dr. Thompson arrived. And he asked me to sit still and not move my head around or we both might get into trouble.

Under his arm, he had a big envelope of x-rays, which up to this point I had not even noticed. He proceeded to open it up and showed me my neck bones and the fracture. It didn't look that bad to me but he explained that I had lost about a third of the height of the body of my seventh cervical vertebra. Looking again at the x-ray, it began to make more sense. He explained to me that a Minerva jacket was a body cast and after a day or so I could walk around in it. He had seen other people with them and it wasn't as bad as it looked. He told me that Minerva was supposed to be a Roman goddess of beauty, and they probably named the cast after her as a sick joke. (I didn't find out until years later that Minerva was in fact the goddess of wisdom.)

When I asked what the other doctor had meant by "tongs" he was somewhat reluctant initially to tell me. But when I anxiously pressed him he opened right up. Tongs were really like ice tongs that one might use to lift a block of ice out of the water. The tongs that they used on people were smaller, but they did indeed have to stick them in the side of the patient's head, and the patient had to lie on a sloping mattress with the tongs attached to a rope with a weight that went over a pulley in order to maintain the correct tension. He told me that he thought it very unlikely that Dr. Thompson would use them on me.

A message came that Dr. Thompson was going to be further delayed, so this young man sat with me and asked me a lot of questions. He even asked me what I planned to do the next year. I told him I didn't really know. I didn't like school that much. I had vaguely thought of applying for pre-med, but I had found high school pretty "crappy." Besides, I thought of myself as more of a physical person. This young intern was very supportive. He was a doctor and still very personable. Unlike my teachers, or our family doctor, he asked me to call him by his first name, "Bill."

> Tongs and the Minerva jacket would not be used now for this type of injury. Instead, various orthopedic appliances have been developed that support the neck, but are much more comfortable to wear.

I told him that, for some reason, I always did very well on exams in school and that even my marks in that dreaded English were acceptable, although they always pulled my average down. He strongly encouraged me to consider going into medicine. It was reassuring having this doctor sitting beside me and distracting me by talking about interesting things. I was much less anxious when Dr. Thompson finally arrived.

Dr. Thompson was all business. He looked very harried and asked to see the x-rays. Then he came over and tapped on my spine at the back of my neck and upper thorax. I said one of the taps felt a little sore. He repeated it and said that that was the broken one and then turned to me. He asked how my parents were, and before I had time to answer said, "A jacket would be fine," and was gone.

I felt pretty vulnerable, but fortunately Bill stuck with me and kept up the chatter and even told me some jokes. The plaster orderly soon arrived and got down to business. He formed a big stocking-net to fit over my upper body; it had armholes, a big hole for my face and two holes for my ears, and he tied the top of the stocking-net in a big knot over my head. Bill served as the orderly's assistant and, fortunately, continued reassuring me. Next, a big bunch of padding material was wrapped around and around me. Finally the plaster arrived in warm water, and roll after roll was wrapped around me, covering me about four inches below my navel to the top of my head. Spaces were left for my ears, my face, and a circular space about five inches in diameter was left over my upper abdomen. The big knot was left sticking through the very top of my cast. At first, it felt fairly comfortable. It was warm as the plaster was drying, but my neck now felt a little sore and I noticed it was difficult to take a decent breath.

Pretty soon the Irishman was back. "I see you didn't get the tongs! A pretty sight, aren't we? A real beauty. Yes sir!" And off he went again.

Bill helped me on with my clothes, although nothing would now fit above my waist and I couldn't even do up my trousers, and took me back to the waiting room where my poor mother had been waiting patiently all this time. Bill even took the trouble to show her my x-rays, my mother always being interested in that sort of thing. He told her if I was having trouble to bring me back to the Emerg. He then put his arm around me and the cast, assured me I was going to be all right, and told my mother he'd had a nice chat with me, and said I should seriously consider going to medical school. As we were going out to our car she said, "If you are going to be a doctor, I hope you will be a nice one, like that young man."

In the car, the cast now seemed cold and very hard. My neck was getting really sore and I was still bothered by the fact that I couldn't seem to take a big breath. I couldn't even see properly as I couldn't twist my body in the car to look out the side windows. In the hospital I had kept up the chatter and tried to maintain a little of the macho image, but I began to realize that I was really quite fearful underneath. I was having a bad day and things were only going to get worse.

I ate very little lunch and even less supper. I just couldn't find

24

a comfortable position. My neck was really sore now. The cast felt very bony and even that large knot on the top of my head was pressing down and getting sore. But the biggest problem was the feeling that I just was not getting enough air. I knew I must be, as I could breathe in shallow breaths as fast as I wanted, but I just couldn't take in a decent amount of air in a proper breath. Giving a sigh was out of the question. I didn't tell my parents though, as I thought I was probably panicking unnecessarily. Perhaps, if I couldn't take the "jacket," they would put me in those awful tongs!

Then that evening, Dr. Thompson phoned to tell my Dad that they had seen something very unusual at the base of my skull. I had had a previous injury of my first two neck vertebrae.

I had apparently been a breech (legs first) type birth, and my mother being very small, the doctors had some difficulty with the delivery. My right arm had been paralysed during the extraction process, and remained so for the next three months. But eventually I got complete function back, although I remained left-handed. My father always joked that they had to sew my mother up like a Christmas turkey after this delivery. In any case, Dr. Thompson thought I probably should not play any more contact sports. I certainly didn't need to hear that.

I went to bed very early that first night, but I couldn't find a comfortable position. If I lay down flat I just couldn't breathe. I spent the night sitting up straight, or trying to lie back at about forty-five degrees. I don't think I slept at all, and I just waited until my parents woke up in the early morning. I told my mother I thought I should go back to the hospital because I just couldn't get used to not taking a deep breath, and it was quite frightening. She took me down immediately, and I didn't care anymore if I *was* the biggest kid in the Emerg.

I must have looked pretty uncomfortable because I was ushered into the plaster room very quickly and the plaster orderly and my friend Bill soon arrived. Bill was going to show me that the little saw that they were going to use to cut the front of the cast to allow me to breathe wouldn't cut my skin. I didn't care at that point if it did cut my skin; I just wanted to take a big breath.

They made a cut in the plaster from the bottom of the face hole to the top of the hole they had previously left over my abdomen. I don't think the cast opened more than an inch but it was enough, and I was immediately a lot more comfortable. The Irishman came into the plaster room and said, "They didn't have breathing problems with tongs!" and then vanished. Fortunately I never saw him again. My friend Bill reassured my mother and me, and said he didn't see why that cut wasn't put in every body cast before the patient went home.

My mother was always polite, but on the way home in the car, she kept asking why the doctors had to be so dumb. After all, breathing was important, and the new cut in the cast didn't interfere with the immobilization of the neck. She also didn't like that "stupid knot" on the top of my head. I didn't like it either. The natural elastic recoil of the stocking-net was still pulling it down on the top of my head, which was becoming increasingly tender.

As soon as we got home, she went to work and untied the stupid knot, pulled the stocking-net material well up through the small hole in the top of the cast and put some household glue around the opening. She then stretched the fabric well down and taped it there until the glue dried. It was a big improvement. The top of my head was no longer tender and my mother said a lot of hot air would now be able to escape. I now knew I was going to live and could probably tolerate the six weeks I would have to wear the "jacket."

My neck remained sore for the next couple of days, but I had few further problems. I missed only one day of school because it was Friday when the cast was put on, and I was okay by Monday. My friends were suitably impressed, but I was quite worried about not being able to play contact sports again. Football was all right, but I really enjoyed wrestling and boxing, and I just knew there had to be some solution to this problem.

One advantage I noticed right away with my new cast was that I could sit forward on my desk at school, and the cast acted as a support; I could actually sleep quite comfortably in class in this position. It was a real advantage, as some of the classes seemed so repetitious. The teachers either didn't notice, or just felt sorry for me and didn't disturb me very often.

Our school was quite formal and, among other nuisances, we had to wear a shirt and a school tie every day. Before my injury, I always seemed to be in minor or major difficulties with the school authorities. But with this cast, I noticed I seemed to get away with some things that weren't previously overlooked. I

Playing the fool in French class, giving my scalp a good scratch.

asked one of my friends to paint a large bow tie with pink polka dots prominently on the front of my cast. These were decidedly not school colours! Our first class the next morning was French, with definitely not my favourite teacher presiding, the much feared Mr. S. To his credit, he said nothing, and even pretended, I think, not to notice my new tie. Even in the Prayer Hall during morning services nobody in authority said anything. I was a bit disappointed.

I think there must have been a bit of a smell to my cast, particularly as the weeks wore on, but fortunately, nobody said anything to me. It became increasingly itchy, particularly at the back of my scalp, but my good old mother was once again up to the task. She produced one of those flexible knitting needles used to knit sleeves in sweaters. I used it to great effect to scratch the back of my head by inserting the needle in one of the ear holes of the cast and out of the other. Because of the very flexible middle part of this type of needle and the straight and stiff ends that are meant to pick up the stitches, when I inserted the needle into the ear holes of the cast and pushed the needle back and forth about an inch, it appeared that I had run the needle through one ear and out the other. It always got a good laugh in class. In fact, some of my classmates couldn't seem to get enough of it and would laugh uproariously every time I used this needle. I was pleased to see it annoyed my French teacher, but again to his credit, he never said anything.

Six weeks later the big day for me finally arrived — the day I was to get my cast off! It had become really itchy and I know, by now, stinky. My good friend Bill was there again. He complimented my mother on getting rid of the knot, the knitting needle and of course the excellent bow tie. I was given an appointment to see Dr. Thompson in a week in his office.

When the cast was finally off, my whole upper body felt strangely light, my head very wobbly, and I didn't have to be warned to take it easy for a month until my neck muscles got used to carrying my head around again. My skin was very scaly, and I owned the worst case of dandruff I had ever seen on anyone.

When I got home I had a bath (we didn't have a shower in our bathroom at that time). When I pulled the plug at the end of the bath, I had to reach in three times with my fingers to pull the dead skin off that little cross below the plug, so the water could run out! I had a bad case of dandruff for about week, and then it cleared up spontaneously.

It had been a Friday when the cast was put on, and it was taken off on a Friday, so again I had two days to adjust before going back to school. I usually rode my bicycle to school, but since my injury I had had to take the bus. The Monday after the cast was off, when I was on my way home on the bus (I wasn't supposed to ride my bike for another month) two middle-aged ladies sitting together were talking so loudly that I couldn't help overhearing. One of them told her companion that last week she had seen this poor high school kid on the bus with a body cast on. He didn't look very well and the cast really smelled awful. With my head covered in heavy dandruff, I didn't volunteer that I knew who that kid was. I was suddenly very impressed at how tolerant my poor friends had been about the smell.

My cast had only been off for about two weeks when I stumbled into Bill Davison, another "Bill." He was three or four years older than I was and had just started his first year of medical school that fall. He had always been a nice guy when he was in high school, and was pleasant to the younger kids like me. He had been on the football team, and was a steward at the school in his day.

Dr. Thompson wasn't very encouraging about my ever playing contact sports again; however, I was absolutely determined to prove him wrong. I started an increasing exercise program. I lifted a lot of weights and did multiple neck bridges in an effort to make up in muscle what I lacked in bone. Weight lifting wasn't very popular in those days and we were always warned that we might become "muscle bound." With my skinny body, I didn't have to worry about that. But with aging, going from age seventeen to twenty and, perhaps all this exercise, I gained twenty-five pounds, and possibly most important for me, my neck went from a size fourteen to an eighteen.

By this time I was in first-year meds and when I told one of our anatomy demonstrators my neck story, he arranged for me to see one of his friends, a cervical orthopedic specialist, Dr. Wallen. This man took numerous x-rays and suggested that I was "pretty good" and, though he didn't want to put it in writing, he at least intimated that I could likely survive contact sports again. I didn't need to hear more. I joined our university boxing team, and played rugby for the Toronto Old Boys.

Strangely, I did eventually suffer another neck fracture, but it had nothing to do with any previous problems. I broke the spinous process (a finger-like bony projection extending back from the vertebra) off one of my neck vertebrae, apparently a pretty common injury, called a "shoveller's fracture," in a wrestling match. This injury has no long term consequences and I made a full recovery.

He asked what I was going to do after I had finished high school. I told him about my neck injury and that I was considering trying to get into pre-med. He thought that was a great idea and suggested that I spend a day with him at med school. I was surprised people were allowed to do that, but, naturally, I jumped at the offer. He suggested I should come down on a morning when he had anatomy class so that I could see all those dead bodies that everyone spoke about.

Soon afterward, during some high school day off, Bill arranged for me to meet him at the bottom of the stairs of the anatomy building. He got a lab coat for me, so I wouldn't be so noticeable, and we proceeded up to the top floor of the building and into a very large room. There on steel-topped tables were about twenty of the promised bodies, all covered with some type of coarse cotton wool and then wrapped in a sort of oilcloth. The smell of formaldehyde was initially overpowering.

I was invited over to his table where his partners were in the middle of a dissection, apparently of the lower arm. It seemed pretty awful, with the smell and all those students practically leaning into the dissection. Everything seemed sort of greasy, and the actual tissues were a nondescript brown colour. Books were lying on top of the portion of the body that was under wraps, and there were more books on the floor. I noticed some of that greasy stuff was even on some of the pages of their anatomy atlases. Everyone seemed to be talking or poking at some bit of tissue; and one student sat on the floor with a bunch of pages spread out before him, reading something out loud from his notes.

An older doctor came over and asked who was I. Bill came over quickly and told him that I was a very good high school student who was thinking of going to premeds the following year. He didn't seem to mind. (I thought that poor Bill and I were going to get into trouble.)

This man, apparently an anatomy demonstrator and, as it turned out, quite a character, took me over to the arm that was obviously under serious demolition and asked me the name of a fairly large muscle he had picked up in his forceps. I of course had no idea, and he then told me it was the "brachio-radialis." He then asked me to take off my lab coat and show him my brachio-radialis. This time I got it right, as I simply had to compare the arm of the cadaver lying there and my own arm. He seemed pleased, and told me that I had quite a big brachio-radialis muscle for such a skinny kid. Then he asked what the muscle did. I tried flexing it in various ways and by forcing my wrist up against resistance was able to make it stand out consistently.

Then, amazingly, he said with a laugh that I must be a big masturbator to have such a well-developed muscle. I took to this man immediately because, despite his age, he talked at my level and didn't take himself too seriously. Entering into the spirit of things, I told him it couldn't be from doing that because I was left-handed. He then immediately asked one of Bill's partners how they could determine whether I was, in fact, left-handed. When nobody seemed able to answer the question immediately, he pulled out a measuring tape, asked me to hold out both arms, and at a specific distance from my elbow crease measured the circumference of both forearms, marking the measurements on the skin of my forearms with his ball point pen. He determined by measuring three times that indeed my left foreman was five millimetres bigger around than my right, and therefore I was probably left-handed. Then, with a big grin, he said I should probably change hands in the middle of things if I wanted to be more symmetrical.

In the course of this conversation, he often referred to other nearby muscles and tendons, discussed the origin and insertion of this and related muscles. And to this day I will never forget the name of that muscle, the brachio-radialis.

What a difference from high school. Here I was in a class ("illegally") and nobody seemed to mind. The teacher had a great sense of humour, I had learned something worth remembering, and medical school could even be fun! Learning all about some uninteresting poem in English class, discussing for hours what the author *really meant*, didn't seem to me in any way as important as the origin and insertion of the brachio-radialis muscle.

Bill's class in anatomy continued till noon, and then there was supposed to be an hour off for lunch before the afternoon class came in to do their dissection on the other side of the body. Bill's group was supposed to wrap its half of the body very carefully and put it to bed, at least before one o'clock.

As we were getting ready to leave, I noticed some of the students were starting to unwrap their lunches, and one of them was actually eating a hot dog. He was sitting on the floor with his back against the wall, his anatomy atlas spread out on his lap as he was reading to the others doing their dissection.

I was a little horrified, but Bill explained that some of the guys were a little behind in their dissection and it was the only way they could catch up. Indeed, he and his group had to stay over the lunch hour quite often. Biochemistry started at one o'clock in the main lecture room and if you wanted to eat at all, you had to do it when you could.

Although I couldn't have known it at the time, exactly three years later I would be sitting on the same floor, my back against the wall, with *Grant's Atlas of Anatomy* spread out on my lap, eating a hot dog. Even that same greasy brown stuff was on some of the pages of my book.

That particular day Bill got off shortly after twelve o'clock and he invited me to his fraternity house for lunch. There was another student there from second-year meds and he asked if they had "opened the chest." Bill said they hadn't gotten into the guts yet, whereupon his friend said they should have a "pre-cadaver course." Bill didn't know what his friend meant by that comment.

His friend explained that the previous year his group had a cadaver that must have weighed two hundred and fifty pounds, and they often couldn't find their landmarks (some of the smaller muscles, tendons and organs in the abdomen were very difficult to find). His opinion was that those people near death, who obviously had nobody to claim them, and hence their body would likely be used for science, should be put on a diet and a weight lifting course, and on the day of their death should be given an enema! He said it would certainly improve the quality of the cadavers that the students had to work with. I was shocked that he would say this to Bill and me; it was my first initiation to the gallows humour of medicine.

In the afternoon Bill took me to that dreaded Biochem lecture. To my surprise, I thought it comprehensible and even interesting. Bill kept apologizing about how difficult it was. I honestly didn't think it was all that bad; some of that inorganic chemistry we had to learn in high school with all those equations was a lot worse. I noticed that some of the students in the class were quietly whispering to each other. And in the hallway, at the very back of the lecture hall, some students who were apparently supposed to be listening were playing bridge at small tables. Nobody seemed to mind, and Bill said a lot of the students had used last year's notes that they got from their friends from one or two years ahead of them. It didn't matter, as long as you knew the information, passed the exams during the course, and the final exams at the end. It all seemed very relaxed, and so much better than my high school experience.

I had stumbled into a player on the opposite football team, and because of that, into these two Bills in medicine. My fractured neck likely was the final straw in getting me to apply for pre-med school, so perhaps my injury did have a silver lining. Without any reservation, I applied to the pre-med course. Fate had enrolled me on a fifty-year course in medicine, first as a student, and then as a practitioner, and ultimately as a patient.

After I had been accepted, one of my dear uncles asked me one day what kind of doctor I wanted to be. I said that I didn't know, but whatever kind I turned out to be, I wanted to be the kind that was nice to the patients and the students like my two friends, both called Bill.

CHAPTER 2

Doctors' Devices, Cardiologists' Contraptions

MONITORS

During the summer of 1960, I was classified as an extern at a small hospital north of Toronto, Soldiers Memorial Hospital, located in Orillia. (An extern was, officially, a medical summer student going into his last year of medical school before graduating.) This was a very nice hospital community and the physicians went out of their way to be helpful to me; I was a bit of a curiosity, as they weren't used to a teaching role. My job was to help out in the lab, to help in the Emerg, and to assist in the operating room.

I was generally given a pretty free rein, but any orders I wrote had to be countersigned by one of the practicing doctors. These guys were really pleased when I wrote histories for them that they had only to sign. Moreover, when a patient came in who was not a local person and didn't have a local family doctor, which occurred very commonly during the summer tourist season, a lot of the GPs were happy not to be bothered during their office hours or during the night. They would ask the nurse if the extern was available, and if he could see the patient first, and then phone them. I really liked this arrangement since it gave me valuable experience, and when the GP came in, often the next morning, he would go over what I had done and give me instructions. I was, of course, completely wet behind the ears and often nervous that I might make a mistake.

I gained a little confidence and, with time, I became semi-proficient at taking out fishhooks and sewing up small cuts. It wasn't that difficult to order x-rays and blood work before the doctor arrived, and doing so, of course, saved the doctor some work and time.

Mid-afternoon one day very early in my time there, I was called "right away" (the word "stat" wasn't in common usage yet) to the Emerg. The weather had become very hot and humid, the sky was ominously dark, and the world seemed strangely silent. Despite being fairly far north, Orillia had its fair share of thunderstorms and this one promised to be a doozie.

Just before I arrived, a forty-two-year-old man had been admitted with a very severe pain in the centre of his chest. He told me that it felt like an elephant was sitting on him. He was sweating profusely. He was a clean-cut, very pleasant person, and he told me that he was a contract electrician putting new wiring in some of the houses under construction in the local area. Fortunately, his GP was close by and came in almost immediately.

I had already started an IV — that was my job — and the GP ordered morphine and oxygen. An ECG (electrocardiogram, a graph of the electrical activity of the heart) was done; the GP told me he wasn't very good at reading these things, but he thought it looked bad to him. I simply had no idea what it showed. All the ECGs were normally sent to Barrie, a larger town about 20 miles south, where they had internists (or diagnosticians) who knew how to read them. In those days there were no monitors, and we had no idea if he was having some serious arrhythmia, apart from taking his pulse at his wrist.

The GP and I were standing on either side of the bed, each holding a wrist and feeling the patient's radial pulse. The morphine had started to take effect and he was now much more comfortable. Because we noted he had a very slow pulse, and would often appear to almost pass out when his pulse dropped to less than 30 beats per minute, we seldom put down his wrist. I think we were both mesmerized by this finding, and it was obviously playing a big role in his symptoms. The doctor ordered Atropine in an effort to increase his heart rate, but it seemed to have little effect.

On a whim, I suppose, he got the technician to hitch the patient up to the ECG again, and we both noticed little rounded waves on his ECG, but no corresponding pulse to match these complexes on his ECG. The patient would have a lot of what looked like a fairly normal ECG complex with a corresponding pulse, but when he had a run of these smaller complexes he would not have any pulse.

Within the next few minutes, the patient's pulse stopped completely. After a couple more minutes, the GP said, "That's it I guess; there's nothing more we can do." He dropped the patient's arm back on the bed and left the room, the nurse closely behind him. They had important things to do. The next of kin had to be notified, those important papers had to be filled out, and the porter had to be called to take the body to a more appropriate place. I just stood there, like a dummy holding the patient's wrist, hoping his pulse would, somehow, mysteriously come back.

I didn't want to let go. I imagined that some form of transparent cement was forming over the patient, and it was hardening rapidly, removing him from our world. As long as I held on to his wrist, I felt I could prevent him, somehow, from leaving. Fortunately, as I was now alone in the room with him, there was nobody to notice how shocked I was.

In the distance, I could hear the rumbling of thunder and see the occasional flash of sheet lightening. The storm moved closer, and the sound and light show became more dramatic. The fury of this storm was somehow comforting, and I eventually was able to collect myself, put down his wrist, leave the room, and join reality. I had never seen someone die before, and it all had happened so fast. He was alive and talking to me, then he was fading in and out of consciousness, and then he was dead. I wondered what happened to his brain, to all the knowledge that he had collected during a lifetime, and where did his consciousness go?

In medical school, we had seen all those cadavers in our anatomy classes, and saw all those human parts in big glass jars in the pathology museum in the sub basement of the Banting Building, but these people and parts were long dead and I had never seen them alive. Somehow I felt detached from this stuff, but seeing the abrupt transition from a viable nice guy to a cadaver was awful.

I had the feeling I wanted to go home, go back perhaps ten years in my life, see my parents and my brothers laughing and talking all at once, and my black Labrador retriever pushing his face into my lap with his tail wagging like mad. I guess this "vision" was my security blanket. Perhaps, I was a bit like Linus in the *Peanuts* comic strip, dragging his blanket around with him wherever he went. But I obviously couldn't just leave and go home, and if I did I probably would never come back. Besides, my older brother was by now living on his own, and my dog had recently died.

I found some solace seeing people in the corridor nearby standing and walking about and very much alive. Later in the day, I went back across the street to the residence. I noticed that the streets were all wet, the humidity had gone, and the air was cool and fresh. Life was starting out anew. But over the next few days, I seemed to seek out human activity, and had a feeling I didn't want to spend much time alone.

It's perhaps a shocking thing to say, but over time I guess I just got used to seeing death. It was never nice, but always there. My job, after the fact, was to try to solace the family and explain what had happened. I had overcome the stench of the cadaver and, after a time, was able to eat my lunch in the anatomy lab, and I guess this was another hurdle to cross. I never hardened up sufficiently, however, to work more than a short time in a children's oncology ward or, for that matter, in an adult oncology unit (oncology is basically the study of cancer).

It seems strange now and a lifetime ago, but it wasn't until March 1962 when two cardiologists, Dr. K.W.G. Brown and Dr. Bob McMillan, working at the Toronto General Hospital, devised a very complicated apparatus that could actually monitor a patient's ECG rhythm strip over a prolonged period of time. These two were the first in the world to do this. They began to find out what was causing the high mortality in the early stages of a "heart attack." They discovered that some patients would show signs of ventricular irritability, often progressing to ventricular tachycardia and fibrillation. They learned that they could take corrective measures by administering different anti-arrhythmic drugs. They could also spot the early stages of heart block, and start an Isuprel IV drip as necessary to speed up the heart rate. Three months later, the Americans, however, followed suit and, because of their

> The son of K.W.G. Brown, Dr. Bob Brown, also became a gifted cardiologist and has worked at the Royal Columbian Hospital for many years. He was one of my esteemed partners.

An Isuprel drip is an IV infusion containing a small amount of an adrenalin-like substance that makes the heart more "irritable" and speeds up the heart rate. In cases of complete heart block where the heart rhythm may slow or even stop, it can be life saving.

huge resources, soon took over most of the new technology for the benefit of *all*.

As young interns, we often cursed this machine because it was always breaking down, and frequently the rudimentary ink pens from the various patients would cross over on each other and jam. It was called a Grass machine and with all the wiggly lines on the paper it did indeed look like "grass." We would be called on the weekends and at night to try to fix these problems. This job fell, of course, on the ward "G" junior and, naturally, as luck would have it, I was one of them. (Ward G was one of three large public medical wards — 60+ beds! — at the Toronto General Hospital.) We would have to scan reams and reams of paper pushing out of the machine into a big box, watching for abnormalities. It was just another job for the overworked junior.

We had no idea at the time how groundbreaking and ultimately important all this was.

Looking back, our patient in Orillia was very likely in third-degree heart block, and those little rounded waves that we saw on his ECG paper were just his natural pacer beats that were not getting through his heart muscle to make it contract. A bedside monitor and an Isuprel drip could, perhaps, have saved his life. Later, of course, a temporary pacemaker would have made saving his life all very easy.

No monitors, no pacemakers, and, basically, apart from a few newer drugs and some fairly heroic surgery, in the early 60s we didn't have much more to offer than they had 100 years previously. Some of the things we did were probably even counterproductive. When a patient arrived with a heart attack, he was put in a darkened room on strict bed rest, sedated heavily, and not even allowed to feed himself. The nurse, backed up in her chores, would sometimes inadvertently rush the patients while she was hand feeding them. The patient was often not allowed out of bed for the first week, and he had to use those infernal bedpans. During the second week, it was strictly chair and bed, now using a commode in his room, if he was lucky enough to get a private room.

Otherwise, it was drawn curtains. The patient didn't go home until at least the end of the third week. Probably the worst thing was that he was cautioned "not to do too much." Sometimes, the patient wasn't back to full activity until six months had elapsed, if ever. Monitored treadmill tests were still very experimental, and even considered risky. Medical "science" at that time, was afraid that too much activity after a "heart attack" could cause the heart to tear open, resulting in sudden death.

Mother Nature (God) help you if you had high blood pressure. Sometimes you would be put on phenobarb and then some ganglionic blocking agent, given in an attempt to further lower your blood pressure, but it could also make you faint if you stood up too quickly. Some doctors strongly encouraged their patients to avoid stress, both mental and physical. This kind of advice often would greatly change a patient's life, not necessarily for the better.

I remember, personally, telling patients that they should avoid using butter, better to use margarine. All those trans fatty acids were better for you than butter?! Trans fats have been chemically altered to raise the melting point so they can be spread like butter — really changing oil into a more solid fat. Unfortunately, because this fat is now "artificial," the body's metabolism doesn't know how to handle it and it may accumulate on the lining of our arteries. With this in mind, one might wonder if some of our current instructions to our patients might also be incorrect!

In any case, cardiology has seen tremendous changes in the last fifty years, and we are now experiencing its golden age. We have progressed from the ineffective treatment of the darkened room (you may as well have been smoking an opium pipe for all the good we did in those early days) to modern medical advances such as angioplasty (plus or minus a stent), coronary artery bypass, or even total heart transplant.

The fantastic advances in cardiology that I have witnessed in my short lifetime are mind-boggling! That young electrician that I saw in 1960 would now have a temporary pacemaker installed, be monitored for three or four days, and then have the temporary pacer withdrawn and perhaps be sent home the next day. If he were found to have a more serious condition, he would likely undergo heart catheterization, and if he had some major blocks in his coronary arteries (heart arteries) he would undergo

To open an obstructed artery, the cardiologist threads a fine wire through the obstruction and then passes a catheter with a deflated balloon on its tip over the wire. The balloon is then inflated and the obstructing material is flattened against the wall of the artery. (In fact, this material is "scrunched" into the wall of the artery). The process of opening the artery by this method is called an angioplasty. If the artery collapses down, or the operator feels that there is a high probability of this happening, he or she will insert a stent of the correct diameter and length in an effort to keep this damaged artery from narrowing down again.

Stents are usually made of various metal alloys that look like a small coil or spring. Usually they consist of two coils that look like springs coiled in opposite directions. The stent, which may measure one millimeter in diameter, is slipped over the deflated balloon. The balloon and the stent on top of it are then reintroduced into the obstructed area of the artery and the balloon is then re inflated.

Minute notches, usually made by a laser, have been cut in one of the spring-like coils so that when they are inflated the coils of one lodges into the notches of the other; the stent retains this new shape, often a much larger diameter of as much as four or more millimeters. The obstructed artery then has a "culvert" placed in it that won't allow the artery to collapse below the diameter of the placed stent.

Many techniques have been tried to stop the subsequent buildup of cellular material in the stent. In the past, stents were coated with various materials that discouraged cellular growth; even radiation has been tried, using short-range radiation in the form of beta particles to blast the area around the obstructed area.

This area of medical expertise is rapidly evolving, and efforts being made to expand this technique for various other arteries that become obstructed, including those supplying the kidneys, brain and bowel.

angioplasty, with or without stenting, and be sent home, likely the next day. If he were found to have arteries that were not suitable for angioplasty, he might be taken to the operating room for coronary bypass — a pretty common procedure now — and still go home within five days of his surgery, or within six days of his original admission.

During my training, two remarkable cardiologists had a huge influence on my later professional life. The first one was Ramsay Gunton, my boss during my fellowship year of 1964–65. Ramsay was like a big teddy bear. He had been the fullback on his university football team and a subsequent Rhodes scholar.

Viewing the patient's heart under fluoroscopy at various angles it was possible to see that some patients had areas of their heart muscle that weren't contracting normally, suggesting damage in those areas of their heart.

He was a mild-mannered, very personable man, and an extremely effective instructor. At that time in his career he was the professor of therapeutics, but in reality he was a cardiologist, and all his patients were basically cardiac patients. Ramsay had a very kindly way with his patients and as an old-time clinical doctor, obtained a great deal of his knowledge of the patient by taking a detailed history and doing a careful physical examination. He was also interested in wall motion studies of the heart muscle, long before it became a popular examination with the advent of ultrasound. He was the reason that I gravitated into cardiology, as I could see that this specialty was in its infancy, and I enjoyed the patients and the medical staff.

Then, between 1966 and 1967, I spent eighteen months working with Doug Wigle, who had become famous not only in Canada, but in the world literature, for his work on the aortic valve and a particular problem of muscle overgrowth underneath this valve. He got me into the heart catheterization lab, and I gradually learned how to push those "terrible" tubes around inside the heart. When I eventually started working in our own catheterization lab at the Royal Columbian Hospital, Doug's lab in Toronto was doing about ten times the volume of our own lab in New Westminster. Statistically, they would likely see equipment problems before we would, and he always took the time to phone me so that I was less likely to get into trouble in our new lab. I don't think there are many former bosses who would think of doing that, particularly someone like Doug who was so busy doing his clinical research and trying to keep up with his active clinical practice.

DEFIBRILLATORS

"Where is Dr Godwin?"

"I don't know, sir!"

"Well, you tell him that when I find him I'm going to SHIT ON HIS HEAD!"

"Dickie" Foulkes was really mad at me this time! He slammed the door and exited the cardio department. Dr. Richard Foulkes was the administrator of the Royal Columbian Hospital, the equivalent of CEO and president in modern parlance. Somewhat affectionately, I think, we called him "Dickie" behind his back. Poor Mrs. McKnight had to take the brunt of his wrath. She really knew where I would likely be found and phoned me immediately. Good old Marjorie McKnight. She was the chief technician of our cardiology department, and was my protector. I often thought of her as my surrogate mother. This time, like many others, she forewarned me so I might have a chance of making some sort of defence.

At first I didn't know why he was so angry. Our little research project to determine if exercise is beneficial for cardiac patients had been running smoothly for several months now, and we had a lot of positive feedback from the patients who had been enrolled; the physio department had its brand new bike, and another one was promised, so why all the fuss at this late date? Marjorie said she suspected that Dickie, who as yet hadn't heard about our project, must have been reading the last night's newspaper, as a big article, complete with pictures, had appeared in one of the inside pages about the very good program that was going on at the Royal Columbian. There, sure enough, were three of my patients sitting on their bikes, happily pedaling away. The background clearly showed the inside of the Royal Columbian's physio department. I was screwed.

A few months earlier in 1972 we had met a nice professor of kinesiology at Simon Fraser University, and he had agreed to measure oxygen and carbon dioxide content of expired air by patients undergoing heart catheterization, necessary in those days in order to calculate the cardiac output (the amount of blood being pumped per minute). If we knew the pressures on each side of a particular heart valve, and how much blood was going through it each minute, there was a magic formula that would calculate the amount of narrowing of the valve. The cardiac output was also useful in calculating how much blood was going across the defect between two chambers of the heart if the patient had a "hole in the heart" problem. Dr. Eric Bannister was very interested in cardiac physiology and he did these calculations at no charge.

One day he asked me if we would be interested in helping him do a study on patients who had suffered a recent heart attack. It was to be a carefully supervised graduated exercise program to see if the performance of these patients could be improved over time. The information could be useful, and certainly it would be good for our individual patients to be put on an exercise program. In the early 1970s cardiac exercise programs were not in vogue, and there was still a residual opinion that it might even be dangerous.

Rather than go through all that red tape that would entail endless committee meetings, and then probably a "No" after all that extra work, I stupidly agreed that we could probably do it after hours.

The cardio department was right next door to the physio department. We often borrowed their Monarch bike if we had a patient on whom we wanted to do a stress test, but who, for physical reasons, could not walk on a treadmill, however was still able to ride a stationary bike. Dr. Bannister held out the "carrot" that if we allowed the study to progress, he would donate another Monarch bike to the department. This promise naturally put everybody on side.

We wanted to do this study in the hospital environment because of the remote possibility of a cardiac arrest occurring during the project. After five o'clock, all those nasty bureaucratic types had gone home, and the evening supervisors just naturally assumed that all that activity in the physio department was approved and was supposed to be going on. Poor Dickie was simply "out of the loop."

What really got his dander up, it was rumoured, was that one of the volunteer board members had phoned him and told him that she was very pleased to read in the newspaper of such activity going on in the hospital — it was very good PR. The administrators are supposed to know what is going on in their domain and, of course, Dickie didn't have a clue. Apparently my friend Eric had decided a little publicity wouldn't hurt the program, particularly because it was running so smoothly; it might even be good for his department and perhaps for our hospital. He had accordingly called in a reporter from the *Vancouver Sun*.

When Dickie finally caught up to me he had settled down. (I always liked him and appreciated the way he spoke his mind.) Unfortunately, we could not continue the program because the hospital's insurance was not structured to accept this type of risk. The study was about halfway complete, so now what were we going to do? It would be a big disappointment for Dr. Bannister, but especially for the patients.

Dr. Peter Richardson came up with the answer. He just suggested that we move everything over to our office directly across the street from the Emerg. The local drug store supplied us with a "crash box," containing an IV set up and all the drugs that we thought we might need in the case of an emergency. We had all the emergency airway stuff but we didn't have a defibrillator. This problem was quickly solved: the emergency department had three of them and we would just take one out each evening for "repairs."

In those days defibrillators were quite heavy, so we just put one on a small hospital cart and trundled it across the street. Funny thing — the defibrillator broke down three times a week and of course had to go out for repairs every Monday, Wednesday, and Friday. It was a pretty quick repair job though, as we always had the machine back in an hour and a half.

Peter and I weren't worried about our insurance; we believed we had all the bases covered from a medical standpoint. If you were going into arrest, what better time than when all the equipment is right at hand and your personal cardiologist is standing by? The bad side was that one of us had to stay in our office from 5:00 to 6:30 p.m. three times a week. We just saved some of our office work to do during this time while Dr. Bannister and his staff ran their project. In the end, the study lasted only another three months in our office and was then transferred to Simon Fraser University.

The risk of having a cardiac arrest during a stress test is very remote. During my twenty-eight years of doing these tests, I can remember only seven cases occurring in our department, and all the patients survived. Each cardiologist in our department would probably average ten exercise tests a week, and when I left the Royal Columbian I had seven partners. In reality, it is far better to have an arrest in the department than at home cutting the grass, particularly if nobody is around to assist and to call the paramedics.

Cardiac rehab is very much part of the program now, but it wasn't always like that. Our patients who went through Eric Bannister's program were totally smitten with the "exercise bug." Thirty years later one of those patients, Walter Fudge, still sends us a Christmas card each year and is still out walking as much as his old legs will permit.

Dr. Terry Kavanaugh started a much better and bigger program at Sunnybrook Hospital in Toronto. A few patients each year, who like ours had suffered a heart attack, were actually trained eventually to participate in the famous Boston Marathon. The male patient in particular is often demoralized after a heart attack and feels that somehow his masculinity is threatened. Used to being the strong man around the house and workplace, now he is a "heart patient." How will he ever be able to go up to his boss and ask for a raise, or take on anything that may cause stress?

In fact, many patients I saw in my later years of practice, after they were put on a supervised exercise program, told me that they were in better shape than they had been for years before their heart attack. Many of them had never done any regular exercise since they left high school. Post heart attack, they had lost weight, gained endurance and muscle strength, and thrown away their infernal cigarettes. Now that they had increased self-confidence, there was no problem asking the boss for that raise. For some, a coronary event was a big wakeup call. Getting annual blood pressure checks and cholesterol tests had become a way of life. Mother Nature finally had their attention, and Dickie and I survived and remained friends.

PACEMAKERS

When I started my junior internship at the Toronto General Hospital in 1961, the status of the lowly "junior" was definitely at the lowest level of the totem pole. However, most of the senior medical staff were very helpful to us — with a very few, but notable, exceptions. We did four-week rotations on various medical and surgical services throughout the year, and a single twelve-week rotation on general medicine.

As a junior, I was enjoying this exalted status on the cardio-vascular service when I was ordered to appear in one of the operating rooms to assist in putting in a pacemaker. As it turned out, this was to be the first "permanent" pacemaker to be implanted in Canada. (Temporary pacemakers were still not on the horizon.) I was scrubbed in, and my big role was as fifth assistant, away down at the far end of the operating table. I remember I actually did absolutely nothing. Even though I was handed a pair of very impressive scissors with a long shank and a slightly curved tip, I never even got to cut a single suture. I was very glad, however, just to be there, and I certainly had a ringside seat for this memorable event. In those days, it was an open-chest procedure, and the little terminals had to be sewn directly onto the beating heart muscle.

Dr. Ray Heimbecker, the doctor in charge, commented on the poor quality of the wire, which was flexing and straightening with each heart beat, and he wondered out loud how long the wire would last. Leaning away to my left I could certainly see what he meant. The technology was still very primitive and, in fact, one of the wires broke within three months and the pacemaker became inoperative. In the United States a number of pacers had already been put in, but also with poor long-term results. However, there was an urgent need for these things and the technology, fortunately, improved extremely rapidly.

Within a few years, the wires were threaded up a vein, and the need for an open chest operation to install one of these permanent pacers rarely became necessary. The pacer wires, which had been fairly straight, were changed to a coiled arrangement, looking like a tightly wound spring. Each coil in turn took a very small portion of the flexing and straightening. The metal used in manufacturing these wires was also changed and they became virtually indestructible. In fact, once the technology was really perfected, the wire was usually good indefinitely. The pacer could be changed each time the battery showed signs of running out, with no need to change the wires. Installing a pacemaker was now a very simple procedure. The original wire or wires were used repeatedly, sometimes over as long as twenty or more years.

Great progress was also made in the field of "temporary" pacers. Originally, when a patient had a heart attack, and the course was complicated by heart block, there was very little that could be done to prevent the heart from stopping intermittently. Fortunately, the stoppages were usually only temporary and after three or four days the heart's natural pacemaker started functioning again. The difficulty was trying to keep the patient alive for those three or four days! Before the days of monitoring, and the advent of using an Isuprel drip, the patient often died, as with our electrician, or was left with brain damage.

The Isuprel drip was a new invention and it fell on the intern in a teaching hospital to sit beside the patient's bed in shifts to run this drip. Isuprel is an adrenalin-like substance that had many uses, but one of its side effects was to speed up the heart rate by making the heart much more irritable. Potentially it was a very dangerous drug, and has been completely replaced by drugs that are much more specific and don't increase heart rate. Only an MD could run this type of IV. (With the advent of the temporary pacemakers, the Isuprel drip is no longer used.) Using this drip was obviously very time consuming, as the intern could not leave the patient's bedside.

My boss, Dr. Arthur Squires, had a very pleasant brother-in-law, and while I was on his service, during one of my senior intern years in 1963–64, this comparatively young man came in with a heart attack. It was fairly minor, but, unfortunately, it involved his natural pacemaker connections. At this point in time, there simply were no temporary pacemakers in existence.

He arrived at the Toronto Wellesley Hospital with the symptom of pain in his central chest, but he had fainted several times during his trip to the hospital. At that time, heart-monitoring facilities were not commonly available, but, fortunately, there was a big American Optical monitor in the emergency department. Our patient was hooked up; we saw he was in third degree block with a heart rate of about forty beats per minute. Intermittently, his heart would drop to ten beats per minute and he would pass out; then his heart rate would come back up to forty or so beats per minute and he would revive again. However, before we could get the Isuprel drip organized, he had a very long pause and had a brief generalized seizure.

We knew we would have to watch him very carefully once we started the drip; therefore, on instructions, I was soon glued to this patient's bedside trying to run the Isuprel drip to keep him out of trouble. I gradually learned his pattern and I found that I could begin to predict when I should start his Isuprel, and get it stopped before his heart started to go too fast and bring on ventricular fibrillation. During the next two and half days I was in his room being spelled off by one of the other seniors, Dr Randy Johnson. We could not leave his bedside during all this time. Fortunately, our patient soon settled down and eventually made a very good recovery.

Over the next few years, this became a fairly common procedure and most of these patients, too, made a good recovery, after the first few harrowing days. But it seemed that they would always come in when we were having a particularly busy day and everything just got further behind.

When the temporary pacemakers came in, they were like manna from heaven. They were certainly not without problems, but they were far more reliable, and the poor patients didn't have to go through multiple shocks and fainting spells. The mortality rate also declined measurably. The pacer wire was threaded up through the femoral vein in the groin and placed in the right ventricle of the heart. These pacemakers became very common in every large Canadian hospital. They were usually inserted by the cardiology intern in teaching hospitals, or by cardiologists or internists in the non-teaching hospitals.

Necessarily, inserting a temporary pacemaker was almost always considered an emergency, and usually seemed to occur after business hours. The hospital had to mobilize an x-ray technician and an extra nurse as quickly as possible. However, the actual procedure of threading the wire up the vein into the heart was usually a non-event. As soon as the wire was in place and tested out everyone could usually relax. And in my case, this often meant I could go back to bed!

In the late 1960s permanent pacemakers were still quite large, about the size of a hockey puck, and worse, were not entirely reliable. It had been the practice in many medical communities to put in a permanent pacer when necessary, but without careful follow up. In some cases, the patient was patted on the back and told to come back in a year or "when you are having trouble again." In retrospect, this was terrible medicine, but pacing was still in its infancy.

In 1968, when I started practice at the Royal Columbian Hospital, I discovered six patients whose pacers were not working properly, and in three cases, not working at all. They were, for the most part, not even aware that they were at risk. We started a "pacer clinic" at that time, but I was quite surprised at the entrenched resistance to this from some of the general internists. Although any physician would be allowed to work in this clinic, some felt that it would give some doctors an unfair advantage over others. In any case, after some struggle, the clinic was established and has had very good long-term success.

I enjoyed working in this clinic because I was keeping track of my patients. Many had become friends, and there was satisfaction in following the very good and evolving technology.

Originally, to test the pacer, we would have to insert a needle into the pacemaker through the skin. There were two "pots" that we aimed at. One pot was to control the rate and the other pot, the output from the battery. This needle (the Keith needle) had a triangular shape and fitted into a slot in these pots much like a mini three-sided Philips screwdriver. Turning the needle clockwise slowed the rate in the rate pot and decreased the output from the battery in the output pot. In order to prolong pacer life, we tried to reduce the output from the battery and, where possible, reduce the rate. These early pacers could not "sense" when the patient's natural pacer was firing, and the pacer would compete with the natural pacer, to the patient's detriment. Eventually, this problem was solved by pretty sophisticated electronics for the time.

In the ensuing years, the pacers gradually became much smaller, going from perhaps the size of a hockey puck, to the size of two Canadian one-dollar coins ("Loonies") piled on top of each other. The pacers have also become very sophisticated. They now have a built-in monitor, so that with an outside programmer that is placed directly on the skin lying over the pacer, the operator can tell what has been going on over the period since the patient's last visit to the pacer clinic. If, for example, the patient reports that on a certain day, perhaps at a party, he felt a fluttering in his chest, the operator of the programmer can "dial in" the date and the exact time the event occurred and get an ECG write out on a paper strip from his programmer. It gives the patient's rhythm strip, even if the pacer wasn't actually pacing his heart at the time. Also, many pacers can have very subtle parameters changed, to improve the patient's lifestyle. Some will change the rate based on the very mild changes that occur during exercise, such as acid-base, temperature, motion, or carbon dioxide and oxygen ratios in order that the pacer can pick up the rate when necessary.

An even more sophisticated unit, the internal defibrillator, can recognize dangerous arrhythmias and block the arrhythmia, or defibrillate the patient as necessary. These units keep track of all this information and when directed, will write it out on the rhythm strip for the doctor. This is pretty expensive technology, in excess of $30,000, but absolutely life saving when appropriately used.

Batteries have also had a quantum improvement during this period. Originally, the batteries were the usual zinc cadmium type. They were bulky and always seemed to have a pretty short life span. Next, we had the mercury types, which were somewhat better.

One company started producing "nuclear" pacemakers, which used plutonium for their power source. They were supposed to last ten years or longer. It was probably the other components that would determine the length of life of this pacer, as the half-life of plutonium was over eighty years.

This power source was never very popular because governments around the world were afraid that if the patient was involved in a major accident, such as an airline crash, the environment could become contaminated. Some countries refused outright to accept people with this type of pacer, and hence these patients' subsequent travel would be limited.

Lithium iodide batteries were then introduced into pacers. They had been used in World War Two for sea mines, but because of problems of a high internal resistance, could not be used in such common things as flashlights, which required a high output. As it turned out, lithium was perfect for pacing because the heart, never requiring much energy to be paced in the first place, uses micro voltage; and perhaps even more important, lithium does not produce gas as the battery discharges. Zinc-cadmium and mercury batteries had to be vented when placed in a closed environment. Unfortunately when gas can get out, fluids — in our case, body fluids — can get in. These fluids would sometimes short out the pacer's components, causing it to fail. With the advent of lithium, it was wonderful to be able to seal the pacer completely, enclosing it in various types of metal alloy "cans."

Lithium also made a long-lasting battery, and the modern permanent pacer typically now lasts ten years, depending, of course, on its output. The older lithium iodide battery has another inherent value in that it really has an indefinite shelf life, meaning that if it isn't being used, the battery will show no loss of power, even over a span of one hundred years. With this development, there was no advantage in nuclear pacers over the lithium types, and nuclear pacers thus became historical relics. Lithium batteries have improved remarkably, and lithium ion batteries can now power flashlights and even motorcars; they hold more energy than the older type batteries, although they are more expensive.

The undertakers, however, now had a problem. Because these new pacemakers did not have to be vented, and therefore were completely sealed off in a metal can, they would explode in a crematorium. This was bad for the undertakers, who consequently had to be more vigilant because they had to "explant" the pacers before placing bodies in the furnace. As you will note in chapter six, however, this explanting provided a good supply of pacers for the veterinarians.

Pacemaker Twiddlers

"Tom, I know that you are not on call, but we have an old patient of yours that came in overnight and her pacemaker is not functioning. She wants to see you, and as she seemed to be quite stable, we waited until the morning to call you."

(If at all possible, the cardiologists that were not on call would usually see their old patients in the Emerg rather than the on-call cardiologist. They would know the history, and the patients always appreciated seeing a familiar face. It also took some of the load off the over-busy cardiologist on call.)

"Thanks, Herb, for not disturbing my beauty sleep. What disaster are you referring to me now to wreck my whole day?" Herb Parkin, our casualty officer, was on call overnight and, as usual, had everything under control.

"Her chest x-ray shows her pacemaker wires are all twisted to hell and one is obviously broken, and she says that she has no idea how her pacer got all twisted up like that!"

This was back in the days when the pacers were a lot bulkier and it often was annoying to the patients because it made a large bump under the skin and sometimes would get in the way of brassiere straps or other pieces of clothing. A Canadian article by

"Witt" Firor had described three cases of Pacemaker Twiddlers Syndrome where patients had "fiddled" with their pacers to the point that they actually flipped them over under the skin. This article described how the patients fiddled with their pacers turning them over and then back again repeatedly. Perhaps sometimes they would forget which way they had turned them and then would over correct the turn. Over several days or weeks, they would turn their pacer over many times more one way than the other, and eventually one of the two wires would snap, rendering their pacer inoperative. To flip one of these pacers over takes a fair amount of force and a little manual dexterity, so it seemed unlikely that it would just happen by chance.

Herb and I were on to this, and we had seen two other cases before this one, either in the Emerg or the pacer clinic. I was curious about why patients would do this, but to my frustration they always denied flipping their pacers. It just magically got twisted round and round. If the patient was totally pacer dependent it could result in disaster, either death or repeated fainting spells. The pacemaker companies were also onto this, and manufactured a little pouch made of a webbing material that the pacer could be put into and then implanted into the patient. Very quickly the body would put fibrous material through the openings of the pouch, which would lock it securely so that the patient could no longer turn his pacer over. This pouch soon became standard for these earlier pacers. When the pacers became much smaller and flatter these little pouches were no longer necessary and the pacer Twiddlers' problems became a relic of history.

My friend Harry, of course, thought this problem was fascinating and he developed his bizarre theory of why patients would do this and why it seemed to be only found in middle-aged and older women. Harry said that men were fortunate because all they had to do was put their hand in their pocket if they wanted to have a "little fiddle." Women, on the other hand, never had this opportunity until they were fortunate enough to have a pacer put in. It was a whole new experience for some of them, and they just couldn't seem to keep their hands off their new toy.

Harry said that we shouldn't be smug, however, because the occasional male is seen in the Emerg who has twisted his testicle over and over and the twisting has then strangled the blood supply to his testicle. This understandably results in a lot of pain and, unless it is quickly corrected, the poor testicle will shrivel up and die. Mother Nature has been onto this too, and usually provides a lot of fibrous material in the scrotum to prevent the testicle from being "fiddled to death." It's the poor chap that has done a lot of fiddling and for some reason doesn't have the usual allotment of fibrous material to hold his testicle in place who runs into trouble.

When I was a little kid my Baptist grandmother was constantly reminding me to keep my hands out of my pockets, I guess for good reason!

Self-Destruct Button?

The various pacemaker companies used to hand out "dummies," which on the outside looked and, in fact, were, the exact replica of their current model of pacer, but, of course, had no components inside. My friend Harry was given one of these dummies, and when I came into the doctors' coffee shop early one morning, he was sitting playing with his new toy. He told me he had come up with an idea for these things that he said was going to "revolutionize society." I had no choice but to listen to another one of Harry's harebrained ideas, because I had already poured myself a cup of coffee, which I desperately needed, and had just sat down.

He was going to have a device built called a "self-destruct button."

"Jeez, Harry, now what? Don't you ever give your mind a rest, and the rest of the world along with it?"

"No, I'm serious, hear me out. These little pacers of yours are completely reliable now, aren't they, since those lithium batteries came in?"

I reassured him that we never seemed to have any problems now with the pacers themselves, and our role had changed. We now adjusted the pacemaker's parameters only as the patient's cardiac condition changed. I think I was becoming an unwitting accomplice to Harry's fertile brain. I had noticed that he had always been curious about "our" pacers when he was supposed to be an oncologist, only doing general internal medicine when he was on call for the internist group.

He also was always strangely interested in these implantable insulin pumps, which at that time were still in their infancy in terms of their technology. I didn't put these two things together, particularly as Harry was always interested in so many things. In any case, I just couldn't think ahead of Harry's rapidly spinning brain.

Harry's idea was, apparently, to marry these two things together, the insulin pump and the electronic abilities of the modern pacer. If this device was implanted, the customer could then, by means of a programmer, adjust his pacer-like machine under his skin. He could make a secret code that nobody else would know and hence he alone could adjust his device to his own bidding.

Harry envisioned that the electronic unit would be attached to this totally implanted pump. The pump would be primed with an irritating agent such as a small bit of alcohol or perhaps a very mild extract of one of the pepper spray materials, and this would be followed by a lethal drug. This latter agent would have to be something that would be painless, but effective. (There are a number of suitable chemicals.) The whole thing would be no bigger than a modern simple pacemaker and would be implanted under the skin on the front of the abdominal wall or the front of the thigh.

"This may sound pretty complicated, Tom, but the basic idea of all this is that the customer can program his device with a pin-number and some other set or sets of numbers that he dreams up, and then with his programmer, and by means of this telemetry, he can program his device or "button" to operate the way it was intended. And nobody, but him, can change any of these parameters."

By this time, I'm starting to smell something really bad. I'm a bit slow.

"Harry, are you trying to upstage Dr. Kevorkian?" (Dr. Kevorkian was a medical campaigner for assisted dying, or euthanasia, and had been jailed for acting on this impulse.)

"Oh no! Not at all! This is the way it would work. Our customer would program his device so that if, for some reason, such as loss of brain function, he did not use his programmer correctly, and if, he failed to do so after a set number of days, the little pump would inject a little "reminder" in the form of a strong local itching or burning sensation, and if, after a set period, the customer failed to program his unit, a second "reminder" might be injected, or it could move on to inject this life-extinguishing substance, whatever was pre-programmed."

In short, this was Harry's "self-destruct button."

"A scenario might be, the customer gets up in the morning, goes to his top bureau drawer and gets out his programmer, dials in his specific set of numbers, places it over the "button," presses the control switch and then reads on the programmer's telemetry window that his 'button' has been programmed correctly. He can relax, and go about his activities. Instead of a daily routine, he can program it to be done, for example every Sunday morning, once a month, whatever suits. If he forgets, say after a period of three further days, a little of this noxious substance would come out and, likely after taking Mother Nature's name in vain, he would run to his programmer and go through his little routine and the button would reset itself. In fact, he would not have to run, because he would have programmed another three days before the button became really nasty.

"In this way, if I had a stroke and could not remember, say my birthday and a simple pin number; then after thirty-three or sixty-three days or any other set period, I would no longer be a nuisance to my family."

I gathered that Harry was allowing thirty days or sixty days for the "little reminder" to be shot in, and then three more days for "the final solution."

"Despite what you might think, Tom, if you are over the age of fifty, and after one or two months you don't know your own name, etc, following a severe stroke or huge blow to your 'coconut' causing severe damage to your brain, there is no hope for you. Alzheimer's is self explanatory and I don't want to hang around with that disease, when I am past remembering the date of my birthday, or whatever numbers I have put on my button. If the customer was very cautious, he could have his button programmed to hold off the fireworks until three months or even longer.

"I believe this type of device could be very simply installed – off shore if our government outlaws it locally – and the cost should be fairly cheap, perhaps $1,000 for the unit and $500 for the programmer. Sticking it under the skin could be done by any physician or trained technician, and should cost under $100. The chance of something going wrong, I believe, would be virtually impossible, as the irritating agent would be well in front of the lethal agent in the pump.

"If someone had this put in offshore and then returned home, nobody could have it taken out without the patient's permission because it would be considered a 'medical assault.' If there was a national disaster and the patient lost his programmer or if there was some sort of a screw up, at worst the patient could persuade someone to take it out, even with a Swiss Army Knife. After all, it is just under the skin in a very accessible place.

"What really appeals to me, is that I would never be a nuisance to my family for more than thirty-three or sixty-three or whatever number of days that had been preset, and all the decisions about mercy killings and Dr Kevorkian, etc., would in fact be my decision alone."

My poor mother developed Alzheimer's in her later years and she had three years that were very miserable for her. She developed a complete personality change and became quite abusive to the nursing staff, something that was totally out of character for her. When she was younger and in good health, she was well aware of these dementias and perhaps because I was the only doctor in the family, she often admonished me never to let her "end up that way." It was very painful not to be able to help this fine lady, and my own mother. In the early stages of Alzheimer's, she was very distressed by being confused all the time, and she kept saying, "Nothing seems to add up." Before my mother had entered this black cloud, I had told her about Harry's self-destruct button. She asked me to "sign her up". We joked about it, but I don't think she was really joking. To see her in the last stages of Alzheimer's was enough to make one weep.

Harry told me that he had not heard from anyone who was prepared to help him in his endeavour. He said he needed some innovative biological engineer who wouldn't be afraid of some adverse publicity. Back in 1984, he said, he had written to all the big pacemaker companies. He had even written more recently to Dr. Kevorkian in prison and not had a reply. So, Harry really was serious. In fact, he only got one reply, apparently from Medtronic, the largest of these companies. It was a very short note: "Sir, we are in this business to preserve life, not to terminate it, thank you."

"That company is run by a bunch of Southern Baptists!" Harry was again at his finest.

He then told me he had discussed this with some of his colleagues, and had "signed up" a number of the doctors in our community. I had noticed that Harry's doctor friends were always a little on the "lunatic fringe" side of things.

Harry then asked me if I would sign up, and I thought about it for all of 30 seconds and said, "Yes."

"Well, Tom, you're my twenty-sixth future doctor customer."

It's nice to know that I now belong. I guess I have joined Harry's list of lunatic fringe associates.

CHAPTER 3

Groin Pains

AV GAS, 100 OCTANE

It was 1967 and the all-too-often dreaded call came in. "Doctor Godwin, they want you in the Emerg right away."

Just the sort of thing that disrupts your whole day. No time to find some other intern to take over, because everyone else is also fully occupied. You just leave whatever you are doing and head downstairs. If you were seeing a patient, you leave the poor nurse to make excuses, and hope another appointment can be made. Often, however, that can't be done under the circumstances, and the patient is left frustrated and waiting.

I was probably at least thirty feet down the hall from the emergency department when I was literally hit by a horrible smell. It reminded me of the smell I had experienced as a kid when I accidentally leaned too far over a campfire and singed the hair on my head. But this smell was much stronger.

When I arrived, several people spoke at once telling me that they wanted me to start an IV. I expressed surprise, because there was an IV team now in the hospital — long overdue — that, in fact, was usually better in starting IVs than the intern staff because they started multiple IVs every day while we were getting out of practice. Nobody said anything about the smell, but by this time it was overpowering.

I was ushered into one of the single Emerg rooms, and lying in bed was a sight that I will never forget. It was a completely charred human being. Everything that was visible was completely blackened except his face and the top of his head. He was even blackened under his chin. Anybody who walked into the room that day must have been shocked to the point of tears.

I found out later from the people who had transported him to hospital that he was the pilot, and the only person on board, of a single engine Otter aircraft fitted with wheel skis. He had tried to land in a snowstorm; one of his skis, apparently the right one, had caught in a snow bank, and he ended up doing a cartwheel. The ski had been followed immediately by the left wing tip, and the plane had landed on its back. The crash had taken place right in front of the terminal building in a small airport north of Toronto. Our patient had been able to exit the plane, but just as he got out there was a great swooshing sound and everything was engulfed in flames.

He was knocked over backwards and lay on his back in the snow, burning furiously. Quick thinking bystanders had suppressed the flames around him and dragged him to safety. However, he was very seriously burned over his entire anterior surface, except for most of his face and the very tips of his feet, which were probably protected in part by his shoes. His entire back, as it turned out, wasn't burned at all, since he had been lying in the snow. After making a quick assessment, the airport staff simply loaded him into another plane and flew him down to Toronto.

What was particularly unnerving was the fact that when he arrived, not only was he conscious and completely rational, but he didn't seem to be in much pain.

They had called me because I was one of Doug's cardio fellows. This was the same Doug described in the previous chapter, and he was world famous for his work in the heart catheterization laboratory. He was my boss and mentor at the Toronto General, and the residents in the Emerg felt that one of his "cardio boys" should be called because, after all, wasn't the groin our "stomping ground"? Even though this area was probably as charred as the rest of the available spots for an IV, there was a pretty big target for a vein under all that burnt flesh.

"What a day to be on call," I thought.

Maybe I should be selling high-end real estate in Toronto's Rosedale or Forest Hill, anything but working here. However, I obviously had no choice now but to get on with it.

At best, the IV was only going to be palliative; it was pretty apparent to us all that our patient had no chance. Perhaps, however, with fluids and IV morphine he would be kept a little more comfortable.

The groin is kind of a nondescript area at the top of the leg, and is pretty clearly defined by the inguinal ligament, a large band of thick fibrous material that runs diagonally across this region just under the skin. The common type of hernia creeps under this ligament. But the groin area also provides a very important portal of entry for the cardiologist when he wants to thread his tubes up into someone's heart; that is, perform a heart catheterization.

There is a large artery about the size of the patient's small finger that slides under this ligament, and a large vein of similar or slightly larger size running alongside the artery, or sometimes indented in part by the more robust artery.

Usually, back in the 1960s and 70s, when your friendly cardiologist came along to perform a heart catheterization procedure, it was done through the groin or, sometimes the front of the elbow. In the late 60s we used the groin almost exclusively, and hence the "cardio boys" had developed a certain level of expertise with this area.

When we wanted to put a cannula, a fairly large plastic tube, in the femoral vein, we palpated the femoral artery, which was usually pretty easy to find because of its size and easily felt pulse. We would put in a quantity of freezing solution and then by just grazing the wall of this artery usually find ourselves in the vein, which was identified by sucking back on the syringe, producing a quantity of venous blood, or more frequently, just allowing the venous blood to flow out of our rather large special needle.

On this occasion, things were very different. The whole area felt solid; it was basically burnt charcoal. I could not feel any pulsation to suggest the femoral artery. I did eventually feel what I thought was a ridge that could have been the artery, only because it seemed to be where I would have expected the artery to be.

Ramsay Gunton, my previous boss, always said, "the bigger the audience, the bigger the disaster." Naturally, I had the usual two or three keen observers, despite the horror of even being in this room. Was it just me? Couldn't anybody else smell this terrible odour? Mercifully, I was in the vein right away and didn't have to poke around. I was just dreading not getting in on the first try, because I had absolutely no idea where I would start "poking" next.

One of my favourite and very knowledgeable surgical intern friends was also involved in this case, my role being very minimal. He was, in fact, the one who had called me down to the Emerg to start the IV.

By this time, over three hours had passed since our patient was caught in the fire. I asked my friend why was he still alive and still conscious. With a "normal" large burn, the patient loses a tremendous amount of fluid into the burned area, and without large amounts of IV fluid replacement, goes into early shock. This poor guy had had no IV until a few minutes ago.

My friend said, "Let me show you something." We walked back into the patient's room. He gently lifted the sterile green sheet that was lying over his legs. (I had only lifted an upper sheet to expose the groin area.) The extent of damage was even worse than I had imagined. There was a flap of tissue over his left knee that had come loose and exposed a portion of charred patellar tendon underneath. (That tendon is the fibrous band that connects the big muscle on the front of our thigh to our kneecap.)

My friend had a short conversation with his patient, who, it was obvious now, was mercifully becoming drowsy. This was likely in part because the IV morphine was taking effect, but also because of the rising toxicity created by some absorption of the burned tissue into his system.

When we left the room my friend said he thought our patient hadn't yet gone into early shock because he was so thoroughly burned that the body fluids couldn't infiltrate the burned area very easily. He also thought that the reason he wasn't in a whole lot of pain was because his sub-cutaneous nerves had been simply fried. He said that this wasn't a fifty percent third degree burn, but a fifty percent fourth degree burn.

An hour later the patient was dead and the Emerg staff were waiting the arrival of his parents.

He was 30 years old, the same age I was at the time.

HAVE TEMPORARY PACER; WILL TRAVEL

When I arrived at the Royal Columbian Hospital in 1968, I was the only person in the entire Fraser Valley who had been trained to insert temporary pacemakers. It was a brand new, extremely useful technique; very often it could be life saving. It was also usually as easy as falling off the proverbial log.

The bad thing for me about all this was if there was a patient in one of the outlying hospitals who for any reason couldn't be transported, I would have to get in my car and, with whatever equipment I guessed I might need, drive sometimes in a great rush, to the hospital, which might be a half hour or more away. There were no ECG monitored ambulance services at that time, no trained paramedics, and no specifically trained Emerg physicians. General practitioners of varying experience in emergency problems covered the emergency departments. The more seriously ill patients would sometimes be transferred from these smaller hospitals to the Royal Columbian with the referring physician and an Emerg nurse, but no ECG monitor.

I wondered at the time why more people didn't learn the technique of inserting a temporary pacer electrode. It seemed so simple. I've noticed that the engineers, it seems, are always ahead of us medical types; we seem to adopt their inventions long after the technology becomes available. For example, stuffing a balloon through a partially blocked artery and flattening the clot against the wall of the artery to allow life-giving blood to get through seems so fundamental. Why did it take so long for this technology to be adapted to our medical problems? There was always the problem of medical ethics, but until perhaps more recently, there seemed to be a real and general medical inertia.

Fortunately for our community, the following year another cardiologist, Dr. Peter Richardson, arrived who was well trained to put in temporary pacemakers, and thus at least *some* of my itinerant travels were partially curtailed.

On May 18, 1971, I was called to the Peace Arch Hospital in White Rock, a community hospital south of the Royal Columbian.

Before World War Two, White Rock was really a summertime community. People living in Vancouver often had a summer cottage in White Rock, and during the summer holidays and weekends they would drive the forty or so kilometres from Vancouver to stay in the White Rock area. It was very attractive because it was close to the seashore with a very large beach with warm-water swimming. The weather was better (having perhaps one-half the rainfall compared to downtown Vancouver) and the on-shore sea breeze made the climate ideal. During the winter months the place was pretty quiet.

After the war, people started moving out to this area in large numbers and started winterizing their homes. Many of the summer cottages had literally started to rot, because they had no proper foundations. The septic systems started to cause problems, if they had ever worked properly in the first place. In those years, White Rock underwent a lot of changes. New buildings were erected, even a few "high rises." By the time of my story, it was clear that the infrastructure just hadn't been able to keep up, including the hospital.

Dr. Paton, the referring physician in White Rock, on this occasion was treating an older man who had just suffered a small heart attack, damaging the bottom of his heart. As monitors were now available, and in common use, it was soon apparent that this poor fellow was in complete heart block.

I knew the physician personally, as was usually possible in those days, the medical communities being so much smaller. I suggested, over the phone, that he put himself and the patient in an ambulance and come directly to our Emerg.

However, he told me that their hospital didn't have a battery-powered portable ECG monitor and defibrillator. He had tried running an Isuprel drip, but he had great difficulty controlling it. The patient had had several episodes of cardiac standstill as well as runs of ventricular fibrillation. De-fibrillation had been required on several occasions.

As usual, I wasn't able to talk myself out of another emergency trip to one of the outlying hospitals.

When I arrived at Peace Arch, there was a small delegation out in the parking lot, and I, complete with my sterile bundles of instruments, monitoring equipment, and portable monitor defibrillator, was led through a small door and down some stairs to the X-ray department. It turned out that the patient was, in fact, a very important White Rock citizen and politician, hence the delegation. White Rock wasn't a big community at that time, and being in their local government wasn't really a full-time job; but he was a very good man and much loved by the community.

That x-ray department seemed like a bad joke. The fluoroscope machine was almost as bad as the equipment that shoe stores had when I was a kid to let you see how far your toes were from the end of your shoes. Modern hospitals had, by this time, image intensifiers that gave a fairly clear picture and a big enough field of vision for orientation, and the image wasn't "back to front." This machine gave a very grainy and small picture. The mirror was very small and made every thing appear backwards.

To make matters worse, the intensity of the image was so poor that for about ten minutes before the procedure was to begin we had to wear red goggles to allow our eyes to become accustomed to the dark. When the test began, the whole room was completely darkened, with the exception of three red lights. The darkened room was to make whatever we thought we saw in the mirror brighter. The pupils of our eyes, which should be wide open now, would let more light into our retina so that we could see the low intensity light coming off the fluorescent plate of the x-ray machine. Our red goggles were removed only after the ordinary white lights had been turned off. (As a kid at my grandmother's cottage in the evening, I had noticed that when we stepped out of a brightly lit cabin to go back to our sleeping cabin, I would stumble around in the dark, tripping over every root. My cousins seemed to be able to see better than I could. The fact was, of course, that my eyes took longer than other people's to adjust to the darkness. This peculiarity wasn't going to make my life any easier.)

I had no idea what I was getting myself into, and the family doctor who had just spoken to me on the phone likely had no idea how primitive his hospital's x-ray department actually was, and hence had not warned me. Not that it would have made any difference.

As I have mentioned previously, audiences are often drawn by such "events." And the larger the audience, the more likely you are to screw up.

This small room was crowded with "important" people: the nursing supervisor of the hospital, the chief of medicine, who was another GP, the chief of the x-ray department, another radiologist, and of course the referring GP who had got me into all this trouble. We even had a reporter from the local newspaper waiting in the corridor.

All I wanted was a scrub-nurse and an x-ray tech to show me how to run this infernal x-ray machine. At the last moment a young scrub nurse did arrive.

Everyone, however, was very courteous to me and I basically kept my mouth shut.

The nice young scrub nurse dutifully unpacked my bundles

and spread my equipment out on a table that took up about a quarter of the available floor space. I scrubbed up and put on a lead apron, and then someone wrapped me in one of those scrub suits that every hospital seems to have. I put on some sterile gloves — something, at least, that seemed familiar.

Our patient, then, just to show us perhaps how mortal we all were, had another run of ventricular tachycardia, which is a dangerously rapid heart rate; fortunately, it did not progress to ventricular fibrillation, a type of cardiac arrest. The Isuprel drip was turned off and he went back, temporarily, to a normal rhythm. But I, of course, knew what was going to happen next if we didn't get that pacer electrode in.

Meanwhile, our scrub nurse had prepped and draped the patient and I began my procedure. As I usually did, I put in lots of freezing and waited a few minutes before I started poking around with the big needle we use. However, I was anticipating the next episode of complete heart block, restarting the Isuprel drip and runs of more tachycardia. At such times, I always try to remember, at least in part, what my grandmother used to say: "Haste makes waste."

I waited less time, however, than I normally would have done just to allow the freezing to soak in, and then started looking for that vein with what I'm sure my audience thought of as a monster needle. My patient was a "good guy" and at least he didn't complain. I found the vein fairly easily.

I thought, "Big audience and no problem. How come?"

I then threaded the guide wire through the needle. This was standard procedure and, as they say on TV, "Even a cave man could do it." The big needle is withdrawn, a little plastic tube is inserted over the guide wire, and then the wire is withdrawn. So far, so good.

Next, I went to insert the pacer electrode, which the scrub nurse had pulled out of its sterile bag. These things are about four feet long and come in various diameters. The electrode was a number "8" and even in the dark, I could feel that something was wrong.

This electrode was too thick! I always used a number "7." And, of course, I had a number 7 introducer already inserted, and I had not brought along a sheath with a bigger internal diameter.

Oh man! I knew that the number 8 pacer electrode wouldn't fit into the number 7 introducer; it was just too fat.

Predictably, I had screwed up big time and, of course, in front of a hometown audience.

In my haste to get to the Peace Arch Hospital, I had for some reason picked up the wrong pacing electrode; the number 8 instead of the number 7, even though it was marked clearly as number 8 on the outside of the sterile bag.

I supposed that I could do a cut-down, (a procedure of cutting through the skin, exposing the vein and then trying to put the pacemaker electrode directly into the vein), but that would be tough as we were still in the dark, with only those three red lights for illumination, and I already had a good sized hole in the vein. I could just imagine all the mopping up that I would have to do trying to expose the vein. Also, it was a long time since I had even done a cut down and I didn't even know if this hospital would have the appropriate instrument tray for this procedure.

Just at this point, of course, the patient had a long run of "nothing on his ECG"; however, the Isuprel drip was immediately restarted, and a normal rhythm came back. I'm thinking, all the while, "I'm going to turn in my badge and sell real estate even if I can only get a job selling a pile of rocks on the Canadian Shield north of Sudbury." But, didn't they say that even if you are up to your ass in crocodiles you must stay calm, or something like that?

Nobody else at this point knew that I had made a big mistake. I bravely introduced the number 8 electrode into the number 7 sheath and, of course, it didn't fit. But I noticed I could, with force, push it in about a half inch past the metal opening of the sheath. Once again, the patient came to my rescue, for he was very thin and I could see that if I chopped the introducer off really short, I might get it back just into his vein. I asked our scrub nurse to put some pressure over the area while I pulled out the sheath, putting the guide wire back in place. I then cut off most of the length of the sheath and reintroduced it into the patient sliding it over the guide wire. With a lot of force indenting the flesh over his groin, I found that I could just introduce this much-shortened sheath back into the femoral vein. I now could get the pacer electrode into his vein.

One of my farm equipment friends had always said, "Tom, in

this business, we never force anything. We just use a bigger hammer!" My very heavy pushing with my fingers was the equivalent of a hammer for this poor patient.

My troubles were by no means over, because now I had to pass this electrode up that big vein that runs along the spine behind his intestines and part of his liver into his heart. Normally, this is a no-brainer. The vein is huge, and the electrode usually slides easily along until it is into the right side of the heart. (Perhaps to the layperson, or even to a GP who has never seen this done before, it may look difficult.) But this time, even though the room was completely dark, except for those red lights, I couldn't even see my electrode until it had passed into the upper part of the chest. The bowel and liver were just too dense for the x-ray machine to see through it all. The relatively slow dark adjustment with my eyesight probably didn't help. And the patient was a skinny guy! I believe at this point I was thinking that selling even a few hectares of ice pans floating in the Beaufort Sea would be preferable to what I was doing now.

Occasionally, the electrode gets hung up in a side branch behind the intestines, but this time, it passed easily into the chest where I could see it. The lungs and heart don't block the x-ray beam the way bowel and other abdominal organs do. This was the only thing, so far, that had gone right. But now, I had to get used to having everything "backwards" because of this archaic mirror arrangement.

With this old x-ray machine, the x-ray gets shot from below the table, goes through the part of the anatomy that is to be viewed, and onto a plate over which lies an unexposed photographic film. The x-ray beam makes a photograph on the film, the standard x-ray film with which we all are familiar. The mirror is inserted instead of the x-ray film if one wants to see what is directly on this fluorescent plate, rather than wait until the film is developed. This plate is lying flat about sixteen inches above the table, so, to make it possible to see the plate, a mirror is inserted above it adjusted at about a forty-five degree angle so that the image can be seen at the side of the table where the operator usually stands. The big problem is the fact that everything viewed is backwards. Because one can leave an unexposed film on this plate for a while, with the patient not moving, enough x-rays get through to make a proper picture.

When we use fluoroscopy, we are seeing moving items and hence we cannot just leave an unexposed x-ray film on the plate to soak up the beam over several seconds to get a clearer picture. Often when viewing moving images on fluoroscopy, not enough x-ray beams get through for us to see properly. Modern image intensifiers avoid this problem completely and use a lower amount of the harmful radiation. Also, because they are electronic, they don't have to use a system of mirrors. I was used to operating only with image intensifiers.

Fortunately, the patient's heart rhythm was still cooperating, more or less, but he was now having a few extra beats and we temporally turned off his Isuprel drip again. Fiddling with this backward image, I eventually got the electrode into the correct position in his right ventricle. When we connected the external pacemaker, it captured his heart rhythm the way it's supposed to and the crisis was over. We now had control of the patient's rhythm; if he went into heart block again, his new temporary pacemaker would take over, and we could now shut off his Isuprel drip permanently.

At the end of the procedure, we always put in a couple of sutures to be certain that the electrode will not be dislodged accidentally, and also bandage it securely. As I was doing these "last rites," the nice scrub nurse who was, in fact, very helpful, said, "Doctor, that procedure was very smooth."

I thought, initially, that she was being sarcastic, but then the referring GP, who I had felt was standing too close throughout the procedure, and was almost in the way, concurred and then added, "I thought the way you sized that introducer to fit the electrode exactly was really neat — it won't bleed around the pacer electrode."

I was saved by the fact that everybody had been in the dark, literally, during the procedure and, as it turned out, I was the only one able to see in the mirror the way it was set up. Also, when I asked the scrub nurse to put some pressure on the groin when I changed the sheath, she had used both hands. I guess she was afraid that she would not otherwise be pressing on the correct spot, and this obscured everyone's view, thankfully.

I mentioned earlier, Ramsay's rule, "The bigger the crowd the bigger the screw up." This case was an exception to the rule; with my entire audience in the dark, I was saved. Abraham Lincoln once said, "You can fool all of the people some of the time, and some of the people all of the time." If people are so easy to fool, maybe I should give up my ideas of selling real estate in the Beaufort Sea and run for Parliament!

At the end of the procedure, before they turned on the white lights, I got my audience to line up to look in the little mirror and stepped on the foot switch so everybody could see, finally, the electrode in the patient's heart.

It was relatively safe now to transport the patient, using the portable monitor I had brought from the Royal Columbian; and because the Peace Arch Hospital, at that time, had no experience with these new-fangled pacemakers, he was, in fact, transferred to the Royal Columbian.

I was glad to get out of that little room and back in the parking lot and fresh air. I had a nice private chat with the referring GP before I left, and I gathered that he was fairly senior on the hospital staff. I explained that I hadn't expertly "sized" the sheath, but had brought the wrong size pacer electrode with me.

I then went on and told him, as tactfully as I could, that they should replace that museum piece of an x-ray machine and get something that was at least post-World War Two. I asked him, in passing, who that really old man was who had been standing silently in the x-ray room throughout the procedure.

I'm not sure if he told me that he was the chief of the radiology department or was a past chief. In any case, although he was alleged to be somewhere in his 60s, he looked as if he had stepped off Noah's Ark. I hoped that he wasn't the one calling the shots with regard to their x-ray equipment, and suggested as much to my GP friend.

As I drove off, I wondered if that guy looked so old because he was either a heavy smoker and/or a big boozer. Or, maybe, it was because he had been standing in front of that old x-ray machine for too long as it spat out radiation all over the place? Perhaps, in retrospect, I shouldn't have let everyone line up to see the electrode in the patient's heart.

My GP friend phoned me a few days later and said there was a big write-up on the front page of their local paper. It was a big event apparently: the first putting-in of a pacemaker in their hospital.

The patient did very well, as usually happens with these

small heart attacks affecting the bottom of the heart, and he didn't require permanent pacing. The pacing electrode was withdrawn a few days later. He continued his political job for several more years before retiring.

When I got back to the Royal Columbian, I told my friend, Harry, all about my sojourn to White Rock. He said in his usual very thoughtful choice of words, "You must have a horse shoe up your ass to extract yourself from a problem like that. I'll bet you are the only cardiologist in North America now that knows that you can fit a number 8 electrode into a number 7 sheath!"

I did, indeed, have a "horse shoe up my ass" that day.

"HEMO-TOMATO"

Mrs. F, a nice lady in her late fifties, was frail and looked much older than her actual age; she could have been taken for someone in her seventies. Also, she had evidence of widespread vascular disease with no foot pulses and loud bruits over both her carotid and femoral arteries.

Mrs. F also had some evidence of emphysema. I had seen her intermittently over a period of several years, but because of her other medical problems, I had been very reluctant to subject her to angiography, thinking she would not represent a very good surgical candidate. Angioplasty at this time had not been invented. But now, her angina had become intractable and she was basically bound to her chair or to her bed. She had, apparently, despite her health problems, until recently been fairly active. With the urging of her family doctor and her own daughter, I agreed to perform this procedure.

The heart cath went fairly smoothly, but her coronary arteries

For the non medical-TV-show watchers, the *carotid arteries* are the big arteries in the front of the neck and they supply the lion's share of blood to the brain. A *bruit* is the noise that may occur when blood runs over a rough surface in an artery and may suggest a partial obstruction. We hear it with our stethoscope and, occasionally, can feel a strange accompanying vibration with our fingers over the point where the noise is the loudest. The reader will now, I hope, be somewhat familiar with the location of the *femoral artery*.

were so badly diseased that there was no way anyone could persuade a sensible surgeon to try to perform bypass surgery. Her arteries just would not accept any grafts. In fact, looking over her films, it was a wonder that she was still alive.

I pulled out my tubes when the procedure was over, and put the usual amount of pressure on her groin, right over the femoral artery. We usually hold it for about ten minutes until the little hole that we have made in the artery seals off. In those days, a large pressure bandage was then applied over the area and the patient, if stable, was sent back to the ward or the short stay area to rest for several hours.

In this case, when I released the pressure I could see that characteristic rising bulge under the skin indicating that my little hole hadn't yet sealed off. (I think, sometimes, that we don't wait long enough; but then, someone is usually yelling at us that we're needed somewhere else.) When it doesn't stop bleeding under the skin we are simply stuck there and have to continue holding pressure.

For many years, the nurses were not allowed to hold the groin and those neat little plugs that a lot of cardiologists now use to plug our little hole were a long way from being invented.

So after several long holds and several quick "look sees," I now, unfortunately, had a good-sized hematoma. Eventually, the bulge was not getting any bigger and I thought the bleeding had stopped. It's hard to tell, however, because in some ways it's like covering the area with a large pillow, and it is hard to know what is going on.

In any case, I made the decision to put on the big pressure bandage, and instead of sending her to the ward we left her in the corridor outside the catheter lab so we could keep a closer eye on her. In the late afternoon, we took the big dressing off and I wasn't sure if the hematoma was marginally bigger, or if it had just spread out a little flatter with time. The scrub nurse took a felt pen and traced a line around the edge of this swelling. This was the routine in these cases, and the swellings usually settled down.

Mrs. F indeed seemed to be settling down and I would normally have sent her home the next day, but she really did have a pretty big hematoma and with all her other health problems, not to mention the bad news that nothing could be done now about her intractable angina, I decided to keep her in another day. But the next day, the damn thing looked bigger, and it was on and off like this for the next two weeks. For two or three days it would look as if it had stopped bleeding, and then it looked possibly bigger again. Gradually, it became apparent that her hematoma was not going to stop bleeding.

If you watch something like this every day, it's perhaps harder to notice any change. When your puppy is growing up, you don't notice much, but when your neighbour comes over he is astounded by how much your puppy has grown. This was no puppy! Because she had an intractable angina syndrome, and her hemoglobin had fallen considerably over this period, we gave her two bottles of whole blood.

My friend Dr. Roy McNeil was called in and he eventually opened up her groin and exposed a huge clot. Some of it was solid and some parts of it had started to liquefy, a quite common development in large old clots, and right next to the artery there appeared to be some fairly new blood. Roy didn't see any continuing bleeding at first, but as he was evacuating the last of the clot, suddenly a very fine jet of blood started pulsing up in the wound. He used a "figure of eight" knot over the bleeding point to seal off this tiny hole.

He noticed that I had apparently punctured a hard atheromatous plaque (a hardened area composed of cholesterol and scar material) on the wall of her artery. He said he didn't think that it would ever have stopped bleeding without this suture. (A strange case…the lab had already done a thorough check to see if she had a coagulation problem, and she had checked out normally in that department.)

I reluctantly told Harry about my latest misadventure and he said he already knew because one of the ladies in the blood bank had told him that an elective patient coming in for a routine (and Harry emphasized the word "routine") heart catheterization had ended up getting two bottles of blood. This was certainly unusual, and Harry said he wondered if I was trying to get into the open-heart business, because there was no surgeon's name attached to the requisition.

You can't get away with anything. Those guys in the lab know when a surgeon takes out a "normal" gall bladder or a "normal" appendix. Worse, they know even before the surgeon does that he has not removed the whole tumour; when they look through their microscope at the frozen section, they see that the re-section line has passed right through the remaining tumour still left in the wound. No doubt they are chatting behind closed doors and speculating about what those wild tube-pushers and ham-fisted surgeons are up to.

When I tried to explain my way out of what had transpired and I mentioned the words "wide spread atherosclerosis, emphysema," and "premature aging," he said, "You mean she was a 'train wreck'?" Harry always gets to the point.

"Yes, I guess she was," I said quietly.

"Tom, another word you used, I think you said, 'hematoma,' like a bruise, eh? Bleeding under the skin? Well I don't like those big non-descriptive words you use. I call those things hemo-to-matoes."

Harry should know. He sees those "tomatoes" all the time, treating his cancer patients with all those poisons they use, which often knock out the platelets and give the patients bleeding problems. But I held my tongue.

Harry didn't ask me why, if she was a train wreck, I subjected her to a potentially risky procedure in the first place. Maybe he was being kind to me for once.

It's a good question though. I know my instincts were against doing this procedure, but the patient's daughter and the family doctor had being seeing her almost daily, had known how active she used to be despite her other health problems, and I think were thinking of "going for broke." If nothing further could be done, then they would somehow accept it.

All of us in this business of cardiology have, from time to time, done heart caths on individuals when our best instincts would tell us to leave well enough alone. We have then proceeded and have been very surprised, sometimes, to find something that was very amenable to a surgical intervention and with ultimately a gratifying result.

So, where do you draw the line? It's probably best to be conservative: "do no harm." My patient spent about three weeks in hospital, and was discharged with a four-inch incision scar over her right groin.

Before she came into hospital, she had been found to not tolerate one of the beta-blocker drugs that are often very useful in managing angina. She was adamant about this, but when I persuaded her to at least try another formula out of the same class of drug, but in a lower dose, while she was in hospital, she found she could tolerate it and there was a slight but noticeable improvement in her angina. That, as small as it was, was probably the only good thing in all of this. About six months later she had a massive heart attack and died very quickly.

IV ADDICTS WILL DO ANYTHING

Because the femoral vein is such a good portal of entry, you would think it might be a good place for drug addicts to inject their drugs. In fact, the only groups that seem to use it are people in the medical profession: doctors, nurses, paramedics, dentists and sometimes laboratory personnel.

During my professional life, I was aware of two remarkable people who got into big trouble using this route. Both, unfortunately, were doctors. One I knew well, and he was a very special person. I did not see him professionally, however, during the course of his drug problems.

Many of us have noticed that doctors who get themselves into trouble with drugs are often super-conscientious and hard working to the point of neglecting their own health. I think, sometimes, that they feel that they are not doing a good enough job, and perhaps feel inadequate to their tasks. Despite their best efforts, their patients may get worse and even die.

They become very discouraged, and depression may start playing a big role in their illness. They become tired to the point of exhaustion and yet are too keyed-up to sleep. Sleep deprivation just compounds the problem and, perhaps to induce sleep, they may start taking something that really seems to help over the short term.

Thus they may start down that slippery slope, and over a period of months, or sometimes years, these drugs become a big problem for them. Often, they don't feel that they have anyone to turn to who will understand their problems. (More recently the various provincial medical associations, fortunately, have started programs that have been very helpful to these members.)

My friend had all of the qualities that make a good doctor. He was very conscientious and driven, but he also had a problem of chronic pain and he tried to self-medicate. He started to inject his femoral vein on a regular basis, giving himself IV Demerol. It certainly helped relieve the pain, but he required bigger and bigger doses. Because he used his femoral veins, the needle punctures didn't show. He was very careful, and as far as I know, he didn't get into any local problems despite the multiple injections.

Very few people even knew that he was taking this drug, because he was always circumspect and knew how to hide his problems. One evening, he overdosed in his office and died. It was a big shock to everyone, a waste of a beautiful human being.

I have often thought that a lot of doctors that get into problems with drugs or alcohol are good people, but perhaps less able to cope with pressure than many of us. Perhaps people like me are better able to keep things in perspective and realize we just can't solve all the problems.

The other doctor I did not know personally until she arrived in the Emerg and I was required to look after her because she had developed a severe thrombophlebitis in her leg (in this case an inflammation in the wall of a vein causing a clot to form near the site of inflammation), directly related to her multiple injections into her femoral vein. On admission, she had a very swollen leg and a bruised area over her right groin. (I have camouflaged this story to avoid any embarrassment to the patient and her family, but the essential story is absolutely true.)

She told me that she had been putting up curtain rods in her house and in trying to loosen one of these rods, she had pulled on it pretty hard and it had suddenly given way and plunged into her groin. She said she hadn't paid it much heed, but over a period of several days it had become quite sore and her leg began to swell. Then on the morning of her admission, she had a sudden episode of shortness of breath that frightened both her and her husband, and they came straight to our Emerg.

Her husband seemed a nice enough man. He was a pharmacist, and fully corroborated her story. I was completely sucked in, and for some reason didn't even think of the possibility of her being a drug addict, or of this leg wound not being the result of stabbing herself with a curtain rod, but, in fact, due to multiple needle punctures. She seemed clean cut, she was athletic, she knew a number of the doctors at our hospital, and I was unaware of any history of previous problems.

The large vein in her leg was likely clotted up and her calf was swollen and tender. The sudden but brief episode of shortness of breath suggested that a piece of this clot (an embolus) had broken off and floated up that big vein along her spine and lodged in her lungs. We ordered a lung scan on admission and this confirmed the presence of a small pulmonary embolus. The area in her groin was indurated (firm, swollen, reddened, tender) and somewhat bruised, but certainly didn't suggest a lot of needle punctures to me.

She was put on the standard treatment of bed rest, elevation of her leg, and high dose IV heparin in an effort to stop any further build up of clots. (This was in the days before thrombolysins that actually help dissolve blood clots.)

Her condition appeared to be satisfactory at first, and she seemed quite comfortable. But, on the third day of her admission, she suddenly became very short of breath, and appeared to be in shock. I was just visiting her at the time and it was all very dramatic. She had some pain in her chest, but her appearance was remarkable with a very definite blue colour to her skin. She was sent immediately for a second lung scan and the diagnosis, this time, of a large embolus was confirmed.

A clot from her inflamed vein had likely loosened and had floated up into her lung, greatly reducing the oxygen content of her blood, and thus giving her skin that frightening blue appearance. She had several repeat blood tests that also supported the diagnosis.

In the 1980s, a special contraption was invented that could be inserted through a vein in the neck, pushed down into the large vein just below the heart, and would then open like an umbrella, blocking further clots floating up from her leg veins. This, however was still in the 1970s and this device had not yet been invented; and so her abdomen had to be opened by the vascular surgeon, Dr. Wally Chung, and the big vein that runs along side the spine was tied shut.

Our patient, overall, did well. But with that great big vein tied off that normally drains most of the blood from the lower half of the body, it takes considerable time before the circulation adjusts; thus the patient has to put up with considerable swelling of both legs for a fairly long period of time.

During her convalescence in hospital, the nursing staff noticed that she seemed to require a tremendous amount of morphine despite the fact that there didn't seem to be any reason why she should be in so much pain. They were now becoming very suspicious, and one of the casualty officers who had seen her when she was demanding more morphine was now convinced that our patient had a drug dependency problem.

When I spoke to her I told her that I suspected she might have a drug problem and that I thought she might be an IV drug user, using that femoral vein that had got her into all the trouble in the first place. She denied this completely, and her husband gave me the impression that he resented my even suggesting such a thing. (In retrospect, I suspect that he was supplying her with drugs from his pharmacy.)

At the time of her discharge we were still suspicious, but had no proof, and she generally did well. Her legs continued to swell for about a year and she was forced to wear elastic stockings. After a year or two I lost touch with her, but then one day a doctor phoned me from another hospital and told me our patient had arrived at their Emerg in complete kidney failure.

The patient had a very tough time, the second time around, even worse than during her previous admission, and for some time was close to death.

During this second admission to hospital, she confessed to her drug problem and admitted, amazingly, that she had gone back to injecting her peripheral veins.

After recovering from her physical problems, she was eventually sent to a hospital in Florida that specializes in rehabilitating drug dependent medical personnel.

I again lost track of her, but about ten years later when she came to visit a friend in our hospital, she was still drug free and doing well. Her kidneys had recovered and she had no swelling of her legs.

Harry, forever the sleuth, knew the main parts of this patient's history and I told him I was shocked to find out that she had gone back to IV drug use after all that had happened at our hospital, and in particular that she had started to inject the other femoral vein.

Harry felt that our patient had probably developed enough collateral circulation that the other femoral vein would carry her drugs back into her general circulation, although it might take a little longer.

Addiction is a hell of a thing. Fortunately, this lady finally seems to have beaten the problem — if, in fact, anybody can truly make that claim.

CHAPTER 4

Paper Pushing and Hospital Realities

During my earlier days practising as a cardiologist, I started seeing more and more patients who were literally on their last legs. The family doctors would call me in just to be sure that, "everything that could be done was done," before their patient ultimately expired. It was often very sad, and there was usually nothing more that could be done.

I would have to talk to the patient and the family and go over all the possible options, and basically cancel out each one of them. In most of these cases, there would not be a surgical solution, only a matter of making a few adjustments in their medications. It would give them a little hope, if some of these adjustments made them a little more comfortable. None of us wanted to give anybody false hopes, however. Sometimes it was a bit of a fine line.

The worst people, I think, are those absolute charlatans who offer false "cures" for a whole list of fatal diseases, particularly the solid cancers. These people come in various guises. Some say they have virtually magical powers; others have "special" medicines that, of course, are very expensive. Some claim to be experts in just about every field imaginable including herbology, acupuncture or acupressure, chelation, hyperbaric oxygen, ozone therapy, etc. Others are into megavitamin therapy, but they have one thing in common.

Their wonderful cures come at great financial cost and they are making large profits, at the expense of the sick and often moribund patient, because their cures don't work. These people are like vultures, but actually worse because they are, in fact, picking the meat off the bones of the patient, while the patient is still alive. (Vultures usually, or perhaps traditionally, wait until the animal at least stops kicking.)

Our role as physicians, in these circumstances, was to assure the patient and their loved ones that "no reasonable stone was left unturned." In these cases, our role was also to protect the caregivers to be sure that everyone involved understood exactly what was going on. As cardiologists, we probably assumed this role more often than other specialists, because cardiovascular disease is still the biggest cause of death in developed countries.

Also, except in a small minority of cases, the patient is not really dead until the heart stops. And the follow-through to that is that as long as the heart is still beating he is still alive. There is always the problem of patients' relatives not wanting to "let go" when it is not in anyone's interests to prolong the agony.

CARDIAC ARRESTS

I was called to many cardiac arrests, I think, because the referring doctors were initially afraid to stop cardiac massage until it was seen to be "kosher" to do so, and that point had to be pronounced by a cardiologist, if one was available. Before 1965, most cardiac arrest routines were, in fact, open chest and this was a horrific undertaking even for the best-trained crews.

Closed cardiac massage was a relatively new thing even in the late 1960s, and the medical community was still a little afraid of it. If the cardiologist was present, and especially if he assisted, everyone felt better, even though, as most often happens with these procedures, there was not a satisfactory outcome. As time advanced, and well-trained casualty officers (emergency docs) and other personnel arrived on the scene, the need for a cardiologist became less mandatory.

Harry, who so quickly gets to the point, told me I should be called "Dr. Butt Protector."

Not very flattering, of course, but possibly he was not far from the truth.

I realized he had a point when one day during my early days of practice, my office secretary told me my "dead file" was larger than my current file.

She had told her husband about this and he had become alarmed. He suggested she should change jobs because she might be implicated if there was ever an investigation. When I went over this with her, however, she was satisfied that the record was legitimate, and her husband's anxiety was relieved.

From the forgoing, one might get the impression that nobody survives cardiac arrest.

Survival depends so greatly on the circumstances. In the 1960s, during heart catheterization, when we first started injecting the coronary arteries with contrast dye in order to see where the blocks were, we used a dye called Hypaque. It gave pretty good pictures, but was somehow irritating to the heart, and the patient frequently went into ventricular fibrillation (a form of cardiac arrest). These patients were easily defibrillated by the use of those paddles that we all see on TV. These paddles are covered in "goop," or special electrolyte solution pads can be used. One paddle is then placed on the left side of the lower chest and the second paddle is usually placed slightly to the right of the front line of the chest and a little higher up. The operator shouts "all clear" and then steps on the foot switch or presses on the two red buttons at the top of the handles, and a very brief high voltage electrical discharge is sent from one paddle to the other. The idea is to totally remove all the electric discharges that have kept the patient's heart in a very rapid irregular contracting state that has totally stopped normal heart function. After this discharge has passed through the heart, it is hoped that normal electrical activity will return. Under these circumstances, I don't recall any patient not coming out of this process called ventricular fibrillation. The vast majority survived without after effects.

Dr. Harold Aldridge, working exclusively out of the Toronto General for a long period of time, probably did more "heart caths" on a day-to-day basis than anyone else in Canada, and was very efficient. He was very talented and worked quickly. We used to call him, "Have catheter, will travel" after the television series "Have Gun, Will Travel."

The well known Toronto cardiologist, Dr Harold Aldridge, sometimes would use this cardiac arrest to his advantage, because when the heart was in ventricular fibrillation it basically stopped beating and slowly dilated, giving a somewhat better x-ray view of the coronaries than when the heart was beating normally. He would purposely delay defibrillation for a few seconds longer just to get better pictures.

A number of our patients would have several bouts of ventricular fibrillation during the test. In fact, if we were too fast with the paddles, the patient would sometimes not yet be completely unconscious and would react violently to being shocked. Hence we intentionally delayed the defibrillation for a few seconds. (If someone did it to me while I was even semiconscious, I would certainly react too!)

When we started using Renograffin dye to inject the coronary arteries, it was found to be much less irritating to the heart, and the number of ventricular fibrillations during heart catheterization dropped dramatically. The contrast dyes have improved further and the image intensifiers are much better now, so that we can get away with using less concentrated contrast material.

All cardiologists have had patients who have come into hospital for various unstable heart conditions, and arrested. Fortunately, most of these people are successfully defibrillated. Sometimes, patients who arrested outside of hospital, and even had had a long course of cardiac massage, would also survive; a small number of these patients subsequently did very well.

Because I was "in the thick of it" for a long time and had seen many patients who survived their cardiac arrest, I was naturally curious about the much-talked-about "out of body experience." Whenever I had patients I had to follow up, I made a point of asking them about this phenomenon. I know people will be disappointed to hear that I found no one amongst all these patients who gave a story to support this concept.

I guess if one considers the matter completely rationally, there is probably little difference between someone who undergoes cardiac surgery, with cardiac bypass when the heart is completely stopped, and someone who has a brief stopping of the heart for some other reason. If there is no circulation to the brain for more than a few minutes at ambient temperatures, the brain, being so oxygen-dependent, starts to suffer damage, which very quickly becomes irreversible.

I just don't know where the people who believe in "out of body experience" can fit their concept into this scenario. Perhaps, those patients who were just starting to get a little brain damage that is still reversible may experience all sorts of phenomena as their brain is being, hopefully, only temporarily damaged.

NOT A PROUD MOMENT

One of the very few occasions when I wished that I had never become a physician occurred when I was a senior at the Wellesley Hospital in 1964.

There had been a cardiac arrest call, but I was not on call for the arrest team that day. At that time the Wellesley Hospital occupied several buildings that had been part of a huge mansion, and one of these buildings, which was occupied by perhaps forty patients, was called the "annex." The biggest room in this building had been a large solarium, and the floor and walls were tiled up to about four feet high, and the rest of the walls consisted of large fancy windows. The ceiling was partly tiled and windowed, and from the floor to the apex of the ceiling the height was about twenty-five feet. This room was bright and airy, and in its day must have housed some pretty impressive tropical plants. Approximately ten patients were arranged in beds around this large room, in a rough circle, each bed head up against the wall. Removable curtains on flimsy trolleys provided the only privacy.

The arrest had been in progress for perhaps five minutes when I arrived. Not being on call allowed me to finish whatever job I was doing at the time. One small segment of the roughly circular room had been cordoned off with these removable curtains. The other nine patients had been moved closer to each other in this circle to provide more room for the emergency team. There were perhaps an additional ten hospital personnel in the room around this one bed.

In those times, the arrest procedures were all "open chest." On each arrest tray there was provided a large scalpel in a glass tube. The doctor was supposed to examine the patient to be sure that there was, in fact, a true arrest, and then according to the protocol, an incision was made in the fourth left interspace (an area just under the left nipple). A rib spreader was placed in this incision, and the crank was turned to open up a suitable space between the ribs. Simultaneously, another doctor arriving on the scene would slip an endotracheal tube down the patient's windpipe and begin "bagging" the patient.

The first doctor then had to thrust his hand between the ribs and start squeezing the heart in a rhythmical fashion. Unbelievably, we were told not to put on gloves, as time was the essence. The bottom of these ribs is quite rough, and invariably we would

83

sustain small lacerations on the back of our right hand. We basically were unaware of most communicable diseases, and there was no thought of hepatitis, and no one had yet heard of AIDS. Perhaps the only thing of which we were vaguely aware in this regard was syphilis.

Basically these open chest procedures, even under the best of circumstances, were a horror show. When I arrived at the solarium, there was blood dripping from both sides of the bed onto the floor. Some patients bleed more than others during this procedure. The hospital mattresses are covered with a waterproof plastic covering and any excess fluid, including blood that isn't soaked up by the bottom sheet, runs easily off onto the floor. The curtains that were supposed to provide a modicum of privacy were considered a nuisance as they only got in the way of all the people coming and going. Consequently, the other nine patients in the room were getting a ringside seat whether they liked it or not.

In this hospital, which was so fragmented geographically, a cardiac arrest in some ways provided a social gathering. People who had not seen each other for several days would be brought together, and they could discuss mutual problems and even socialize.

As I could see that the procedure was winding down, I just stood in the doorway and watched. It was horrific. The other patients in the room were traumatized seeing all of this happening to one of their own guys. Yet despite the fact that this patient was not going to make it, there almost seemed to be a festive air in the room. While I was standing there, a couple of interns moved away from the bed talking and laughing as they walked through the doorway.

The defibrillator had a problem and each time the foot switch was depressed the machine made a loud moaning sound. There was a short pause and then everyone would laugh at this peculiar sound. It must have happened five or six times, each time followed by a short pause and then peals of laughter.

I continued to stand in the doorway watching the other patients in the room and they were obviously horrified. After a short time the staff started to drift away, laughing and talking, and pretty soon there were only two nurses left to clean up the mess and wheel away the bed on which the dead patient now lay covered with a partially bloodied sheet. The floor cleaner soon arrived and mopped up the floor. The remaining beds were pushed back to their original position and a short time later a new patient was wheeled up from the Emerg.

I fully realized that the only reason that I was not part of this scene was that I had been late arriving and was not part of the arrest team that day. Otherwise, I would have been just as culpable as the rest of the staff. Part of the problem, of course, is the terrible accommodation in these old hospitals, but we have absolutely no excuse for being so callous.

I hope I learned something that day.

WHEN DEAD IS DEAD, PART 1

At two o'clock one morning in 1964 while I was working at the Wellesley Hospital, a police van drove into our emergency department and they wanted an MD — any MD, me, the lowest guy on the totem pole — to sign the appropriate papers so that they could transport their customer, who was lying in the back of their van, to the Toronto Morgue.

I was called to the Emerg and, of course, was "volunteered" to fill out the appropriate papers. It seemed pretty routine. The patient, a young man who I subsequently gathered was part of a gang, had been sitting in the driver's seat of a convertible when one of his contemporaries took an axe and literally bashed in the whole right side of his head.

I crawled on my hands and knees to the front of the van and quickly inspected the damage. I did the usual routine of listening for heart and breath sounds and felt for any pulses, pulled up and down on one of his eye lids to see if he had any pupil response to light and then climbed out and filled out the two papers that our emergency department always had available.

The guy was dead, that was for sure. Somebody had hit him so hard with this axe that his brains were quite visible on the back of his neck and mashed into his hair and the collar of his shirt. I thought this was an easy one. So back to bed for, I hoped, a bit more sleep — a scarce commodity when you're an intern on Emerg duty.

I completely forgot about this incident until almost three years later, when I received a subpoena in the mail directing me to ap-

Doctors are trained to fight the disease. There's no question that we have full public support in this regard; it's almost a question of good against evil. Nobody would think of standing up for the disease process. Doctors tend to be right of centre and are sometimes shocked when they see some of the light sentences that are handed out by the courts in modern times.

pear in court on a certain date at 10:00 a.m. — bankers' hours!

Like most doctors, I had reservations about our justice system.

This subpoena was going to put a huge hole in my day, and already we didn't have enough time to do our jobs, not nearly enough time to serve our patients properly. Sure enough, I was there before 10:00 a.m., and trying to find out exactly what I was supposed to do. In the medical records department of the Wellesley Hospital I had found and read over the notes that I had made on the night of my encounter, and I thought that my testimony would be very brief and that I could get the hell out of there and back to work.

A very nice court clerk told me that I was the first witness, and likely all I would have to do was to confirm that I was the doctor who had signed the death certificate and then leave.

As it turned out, however, his honour, the judge, was late. And then I wasn't called all morning, and (can you believe this?) they announced a *two-hour* lunch break! I was told to be back by two o'clock.

There I was waiting, chomping at the bit, and there was another delay. Four o'clock arrived, I still hadn't been called, and they shut the place down at four o'clock. At four o'clock in the afternoon!

Their day was finished, and I was told to be back at ten o'clock the next morning.

It took me almost until midnight to catch up on my work at the hospital, and I wasn't even on call. I dutifully appeared the next morning at ten o'clock, only because the nice court clerk told me about the penalties for not obeying subpoenas.

The next morning, "his highness" was on time and I was ushered into the court. I think I was too frightened to notice much, but there was someone in the prisoner's box, and a bunch of well-fed men in expensive suits sitting around a table in the front of the court room. I was led in and I had to put my hand on the black book and mumble something.

The initial questions seemed pretty straightforward. But when the man in the most expensive suit got up — I gathered he was the defence lawyer — and started asking me questions, I didn't like the tone of his voice.

He asked me how long the patient had been dead when I saw him. I told him that I had been asked to determine if he was dead, and only asked to then fill out the death certificate and one other form that goes with it. I specifically told him that we never determine the time of death in the Emerg because that was the responsibility of the coroner's department.

He then asked, for some reason, how I knew that the victim was dead. I told him, among other things, that I could see that his brains had been mashed into his scalp and the back of his collar. At this point, the judge said that was enough — I guess he had a weak stomach — and I was finally allowed to leave. It was almost twelve o'clock. What a waste of everybody's time. I'm certainly glad I didn't decide to become a lawyer. Fortunately my lack of language skills would have precluded that choice anyway. Certainly, if I had had the choice, I would have volunteered to sell those ice pans floating on the Beaufort Sea rather than become a lawyer.

One amazing coincidence occurred with this court case.

The day before I went to court, I had been working in the heart cath lab at the Toronto General. The last two cases that afternoon each had a small stroke during the procedure, and I was basically the chief operator.

Very fortunately, they both made a good recovery, but I was the doctor passing the tubes in these two cases. Understandably, I felt horrible and kept going over in my mind what I might have done wrong to cause these strokes. Nobody said anything to me, but I am sure they might have been wondering too.

I was supposed to do the first heart catheterization the next morning, but because of this inconvenient court appearance, one of my colleagues took over. Sure enough, this patient suffered a small stroke as well. The rest of the cases that day were cancelled.

Having this happen to two different and consecutive operators pointed to a mechanical problem, and not to something that I or my colleague had done wrong. All the machinery was taken apart, and it was felt that the problem was likely in the injector.

We used this machine to inject a fairly large quantity of contrast dye over a short period. The machine was changed and the problem went away. If I had done the next case the following morning, I might have looked incompetent, especially as a definite defect had not been conclusively found.

Maybe, after all, that lawyer in the expensive suit was doing me a favour by asking all those questions.

WHEN DEAD IS DEAD, PART 2

It was 1974, and to satisfy the bureaucrats I had to sign those papers again. How often had I signed these papers by then? The bureaucrats have to have all their little ducks in a row, and I have to "cover someone's butt" by signing these papers.

I don't believe in ghosts, but one day I had a frightening experience when I was signing these papers. It was very early in the morning, and I had just arrived at St. Mary's Hospital in New Westminster to see a patient.

I usually went very early in the morning, to avoid seeing any of the GPs. If I ran into any of them, what invariably happened is that they would say, "Oh gee, I'm glad to see you, could you just have a peek at my patient in room so and so while you are here?" They were always very nice about it, but a "peek" was another hour out of the day, and my new partners and I were already too busy. Most of the time, the family doctor in these cases would manage without a consultation, and if he really wanted one he could ask and one of us would come back. The trick was to be out of there before seven o'clock in the morning.

On this particular day, when I arrived the night supervisor asked me if I would pronounce one of her patients dead. Because St. Mary's had a large chronic care population, a death during the night was quite common, and I had done this duty before.

I was told that both the family doctor and the patient's family had been informed, and the supervisor was anxious to take the patient off the ward and place him in their temporary morgue in the basement of the hospital. They just had to have some MD — again any MD — sign the necessary papers.

The patient, by this time, had been placed near the elevators on the fourth floor in a very small, quite dark and narrow room, with only a small desk lamp on a small table at the far end of the room. He was on a stretcher, positioned so that I had to squeeze along a very narrow passageway to get to the table where the papers were spread out for me to sign.

I was very tired from a busy night before, probably still half-asleep and, in fact, I hadn't had any coffee or breakfast. I did the usual things, probably almost by rote. I looked at the name band on his wrist to see that it matched the name on the death certificate. I fished out my stethoscope and listened to his chest for any heart or breath sounds, and as is my custom felt for both his radial and carotid pulses. I also checked his pupil response with my pen-light. There was no sign of life, the supervisor had told me he had been dead for several hours now, and he indeed looked dead.

With just the patient and me in this small dark room, I sat down and was signing my name to one of the two familiar papers, when, suddenly, the patient let out something between a big moan and a long sigh.

I think the hair on my back stood up, and I became very sweaty. I have no idea what had happened. The patient still looked quite dead. I took out my stethoscope again, likely with very shaky hands, and felt for his pulse. Nothing seemed to have changed. Was it gas? Who knows? It never happened to me again. Good thing!

I probably laid down another layer of cholesterol on my coronary arteries that morning. I finished signing the papers, but I felt very jumpy for the rest of the day.

COMMON SENSE BACKFIRES

Some patients' loved ones will not accept death under any circumstances.

This response seems to be Nature's way of softening the shock, but sometimes the response may be inspired by guilt.

I think most doctors have seen this type of case. One that will be forever in my mind concerns two daughters. The daughter who had been looking after mother for the last fifteen years or so was quite agreeable to being "conservative" in mother's management. The other daughter, for various reasons, had really not paid much attention to mother's problems, but at the last moment of her mother's illness came "riding in like a knight on a white horse."

This daughter now wanted every thing done, even if it was not only impractical, but would, at best, only prolong her mother's suffering. In this particular case, we ended up doing some investigations that were, in my view, not only unnecessary, but not in the patient's best interest. The family doctor felt that he was forced to do some of these tests for self-protection, but also, in some way, to placate this very aggressive daughter.

The two daughters almost came to blows over their mother's management. Our poor patient ended up in the cardiac care unit and sustained multiple cardiac arrests before she died. Fortunately, she was unconscious for the last three days for the worst of this horrific and useless exercise.

On a different occasion, our office had been following a patient intermittently — and only at the request of the family doctor — from 1974 until 1995, when he died in hospital.

He was a pleasant man, but like so many of our patients, didn't follow our advice too well. He had started smoking at an early age and just hadn't been able to stop until 1991, when he finally got the message. He was on a long-term anticoagulant, but wasn't really conscientious with this potentially dangerous drug. Warfarin is not called "rat poison" for frivolous reasons, and, in fact, when I was a kid it was commonly used to poison rats in my parents' barn.

To make matters worse, he also drank alcohol, sometimes quite heavily. This can have a profound effect on the bleeding problems associated with anticoagulants.

Three years before he came to our office, he had a Starr-Edwards valve (a "ping pong ball in bird cage" type of valve) implanted in his aortic area and he had subsequently suffered two separate embolic episodes. This problem occurs when clot material builds up on the valve and then floats away in the blood circulation, causing major problems. We had therefore kept him on this "rat poison" to reduce the chances of further embolic events.

I didn't see this man personally until 1980. I saw him on three further occasions until 1994, just prior to a hernia repair. The only real problem with planned surgery was what to do with his anticoagulants. There is a well-established protocol for this, which involves switching to a short-acting IV preparation — heparin — just prior to surgery.

Over the years, many types of artificial valves have been used to replace the original natural heart valves that are no longer functioning adequately. One of the earlier types was the Starr-Edwards valve, opening when the pressure below the ball was higher in the heart chamber behind the ball, and then closing when the pressure down stream was higher, forcing the ball back onto its seat. This assured that the flow of blood continued in a forward direction. The cage around the ball kept it properly aligned so that it could fall back onto its seat. This mechanical-type valve opened and closed with every heartbeat, perhaps sixty or more times a minutes, and over several years the structure would take an awful bashing. This and many similar valves ultimately failed, resulting in many disasters. Also, since it was made of foreign material, blood clots sometimes formed on the valve and would float away, sometimes to the brain, causing strokes. Bacterial infection on the valve was another very serious problem.

The patient went through this operation without any problems, but the next year he was back with cancer of the bladder. The "butt protector doctor" was not asked to see him prior to this surgery, because I had already outlined the schedule for his anticoagulant on his old chart, and from a cardiac point of view, his condition, had not changed.

Unfortunately, at the time of the surgery, the surgeon found that the cancer had advanced too far for the operation to be successful. By the time the surgery took place, the cancer had spread from his bladder to his pelvic wall. He had part of his bladder and the obstructed kidney removed, only for palliation, and then he was closed up.

Even though his short-term future was going to be poor, he did well for the first post-operative day. At this point, I think only because of family pressure, I was now asked to see him. I felt that he was doing as well as he could under these unfavourable circumstances, and basically agreed with everything that had transpired.

His anti-coagulants had, of course, not yet been restarted. I said that I would only see him again if I was called, and expected him to be able to walk out of hospital once he had recovered from his surgery.

The next day, over a short period he started to look bad, his blood pressure slowly but steadily dropped and his pulse rate went up. I was called back, and saw him as an emergency. I strongly suspected that he was bleeding somewhere, and I ordered the usual protocols, including four units of whole blood.

Then in front of my eyes, he looked to be on the point of arresting. I called for a "code 21" (the cardiac arrest routine), and although he was not yet unconscious, I knew that in a few more moments I would have to start cardiac compressions. Just at this point, he vomited a huge amount of blood.

I immediately called off the cardiac-arrest routine. What was the point? Once the patient has lost the greater portion of his blood volume no amount of cardiac compressions will help. Without blood in the system, the heart cannot pump out the necessary blood volume and therefore insufficient oxygen reaches the brain. The blood volume would have to be replaced immediately, and the open wound that had resulted in all this blood loss in the first place, would have to be sealed up. I felt this patient had likely developed a "stress ulcer," which happens sometimes in the post operative period, particularly in older, very sick patients. This type of cardiac arrest is sometimes called a "traumatic arrest," and unless the patient was already hooked up to an open-heart machine, with lots of blood volume standing by, there is no hope.

> Stress ulcer is an erosion in the upper gastrointestinal tract, which may erode into an artery and can be responsible for massive blood loss. It is more common in older patients with other severe medical problems.

Most unfortunately, the patient's wife — very concerned that the other doctors had not called me before the surgery had taken place — was angry with me because I had called off the cardiac arrest procedure.

She was worked up sufficiently that she complained to the BC College of Physicians and Surgeons, and many people were named as defendants in this case: the family doctor (who was about as conscientious a guy that there could ever be), one of my partners who happened to be peripherally involved, the surgeon, the anesthetist, and me. Undoubtedly, the hospital and the nursing staff would also have been named as defendants.

This problem didn't filter down to me until two years later. In the meantime, I had been forced to retire, was myself on heavy chemo, and really not ready to put up with this. To me it was obvious that none of the doctors had done anything wrong, and that should have been the end of it.

I had never been "in trouble" with the College before, but now the lawyers were involved and undoubtedly making money from this patient's estate. If these lawyers, after getting all the facts, had sat down with the lady and explained what had happened, or had asked the family doctor all the circumstances, and asked him to re-explain them, all this could have been avoided.

I offered to talk to this lady, and her lawyers too, but they didn't reply to my letter. To the College's credit, however, a full explanation was eventually given in writing, and it is to be hoped that the poor woman was finally satisfied.

Of interest, the incidence of bladder cancer is three times more common in someone who smokes compared with the non-smokers. If anyone still thinks that the carcinogens don't get around in the body after cigarette smoke gets into our lungs, they probably still believe that the world is flat!

This patient's cancer had spread to the pelvic wall and was impossible to remove, but that wasn't the reason that I called off the procedure. I must say, however, that if I, or one of my family members, had arrested under these circumstances, I would hope that the prognosis of the cancer alone and the inevitability of the subsequent suffering would have in itself been enough reason not to continue with an arrest procedure.

To return briefly to "traumatic arrests," there are some interesting points to make. Victims who have been in severe traffic accidents that have resulted in massive bleeding causing cardiac arrest just don't survive.

Princess Diana was alleged to have suffered a torn pulmonary artery. This artery is about the size of at least our ring finger, and if it has a serious tear, the majority of our blood volume will exit into our chest cavity in a matter of a few very short minutes. Those poor French doctors, although they made heroic attempts to save her life, didn't have a chance. It is very frustrating to see such a young and vibrant person die so quickly.

In the early days of my practice at the Royal Columbian, I saw a young man who had sustained a severe chest injury resulting when the old non-collapsing type steering wheel had been rammed against his chest.

When he arrived in the Emerg, he was fully conscious, but basically had no blood pressure and a fast and very weak pulse. He told me that he was dying, and I knew that he was probably correct. I actually lied to him telling him that he would likely recover, and will always feel guilty for it, but what else could I do? I didn't want to abandon him and take away any lingering hope that he might have had. He just ignored me and wanted to talk to his father. Fortunately, his father was there for about the last two minutes of his life.

Our working diagnosis was a massive internal bleed into his chest, and although we went through the motions, calling the cardiovascular surgeon, setting up the OR, and ordering massive amounts of blood, there was nothing we could do, and he was dead within five minutes of his arriving in Emerg. All that blood work was cancelled.

I have no idea how he could be so definite about his impending death. Because it was a traffic death, there was a mandatory autopsy, and this showed that he had suffered a torn pulmonary artery.

HOSPITAL REALITIES AND ADMINISTRATION — THE LORD CASE

Hospital administrators have a very difficult job. At the beginning of their fiscal year, they are given a certain amount of money and are told that they cannot spend a penny more of that amount of money during that year. This is their global budget.

If the cardiologist says we have to put in more pacemakers even to keep level with the demand, the administrator says, "Well, I guess then we will have to cut back on the number of artificial hips that we put in."

Many administrators are also in a bit of a straitjacket because they have to stick to certain standards, and cannot go against demands of the various unions. They can only increase their efficiencies to a certain point.

In April 1977, the hospital plumber was called because water was dripping down from the ceiling onto the floor below. When he arrived, he noted the now steady stream of water and went immediately up to the next floor. He found that the spot directly above the leak was a patient bathroom with the door locked. He asked at the nearby nursing station for a key and a nurse to accompany him.

When they opened the door, they found that the bathtub was completely full to overflowing. A pair of knees was sticking up in the water; the rest of the patient was completely submerged. The unfortunate patient was hauled out, and an immediate "code 21" was called.

I was assigned to the catheter lab that day and one of my cardiac colleagues, Dr. Peter Richardson, went to the call. He started immediate cardiac compressions and, after a long while, the arrest team was able to detect a pulse, and the monitor showed that the patient was having a spontaneous cardiac rhythm.

Eventually she was transferred to the intensive care unit on a respirator, continuous cardiac monitoring and the usual supportive IV therapy. She remained unconscious, basically in a vegetative state.

Just fifteen years of age, this young lady had been admitted to the neuro sciences ward for investigation of her longstanding epilepsy, which was not being well controlled at home.

The usual custom with these difficult cases is to stop all the current anticonvulsant therapy and observe the patient closely according to a strict protocol that includes careful monitoring of the patient, and then start the anticonvulsant therapy in a very graduated, organized manner. The choice of agent, or in most cases combination of agents, may take some time to sort out, and demands a lot of patience on the part of the medical staff and, of course, on the part of the patient.

On this particular morning, as the nursing staff were about to begin their morning report, one of them noticed this patient walking down the hall carrying a bath towel. She was told to go back to her room and wait for one of the nurses to assist her in her bath after report. Apparently the patient headed back to her room, and the nurses began their morning report.

At some point however, this patient must have decided not to wait, and returned to the bathroom, unobserved by the staff, and drew her bath. One can only assume that she must have had some sort of seizure in the tub and gone under water and basically drowned. By the time she was discovered, although successfully resuscitated, she had sustained severe and irreversible brain damage.

What had happened was, of course, a huge tragedy and was thoroughly covered in all the newspapers. When it eventually went to court, it was again in the papers and on the news across Canada.

The defendants in this case were just about everybody even remotely involved, the lawyers deploying the traditional "wide net" approach. The neurologist who had admitted this patient, written and signed the standard protocol for the management of this type of patient, was caught in this wide net.

It did not seem to any of the medical staff that the doctor who had admitted the patient and signed the protocol should be responsible for what happened to this unfortunate girl. In fact, Dr. Mort Knazan, one of the associates of the neurologist involved, asked our administrator during a medical staff meeting if he felt that this doctor should be held responsible, and this administrator very clearly said, "No."

I was sitting right behind Dr. Knazan and there was no doubt what our administrator had said. It was then a surprise that when this case went to court, this administrator, Dr. M S, said exactly the opposite to what he had said at our staff meeting.

We were all shocked. But I guess that Dr. M S was trying to "protect the butt" of the hospital. The nurses are considered employees of the hospital; if they are found culpable, then the hospital insurance has to pay the costs.

If, however, the doctors can be found culpable, then the doctors' insurance has to pay, because we are not considered employees of the hospital. The courts decided eventually that the patient's doctor was responsible, and the settlement was something in the neighbourhood of seven million dollars, a simply huge settlement at the time.

So that was that. None of the doctors were very happy with this contradictory behaviour by our administrator. But certainly by his action he had made one thing very clear. If there is any trouble, and it might cost the hospital anything, don't look for any backing from the administrator — at least not this one.

Several months later, an apparently psychotic patient pushed an entire window frame out from the third floor of the hospital and it fell on my car, which was parked legitimately in the doctors' parking lot, doing considerable damage to the hood.

When I phoned the hospital's insurance company, I was told that I would have to pay my "500 dollar deductible" and my own car insurance would pay the rest.

In other words, the hospital's insurance company wasn't going to take any responsibility.

I must confess my ire was aroused. I said I would take whatever steps necessary to make them pay.

My anger was no doubt stoked by the recent, still-simmering memory of our administrator's contradictory behaviour, and I went on to say that I felt that M S had perjured himself in court to protect this same insurance company that was now trying to screw me.

I told this insurance man how M S had previously stated publicly at our medical meeting that the doctors were not responsible for the terrible injury suffered in the Lord Case, but then in court he had said just the opposite.

Within ten minutes, M S was on the line. The hospital insurance was going to pay for the repairs to my car, he said. But he was now going to sue me for defamation of character! He arranged for me to meet him Monday morning in his office to discuss the matter further.

I worried over the weekend. But the more I thought about it, the more confident I became. There were perhaps one hundred doctors who had heard him say that he didn't think the doctors were responsible in the Lord Case and it was on record that he had said the opposite in court.

When we met in his office on Monday, he told me that he had decided not to sue me. I said that that was a good idea because I had been going to say in court exactly what I had told his insurance agent, and everybody would know that I was telling the truth.

Then, unbelievably, he asked if I would like to have a cup of coffee with him. Did he think that we could just "kiss and make up"? I told him I only like to drink coffee with my friends and walked off.

I would not have defied my president and chief executive officer just for the sake of doing so, but subsequently, fate would make it seem like that was the case.

BECOMING THE FALL GUY

A short time later, Dr. M S was on the news again. This time he was quoted as saying that patients were not waiting in the Royal Columbian Emerg for as long as three days before a bed could be found for them upstairs, as had been reported widely in the local news. He was even reported to have said that the wait was less than twenty-four hours.

I had been on call often over that period. I knew that I had three of the five patients who had, in fact, unfortunately been waiting longer than three days.

Dr Dave Hilton, who luckily was born with an overdose of Harry's "shit-disturber" chip (see chapter six), decided on my behalf that we should both go together to see our local MLA, Dennis Cocke. Cocke had been the minister of health in the previous BC Provincial Government, but was now in opposition. Dave set up this meeting the same day.

Dennis Cocke turned out to be both a well-informed and approachable man, and because of his previous experience as minister of health, he knew exactly what to do. He phoned CTV, a local television news station, said he had a story for them, and suggested I meet their crew outside our Emerg.

Now I was worried, and wondered if M S would shoot me after he found out. As I had been the consultant on three of these long-waiting patients, I was, unfortunately, going to be the fall guy. But it was too late to retreat. I spoke to my three patients in the Emerg to inform them that a TV crew was going to be in the Emerg in the next half hour and would like to interview each of them.

Surprisingly, all three seemed eager for the experience. The entire Emerg staff was on side. Its members were equally fed up with all the lies, and they felt that they could not look after their patients properly.

The TV crew arrived on time. They were extremely professional, came directly into the Emerg and asked each of these patients the right questions. One patient even turned up the edge of her two-inch rubber mattress to show the viewers the poor accommodation, and said that she thought she was getting a bed sore.

Another patient volunteered that he couldn't get any sleep, because the lights were always on and the place was "too darn noisy"! They all confirmed that they, indeed, had been waiting in the Emerg longer than seventy-two hours.

Dr. M S was protecting his butt by misleading his board and the public. My friend Dave Hilton commented it is difficult to solve a problem if you deny that the problem even exists.

Sure enough, our Emerg problems were the leading item on the CTV news at six o'clock and the item was repeated at ten.

This time, I had only one night to sweat it out and not a whole weekend. As expected, the next morning my name was repeatedly paged over the hospital's loudspeaker system and I was advised to report immediately to the boardroom. An emergency meeting of the entire hospital board had been called, and when I arrived the meeting had apparently already been in progress for some time. My "friend," Dr. M S, was conducting the meeting.

As soon as I arrived, he asked me who had authorized the TV crew to come into the Emerg? I told him I had "suggested" that they see for themselves what was going on. He was about to say something, but I over-rode him, and said that our hospital was a public place, and the public had a right to know that they were being misled by false statements by our chief administrator.

That shut him up, but only temporarily. He then said that I would be served with an injunction, and if it ever happened again, I would find myself facing a contempt of court charge. It was an idle threat. I was never served with an injunction.

In fact, by this time I was furious, totally outraged by this man's behaviour. I asked if he had anything else to say. And he said, "No."

I told him I had a lot of sick patients to see and walked out.

Some of my friends called this man "the little corporal." He even had the appropriate little moustache. Quite fitting, I thought.

Two years later, I met Mr. Neil Russell at a hospital function. He was the Chairman of the Board when all this was going on, and had been in the boardroom when I was told that I was going to have an injunction served against me.

He said that the board at that time was already coming to the conclusion that M S "had to go," and I had made their job a whole lot easier.

I was glad to see him go; I think we all were. He had lied to us on two separate occasions just to save his precious butt.

Much later, Harry said during a discussion, "You didn't seem to get along too well with the 'little corporal.' Is it because you just don't like hospital administrators? I seem to recall that Dickie Foulkes was going to 'shit on your head.'"

"Harry, I actually liked 'Dickie.' He would explain why he couldn't accommodate our wishes. In fact, during my time at the Royal Columbian I liked all our administrators, with the one exception of Dr. M S. He was overly legalistic, and never took the trouble to find out what our problems were. He threatened me with a defamation of character lawsuit, and then with an injunction, and I think he put our hospital behind the 'eight ball' with the provincial government.

"Harry, I would actually prefer someone to shit on my head, than to put all that time and expense in court."

Harry smiled and lifted an eyebrow. "Well, Tom, I can see why, because with that billiard ball head of yours, you would not even have to shower and shampoo afterwards. You could just wipe it off with a damp cloth!"

Good old Harry, he always has an answer for everything!

My favourite administrator by far was Mr. Jim Fair, who took the trouble to keep his finger on the pulse of the hospital. He visited the various wards and sat down with the assistant head nurses to ask what he could do to help. He was always approachable, and he got results for the hospital.

Some administrators become mini-dictators. They surround themselves with generals (five or six "vice presidents") of a like mind-set, and then never listen adequately to the troops in the trenches. The problem is that the vice presidents never come around either.

The people who really know what's going on with the patients are the assistant head nurses on the ward, the on-call doctors in the Emerg, and the staff in the OR. These people know what the day-to-day problems are.

The people who work in the administrators' offices, although necessary, really will never find solutions unless they know where their focus must be — *on the patients.*

Perhaps we should all go down to the Mayo Clinic, discussed in chapter 14, and get some of their ideas on how to run a hospital efficiently. They don't seem to have lost sight of their reason for being in business, and that is to serve the patient.

CHAPTER 5

The Emerg

During the summer of 1960, I had just finished my third year of medical school and at this point had received very little exposure to clinical medicine. In short, I knew almost nothing that was of any practical value for work in the Emerg. Oh sure, I had been shown how to take a history, inspect, palpate and had a very limited idea of how to use the stethoscope. But not much more.

STOMACH PUMP

It was my first day as an "extern" at Soldiers Memorial Hospital in Orillia, Ontario. I was called an extern because I had one more year to go before I graduated from medical school. Fortunately, this particular hospital wasn't completely aware of what an extern really was because they didn't ordinarily have any resident staff. They were extremely pleasant to me, but on the other hand, they assumed that I would know at least something!

Having received the very first call in my life to the Emerg, I arrived to find a young woman tied into a straight-back chair, her arms thoroughly trussed up behind her, and her legs tied individually to the front legs of the chair. A big orderly was standing behind her to be sure that the chair didn't over turn. The poor patient seemed pretty upset and was putting up an intermittent struggle. I had never seen anything like that before, and asked the large matronly nurse standing there with her arms crossed what was going on.

"Oh, the usual," she said, "another overdose. Your raincoat and rubber boots are in the closet over there. You'd better hurry because those sleeping capsules are dissolving."

I hoped she knew what she was doing, because I certainly had no idea. Besides, she looked like a "take charge" type of woman and I rushed over to the closet. I was glad I knew at least how to put on a raincoat and rubber boots; I'd had lots of experience doing that on the farm. But I dreaded what the next order might be. The "raincoat" was in reality a large plastic apron that extended from my neck down well below my knees.

I arrived back in front of the patient and was handed a big rubber tube with a strange rubber ball in the middle of it. At one end was a funnel and the other end was slightly tapered with a lot of holes in the sidewalls.

The orderly inserted a rubber gag into the patient's mouth and with the ratchet device on the side, cranked her mouth wide open. I then realized, with alarm, that I was supposed to put this tube, which probably measured at least eight millimetres in diameter, down her gullet. At some point along the way, my matronly friend told me that the patient's family doctor was on his way and had told her to get the extern "to get on with it."

I remember asking her, plaintively, what if the tube went down her windpipe? To which she replied, "Not a problem! If it does, the patient starts coughing and turns black. Well not completely black, but certainly a dark blue and it's quite obvious. You just pull the tube back and every thing goes back to where it was and you try again."

Fortunately, the tube went down surprisingly easily. The orderly had come around to the front and got me to hold that little funnel up above the patient's head. He started pouring some type of liquid into it from the smaller bucket. I hadn't noticed, but the orderly was standing as far back as he could and still be able to pour. Without warning, the patient vomited, and my tube literally rocketed out of her gullet and there was debris all over the floor.

The charge nurse was delighted, and showed me the half-digested capsules in the mess on the floor. I could see now why I was wearing a raincoat and rubber boots! The orderly took me outside onto the driveway, and hosed me down before I took the apron and rubber boots off. I guessed they wanted them to be clean before hanging them back up in the closet.

Dr. M (I can't remember his name because I was not taking notes at that time, but I remember him as a very helpful, sup-

The stomach pump and I get hosed down on the emergency department driveway.

portive guy) arrived just as we were cleaning up. The matron told him what a good job I had done, and went back to the main desk. The patient, I was very relieved to see, seemed no worse for wear and didn't even seem to be mad at me. The family doctor took charge, and when he had a free minute introduced himself and showed me how to use that brutal tube. By sticking the perforated end of the tube into the small bucket, he demonstrated how to suck the liquid back up again from the stomach using that rubber ball. That apparently was necessary only if the patient didn't vomit. The liquid in the small bucket was usually water, but some of the doctors used a mustard solution or a weak salt solution. We weren't, of course, supposed to use this method if there was a suggestion that the poison ingested was in any way corrosive.

I had to use that brutal tube several more times during that summer. It was important to be sure that the patient was wide-awake to reduce the risk of aspiration (inhalation of gastric contents into the lower airways). Although I was told that the pills were dissolving as I was speaking to the patient and that I shouldn't waste any time, it helped to have at least minimal co-operation from the patient. In those days, I don't think informed consent was ever even considered. Now, with Mr. Trudeau's rights and freedoms, we probably wouldn't be allowed to do this if the patient had any reservations.

The head nurse at the desk said that although that big tube seemed brutal, it worked, and they seldom had repeat customers. No wonder! However, there is always an exception to the rule, and at the end of the summer one of our overdose patients was back. She even came back with the same boyfriend and got into the famous chair without being asked, and we didn't even have to tie her up. Patients have always continued to amaze me.

However, this lady's repeat performance had likely been a suicide gesture and not a genuine suicide attempt. She likely ac-complished what she wanted; she certainly had her boyfriend's complete attention when she came to the Emerg on that second occasion. Undoubtedly, she was hoping that he would feel re-morse for all the trouble he was causing by not being "nicer" to her.

These gestures can be dangerous, though, depending on what pill, or series of medications, that the patient has taken. Some of the chemicals that patients have taken in an apparent suicide gesture can be lethal or cause permanent damage. Cor-rosive chemicals and other common stuff around the house, like antifreeze, can have disastrous consequences. Marilyn Monroe's likely suicide gesture went astray because she got too sleepy too fast to make that very important last-minute phone call.

CAN'T EVEN FIND HIS HEART

A few weeks later I was working in this same Emerg when the desk received a frantic call from a woman whose boy friend had just shot himself. She gave the address, and the ambulance, which was not stationed at the hospital, was informed and duly dispatched. The nice lady at the desk said, "That address has to be right across the street. Why don't you run over and see if you can help?"

The front door was wide open when I arrived. I went straight in and yelled from the bottom of the stairs, and a very anxious woman's voice answered from upstairs. I ran up the stairs and saw a man lying on the floor beside a bed. There was blood on his pyjamas but he didn't look as if he was suffering that much. A .22 gauge, single-shot, bolt-action rifle was lying on the floor beside him. He didn't seem threatening in any way and told me he had just shot himself in the heart. I lifted up his pyjamas' top, and sure enough there was a small dark hole in his lower left chest.

Turning him on his right side, there was another small hole at about the same level but a little further lateral. He didn't seem to be in any distress and I don't think there was any evidence that there was a sucking wound. In fact, the wife or girlfriend was more of a problem than the man lying on the floor.

I felt as useless as the proverbial "tits on a bull." I tried to re-assure the poor woman and told her that I thought he just missed his heart and probably had only a small wound in the lower part of his lung. I also suggested that he probably wasn't bleeding much at the moment, as he had a normal pulse. Fortunately, the ambulance arrived and he was transported across the street to the hospital. It turned out he was a bad shot, couldn't even hit his own heart, and made an uneventful recovery.

The next day there was a big write-up in the local paper saying that I had saved the life of a local Orillia citizen. I was alarmed at what I read. It was a complete fabrication.

The source, according to the article, was the administrator of the hospital. I went to see him right away, as I knew my new friends in the Emerg would know that the story was not true and it would make me look bad in their eyes.

And what was his response? He told me not to worry. It was good PR for the hospital!

A strange world we live in!

WRESTLING TEAM

In 1965 I had reached the exalted rank of "senior medical intern" at the Toronto General Hospital. That would correspond roughly to the rank of head wall washer or floor washer in the hospital hierarchy. We interns, however, were fortunate. The head nurses, although higher up the ladder in this hospital, took a motherly interest in our welfare, and were always a constant source of help and information.

I always had a tight feeling in my stomach every time I got called down to the Emerg, and even thirty years later, I don't think I ever lost that feeling completely. It wasn't that it was a bad place to work — quite the contrary. But the variety of problems and their urgency made it very easy to make mistakes, and a patient might suffer tragically as a consequence. However, despite my best intentions, it was going to be another "amateur night" in the Emerg.

It never failed. I had just left the Emerg, got into bed, and the phone rang. The junior intern wanted me right back as there was now a psychotic patient in their department who obviously had to be admitted.

For reasons I never understood, the senior intern on medicine saw these patients in Emerg, assessed them, did a physical exam, wrote a history and orders, usually including adequate sedation, and then the psychiatric resident would see them in "civilized" hours later the next morning. It did nothing to foster good relations with the department of psychiatry, but most of us never considered them "real" doctors anyway.

I struggled back down to Emerg again, a little sleepy, and was ushered into a large side room. Standing in a corner was a tall, young man who had a very wild look in his eyes. That should, of course, have been a clue for me, but I failed to take heed. There were two good-sized orderlies standing on each side of him and, sensibly, they were keeping their distance. He looked menacing, refused to talk, and made a threatening move towards one of the orderlies.

I noticed that the patient, though quite tall, was a little on the fat side and obviously not in good shape. I was still playing rugby, and this was going to be just another scrum, wasn't it? What was wrong with these orderlies anyway? This patient should be no problem. We just had to subdue him, sedate him, and put a call into that psych resident to see him in the morning. Then I could get back to bed.

I moved in, and before I knew what happened I found myself in a monster bear hug, well off the ground and could only intermittently get even one toe on the ground. I should have known by now that fat people often have a lot of muscle under all that camouflage. I had also failed to notice how really tall this big bear was, and now I realized why I was so far off the ground.

We staggered around for a second or so, and then the two orderlies came to my assistance and the four of us landed in a big heap on the terrazzo floor. Very fortunately, the patient was temporarily on the bottom of the pile. Two other interns arrived and sat or lay on whatever part of him was available. The poor patient was still struggling, moving any part that wasn't being kneeled on and or sat upon. Both his strength and stamina were very impressive.

Starting an IV at this point was out of the question, unless somebody had a tranquilizing dart. I yelled to nobody in particular to get ten millilitres of paraldehyde. A very efficient nurse quickly arrived with the medication in a syringe.

At this point, only an intramuscular shot was possible. We tried to pull enough of his pants down to be able to give him a gluteal muscle shot. We had to be careful to give it in the upper outer portion of his butt, and we wanted to be sure that that the needle had not entered a vessel in that large heaving mass that presented to us.

By this time our poor nurse was also trying to restrain him with one hand and had the needle poised above that big "rump roast" that was, amazingly, still refusing to lie still. By pushing down with my hand on his butt cheek, I thought I could assist the nurse in getting in her shot. The needle plunged down and went right through the web and muscle between my right thumb and forefinger.

No injection was made, fortunately, and she pulled the needle straight out and before I could even think, she plunged it down again, this time on the mark. She withdrew expertly, saw no blood in the syringe and injected the contents into the muscle.

I remembered waiting for what seemed a long time, but this guy just hadn't read the book, and showed no signs of settling down. During all this, a chief resident in medicine, Dr Allan Hart, came along and suggested we give him a big dose of chlorpromazine (Largactil). I don't remember the dose, but it was a lot. Of course, he was a big, big patient.

Our nurse, now full of apologies, was soon back with another

Doing it the old-fashioned way. Where was the taser when you needed it?

syringe, and I suggested that this time she put her hand on the rump roast and I could hold on a little lower down. This medication was soon injected. Once again we waited and waited, and eventually we noticed that he seemed to be struggling a little less. We weren't sure if it was because he was just exhausted, or whether our medications were starting to kick in.

Our chief resident felt that because of all the difficulty this patient had caused, it would be justified to call the psych boy, Dr. JP, down for his assessment rather than wait for morning. This brought a big smile to my face, of course. The first bit of good news I had since I got that last phone call.

By this time the patient was showing a little, but a definite, effect of our drugs, and, one by one, we cautiously climbed off him. A policeman who came into the room about that time kindly offered us his handcuffs, and we locked the patient's hands around a heavy metal pipe that connected to one of the in-wall radiators. His legs were tied up in bandages. Soon we had him sitting up and things seemed temporarily under control.

The policeman was full of apologies. He said he had brought the patient in and thought that the man had settled down. He had then gone to talk briefly to his chief on the phone, and when he got back had seen this big pile of humanity on the floor.

He said it had all started when he had responded to a call downtown to apprehend a big man who seemed to have gone completely wild and had injured another man without provocation. He said he and his partner had just stepped out of their cruiser to talk to this man when he suddenly punched his partner, who promptly fell to the ground with a massive nosebleed.

Not knowing what to do, he called in the tactical squad and he and his partner stayed at a safe distance watching our man. His partner continued to bleed, but the wild man seemed to be talking to himself now, and didn't seem to be an immediate threat. The tactical squad arrived and, strangely, the patient was fairly co-operative. They therefore decided not to handcuff him, and loaded him into the back of another squad car putting him in the "dog compartment." The two tactical police cars then followed the patrol car to the emergency department. When they arrived, the patient seemed quiet; he was still talking to himself, but remained co-operative. The tactical team remained a short time and then drove off.

The poor policeman with the bloody nose just kept bleeding and was put directly onto a stretcher in our Emerg. Suspicious that this wild patient might still be a problem, our nice policeman decided to hang around. But, as luck would have it, it was when his chief had called him away to the phone to see how his partner with the bloody nose was making out that action re-commenced.

I remember our policeman also told us that his partner had made a big mess in the front of his cruiser, and in fact had sneezed twice. There would also be a lot of dry cleaning. (I guess getting a history late was better than never getting one at all.)

Dr. JP dutifully arrived. Without asking any questions, he immediately stated that the reason the patient was so agitated, was that we had tied him up. Dr. JP wanted his handcuffs off. I protested, but who was I but a dumb medical senior.

The policeman, I could see, had his reservations too, but he did as Dr. JP directed and unlocked the handcuffs.

Just as soon as the handcuffs were off, the patient's hands shot down to his feet and he had his feet untied and was running down the hall almost in one motion.

I was standing further back in the now-crowded room, and in the mass exodus after the patient I was crowded out at the doorway. About fifty feet down the hall, there was a big crash as the team made the tackle. That nice policeman reproduced his handcuffs (I don't think he'd even had time to put them away) and the patient was now, officially, a "psych patient," and hence — and to my great relief — no longer my responsibility.

He received his third intramuscular injection.

I heard he slept for almost a day after his experience in the Emerg.

BUT I DID FIND MY HEAD

A few months later, another of Dr. JP's patients who had come in through the Emerg was now on our medical ward. This poor soul wandered around for several days, telling the other patients that the doctors were trying to poison all of them.

He was obviously a real concern, and upsetting to the other patients on the ward, but because of the usual bed shortage, there didn't seem anything that anybody could do about it. He was on our ward for several days. I didn't know that he had finally been sent home that morning. But that same afternoon, when Dr. JP and I were sitting at a small table and writing up our interminable notes, one of the nurses handed him the phone.

Soon Dr. JP was yelling into the phone, "Don't do it, sir! Don't do it, sir!"

I was sitting right beside him, because it was a very small table, and I heard what I thought was a muffled explosion over the phone.

There was a pause, and then Dr. JP put down the phone, and turned to me and said, "I think he shot himself!"

Sure enough, when the police arrived at his address the patient was dead, shot through the head.

I guess even the professionals — let alone the patients — can have a bad day.

MORE WRESTLING

In case the reader thinks that I was always being beaten up, or worse, that I was beating up on some of these patients, let me tell you about Dr John Steele.

He was a very dignified and very hard-working neurology resident who, even under the most difficult circumstances, carried out his duties impeccably. His work was excellent and he never raised his voice. He had one of those fancy English accents that you just knew meant he came from "good breeding." Even his clothes seemed to never be wrinkled. He was two years ahead of us in his residency and he was almost ready to write his fellowship examinations in neurology.

Compared to Dr. Steele, the rest of us were mere peasants.

One afternoon, I heard that very distinctive voice of his, but it was much louder than I had ever heard it before, and I could even detect some excitement in it. Indeed, this was very unusual. Down the hall I could hear someone running and then, amazingly, an old man flashed by. He was very thin and looked far too old to be running anywhere near that fast.

Dr. Steele suddenly appeared, at full gallop, crying "Sir! Sir!" Two interns and a whole covey of nurses followed him. Shortly after, I heard the typical thud that comes when a good tackle is made on a hardwood floor.

Before long, John reappeared, perhaps somewhat triumphantly, at the head of a procession made up of John holding a very skinny leg, walking beside an intern who was holding the other skinny leg, and two young nurses each holding a skinny arm. The patient was facing up and about three feet off the ground.

Dr. Steele spied me and yelled for me to get ten milliliters of the infamous paraldehyde. Pretty soon I was sitting under the patient on my buttocks, looking up, trying to find the famous outer quadrant of the patient's buttocks. Somewhat inexpertly, I injected the poor guy as he faced the ceiling above.

We were all amazed at how quickly he settled down. In fact, we had over-dosed him to some extent, considering his age and relative lack of body mass. He slept all night, under close observation, as we wanted to be sure he didn't get into respiratory difficulty.

Fortunately, when he awakened the next day, psychiatry took over. I just draw this little story to the reader's attention to try to show that even the best and most dignified doctors have difficulty with some of these patients.

The medical residents always felt more comfortable when these poor psychiatric patients arrived with a genuine medical problem.

If they had overdosed on a drug and were unconscious, they were given supportive care, and usually "intubated" (that's the big rubber tube, or more recently plastic tube, with the little bag on it that is shoved down the windpipe through the vocal cords to keep the airway open). The usual blood work and physical was done, and what history that could be obtained was written laboriously on the history sheet. Depending on the type of poison, when known, special orders were instituted.

From our point of view, the real problems arose when the patient woke up. Once the patient was considered physically stable, he was handed over to the psychiatry department, like a hot potato. This also freed up one of our precious beds, and we could then get another patient transferred up from the Emerg.

Although people forget, there has always been a bed shortage, even forty years ago, and patients "piled up" in the Emerg or the Emerg holding area.

MAGGOTS

During the winter and spring of 1964, I always walked from our little apartment to the Wellesley Hospital in downtown Toronto, a distance of about ten blocks. Quite often, I would pass an older man going the other way. He was unshaven and generally unkempt and always wore a thick scarf around his neck.

Because I saw him so frequently, I started to say "Hi" to him every morning. He usually responded, but sometimes he seemed to be lost in his thoughts, and when he was like that, it was as if I had never existed.

In those days, street people were never talked about. There were a few hobos, but they seemed few and far between. Certainly in the 1960s, this area of Toronto was a little run down and was reputed to have a large red-light district.

As the winter faded to spring and then towards summer, I noticed that this poor guy was still wearing his thick scarf. In May, in downtown Toronto, the heat and especially the humidity can sometimes be unbearable. When I passed this man on one of these terrible days, he was still wearing that old and very soiled scarf.

A few days later, I saw him lying on a stretcher in one of the single Emerg rooms and I walked over to say "Hi" to him again. He was considered a surgical patient and was not my responsibility.

As I got near his bed, I was suddenly aware of a terrible smell like rotten flesh. On the front of his neck he had a large hole measuring at least 5 centimetres across; the whole mass looked like rotten meat, and was crawling with maggots!

It turned out that he had a carcinoma (an invasive cancer) of his thyroid, and he had never sought medical attention. He had likely had an open sore for several months, but because of the cold weather during the winter months there were no flies. As soon as the hot weather started, the flies would find this raw sore and land on it, and of course lay their eggs. These eggs would soon hatch into maggots.

The tumour, to this point, had spared his trachea and his large carotid vessels. He had apparently collapsed on the street, and was brought to the Emerg about an hour earlier. I was surprised to see how emaciated he was; this hadn't been obvious under all his clothing.

He was cleaned up, as much as possible, and was admitted to a surgical floor. The surgical staff found him inoperable. Some type of radiation was being considered, but perhaps mercifully, he died quite suddenly.

I had never seen maggots in a human wound before, but I understand that "sterile" maggots have now made a comeback for cleaning up some types of wounds.

PING PONG BALL IN A BIRD CAGE

In 1968, I met a hard-working architect who had a severely narrowed aortic valve. This is the valve at the top of the heart that stops the blood from falling back into the main pumping chamber when the heart relaxes prior to the next beat. The aorta is the largest artery in the body and is about as thick as the base of our thumb. As the valve narrows, the heart has to work harder and harder to get the blood into circulation. The result is that the muscle of the heart gets thicker and thicker, and it eventually fails.

The patient may also be prone to sudden death due to arrhythmias. The narrowing has to be pretty severe for this to happen, however, and frequently these people are successfully followed under observation for many years. My particular patient was getting into the danger zone, and I referred him down to St Paul's Hospital in Vancouver because at that time (fall 1969) we didn't have open-heart services at the Royal Columbian.

He underwent successful surgery, and I saw him periodically for follow-ups. His aortic valve had been replaced by a Starr-Edwards valve (described in chapter 4).

As the patient was an architect, and after he had recovered well from his surgery, my wife and I interviewed him to design and build a house for our growing family.

Before we had made the final arrangements, I got a sudden call to the Royal Columbian Emerg one evening. Our architect had just been admitted with no blood pressure. When I saw him, I could hear only very muffled heart sounds. Although I tried several times, I could not reliably take his blood pressure. He had a very weak carotid pulse, but was still conscious. I had no idea what had happened, and he died within a few minutes.

A subsequent autopsy showed that the ball had got stuck at the top of the birdcage and hence had made his artificial valve inoperative.

For some reason, these balls were not standing up to the flinging back and forth with every heartbeat. Apparently, some of the balls were breaking into pieces and causing emboli (that is, broken ball bits would be blocking arteries) in various parts of the body. Some of the balls were swelling up, and getting stuck in their birdcage, as with our patient.

These balls were originally made with a rubberized plastic material. After a number of these disastrous incidents, the manufacturer started making the balls out of carbonized stainless steel and, overall, had long-term success.

In the mid-sixties at the Toronto General Hospital, we followed all the patients who had undergone aortic valve surgery and 50 percent were known to be dead within three years following their surgery.

It's always strange and unsettling to look back and remember these cases. Almost always they were really nice people who would very likely have survived, if only the technology had been there at the time.

Starting in about the 1980s, the more common practice for aortic valve replacement was using animal tissue, particularly a heavily modified and chemically treated pig's aortic valve. The advantage of using animal tissue in the aortic area was that it reduced the chance of emboli forming on the material. Most of the patients with this type of valve in the aortic area can get away without using blood thinners (warfarin).

Things have come a long way in valve construction, in the anesthetics at the time of surgery, and in the overall post-operative management.

FAITH AT ODDS WITH MEDICAL PRACTICE

One day in the early 1970s, a young lady suffered a severe laceration on the back of her leg, cutting the popliteal artery (the extension of the femoral artery crossing the back of the knee). This is a very large artery and supplies the blood to the leg below the knee. (If you feel very carefully behind your knee, you may feel this pulsating artery, but it's often quite difficult to find without practice.) She was rushed to the Royal Columbian Emerg and had lost a great deal of blood.

This woman, who had a young family, was a Jehovah's Witness and refused blood transfusions. She stayed in our intensive care unit for about fifteen days and I watched her gradually deteriorate. Because she didn't have enough blood, and therefore hemoglobin, to carry sufficient oxygen to her tissues, she gradually declined and in the end died. Her decline was much like what you would see if you cut through a branch on a tree so that the sap could no longer run up the branch.

Her extremities became very cold and she was as pale as I can ever remember seeing anybody. She was close to being the same colour as her sheets. Often, when the body is in a crisis like this, it will shut down the blood supply to most of the not immediately vital areas. Her limbs became very cold and we could not, after a while, feel any of her peripheral pulses. When I lifted any one of her limbs, I don't think she could even feel them. She was still conscious, but almost in a dreamlike state. If we had warmed her up with heater blankets, it would likely have increased her metabolism and resulting in her dying that much sooner. Her vital organs, such as her kidneys and her liver, were also not getting sufficient oxygen to function adequately. The kidneys would function in the short term, but if left in this state for long, would suffer irreversible damage. In retrospect, it might have been interesting to have her placed on high-pressure oxygen (hyperbaric oxygen) if it had been available.

Over the next few days she simply deteriorated and died. The process seemed very strange and would have been totally preventable if she had not refused blood transfusions.

This strange shunting of valuable resources away from other areas to preserve brain and cardiac function is a little reminiscent of the phenomena that we saw when that young man came into our Emerg with the torn pulmonary artery, described in chapter 4.

In the corridor outside of our intensive care unit, while all this was going on, there was always a large crowd of people. In fact, the crowd got so big that the hospital security had to get involved to be sure that there was enough room to move stretchers and equipment in and out of the intensive care unit.

It did show the concern of the Jehovah's Witness community, but her death seemed to me a terrible tragedy.

During my years at the Royal Columbian, I got to know a lot of these Witnesses when they developed various forms of heart disease. Their dedication was simply remarkable, but — from my point of view at least — seemed tragic.

OPEN HEART SURGERY WITHOUT BLOOD TRANSFUSION

His name was Mr. H, and he was a Jehovah's Witness (JW). He was the sort of person everyone likes, and he was very open about his belief.

I saw him in the office in 1980 because he had aortic stenosis (narrowing of the aortic valve at the top of the heart) and he was gradually getting into trouble with shortness of breath on exertion. Because he was a Jehovah's Witness and would refuse blood transfusions, his family doctor was a little hesitant to refer him to a cardiologist. Up until then, the JWs had been allowed to "donate" blood three weeks before their surgery and then again one week before surgery.

The body was almost able to make up for these two donations before the surgery, so there would be two extra units of the patient's own blood available — about 500 millilitre per unit — at the time of surgery. Then, during their surgery they could have this blood infused back into them to load the pump. Like most pumps, there is a "dead space" to account for the space in all the tubing, the pump mechanism, and the space in the blood oxygenator. This amounted to roughly two units. If the patient didn't lose blood because of the actual surgery, after most of the contents of the pump were drained back into him, he would theoretically end up with about the same hemoglobin that he started with before surgery.

The open-heart surgeons, of course, tried to avoid blood loss as much as possible during surgery, but some blood loss was inevitable, even in the best of circumstances. For reasons that have still not been entirely explained, some patients just seemed to "ooze" more than others. It was possible to filter some of the blood that had oozed out during the surgery and transfuse it back at the end, and even during surgery.

Despite all these advances, there was usually a "deficit" at the end of the procedure, and in normal circumstances this deficit, depending on how severe it was, was made up with donated blood.

At about this time in history, the head of the JWs decided that even receiving the patient's own blood back during surgery was, for some reason, not acceptable. Understandably, being unable to accept blood transfusions increased the risks of open-heart surgery considerably. At that time in Canada we did not have a lot of experience operating on these people when we could not give them that extra blood when necessary. There were two centres in Texas that specialized in these types of problems, and we occasionally sent patients down there to at least partially reduce the risks.

My poor patient knew all these issues, and was understandably reluctant to undergo surgery until there was no other choice. I followed him along, and because of his continuing deterioration, we eventually performed heart catheterization on him. He was found to have a very seriously narrowed aortic valve, while the other valves of his heart and his coronary arteries were normal.

Under normal circumstances, we would have recommended him for surgical replacement of this defective valve. However, he suddenly gave us no choice, because he arrived in our Emerg one evening shortly after his heart catheterization, in heart failure, with his lungs full of fluid. With great difficulty, he responded to our treatment with drugs and was again comfortable. However, once a patient goes into failure with this problem, it is likely that he will not be able to live much longer without having this valve replaced.

His congregation and his pastor were extremely supportive and were agreeable to sending him down to Texas for this very dangerous operation. At that time, replacement of the aortic valve had become fairly common, but not without blood transfusions. A trip to Texas seemed to be his best chance for survival. It would be a very expensive undertaking, but his pastor had agreed to pay for the surgery in Texas. He certainly had his entire congregation onside.

By this time, I had got to know this patient quite well and liked him a lot. And although I disagreed with the JW doctrines, I admired his conviction. Indeed, it would be difficult to find a more dedicated and moral community.

Mr. H said to me, just before he was transferred from the Royal Columbian to Houston, that he hoped that he would survive and do well. But if he did die, he hoped that it would be early in the post-operative period, because he knew that it would be very expensive to lie in their intensive care unit day after day and then expire. Even at that time it was about two thousand American dollars a day to stay in their high-tech unit.

Unfortunately, Mr. H spent thirty days in this unit post-operatively and then died. His congregation paid a huge sum for all this without a whimper. I felt very unhappy about this, but there hadn't seemed to be any alternative.

The JW community is a very tightly knit group. If they like the doctor then it seems that doctor will get to see more and more members of the same group. For some reason, I gradually became the "JW doctor" for our area.

Dr Miyagishima, at St. Paul's Hospital in Vancouver, subsequently developed expertise in the area of handling open-heart cases without the use of donated blood. We didn't have to send any more of our patients down south at tremendous expense for the patient and their community. I think that for some period I was sending him more JW patients than all my colleagues combined.

On the positive side, this situation forced us to be more conservative with blood and encouraged the development of "primeless" open-heart pumps and other techniques to make "bloodless surgery" more of a routine.

This became increasingly important with the reluctance of people to donate blood and, of course, with the newly found risks of AIDS and hepatitis B and C in donated blood.

MARIJUANA IS HARMLESS?

For lack of a better name, we will call him "Hippie Mack."

He was in his early 40s and definitely a hippie. He was long-haired, I would guess hadn't had a bath for weeks, and his beard was matted.

Around his mouth was the usual brown ring that we see on someone who is a heavy smoker and never washes his face. Mack had been driving his pick-up truck and apparently crossed the centre line of the road and went head-on into a car coming in the opposite direction.

The driver of the other vehicle was killed immediately and Hippie Mack suffered a broken sternum (breast bone). He also had a cardiac contusion; that is, he had bruised the front of his heart, and the sac around his heart was rapidly filling with blood.

This crash had occurred in the municipality of Surrey, a relatively short distance from the Royal Columbian Hospital, and when Hippie Mack arrived at our Emerg, he was desperately ill. This was in the days just before echo cardiology (use of ultrasound to provide image of heart's internal structures) and we made the diagnosis of cardiac tamponade mostly on the basis of the physical findings. (Cardiac tamponade is caused by fluid building up in the sac that we have around our heart, and this fluid, if under pressure, can squeeze the heart and stop its normal function.) The ECG and chest x-ray were helpful, but it was the physical findings on people like "Hippie Mack" that determined how we should act, and these findings can, indeed, indicate an absolute emergency.

In an emergency situation, a large bore needle is put through the chest wall into this sac, and the fluid is extracted. Most cardiologists don't relish this procedure and there are, understandably, some hazards in performing it. When Hippie Mack arrived he had virtually no blood pressure and his neck veins were very prominent. I had no choice but to "get on with it." Once I had taken off a small amount of this blood in his pericardial sac, he improved very rapidly, but later that afternoon I had to tap him again.

Over the next few days, his other injuries improved and within a week he was put onto a medical ward. Unfortunately, he developed one of those so-called "auto-immune" reactions, and every few days I would have to tap him again. The fluid went from blood red gradually to straw-coloured, and with time, the taps became less and less frequent.

Because of these multiple visits, I got to know Hippie Mack a little better, and he told me about his life and his personal experience with drugs. He was not what you would call a very savoury character. Besides his welfare checks, he supplemented his income by selling drugs, mostly marijuana, to school kids. Sometimes, he got his hands on other drugs that he sold, but he insisted that he didn't use these other drugs himself.

When he was driving his truck and was all "toked up," he noted that sometimes he would come to a stop sign, stop his vehicle, and then he would realize that the stop sign was still 100 yards off. He would then move his truck forward and stop again, only to find that he was still twenty-five yards from the stop sign. His depth perception was obviously very poor or non-existent.

I have no doubt that Hippie Mack's horrific accident was at least, in part, caused by his toking up.

He didn't seem to show any remorse over being responsible for the death of a young man — perhaps the sign of the true psychopath?

I lost track of Hippie Mack, but I wouldn't be surprised if he caused further disasters.

I think the majority of physicians would think it cheaper to incarcerate these people indefinitely until they can prove that they will no longer be a menace to society

.

PEOPLE FROM VENUS?

The next three episodes from the emergency department are of a sexual nature, and the reader may not be interested. However, the Emerg sees its fair share of these problems, which are just part of the human condition.

Urinary Catheter

In 1962, while still a junior at the Toronto General, I was on my four-week rotation in urology. Like most departments, it was a very busy place. I was ordered down to the Emerg to put a urinary catheter in a young man's bladder. It didn't seem to matter if we were on our very first day in the rotation, or our twenty-eighth day, we were expected to know and do all the functions of our job from the start. I, naturally, tried to do what I was told.

This young fellow claimed that he suddenly couldn't pass his water. Because he seemed to be in some distress, the senior surgical intern had requested the junior on urology to come down right away, with the usual instructions of "get on with it." Fortunately, both for me and especially for the patient, I had passed these catheters in my extern job in Orillia the summer before.

When I saw my patient, a young man in his early twenties, I vaguely wondered why he was having trouble. He looked far too young to be having prostate trouble. Could it be a bladder stone, or severe gonorrhea? I had no idea. In any case, with the words "get on with it" still very much in my mind, I started to pass the rubber tube up his penis. I was a little timid and glanced at his face to see if I was hurting him. Much to my surprise, he had flopped his head back, and he was rolling it side to side with his tongue hanging out. I was soon in his bladder and there was very little urine. Moreover, passing the catheter had been very easy, suggesting that there was no obstruction.

It seemed this poor fellow was getting his "jollies" by being catheterized! This incident occurred at the change of shift, and the next shift recognized him. He had apparently been in on two previous occasions that same week. Likely, when he had worn out his welcome in one hospital, he would move to the next. My mother used to charitably say, "It takes all types to make a world."

Vibrator — Get with the beat!

Early one morning, years later, I was just leaving the Emerg at the Royal Columbian, when a nurse said, "Oh doctor, you forgot your lunch."

I should have been on my guard because this particular nurse was always playing tricks on me. I told her it wasn't my lunch, and she said, "Open it anyway." I didn't see much harm in opening it. It was just a brown paper bag and did look like a small lunch bag.

When I opened the bag, there was a large vibrator inside. Unwashed, I might add!

Cory Brown was the emergency doctor during the night shift and had not yet left the Emerg. He told me that a young man had come in with this object stuck in his rectum. It measured about eight inches long and was about one inch in diameter. The back end was flat and there was a small switch low down on the side.

Somehow, the patient had shoved it too far up, the blunt end had passed through his anal sphincter, and now he couldn't retrieve it. Poor Cory had to try to get it out with the various instruments that are available in the Emerg. Removing it was pretty important, because if it couldn't be retrieved, it would be necessary to perform abdominal surgery (a laparotomy). Cory told me that in the course of trying to get this damn thing out, his manoeuvres had inadvertently turned it on and off several times.

When he finally did get it out, the patient was so embarrassed he "forgot" to ask for his vibrator back before he left.

I wondered if you could get any money for it at a garage sale!

Beer Bottle

Another morning, in 1995, I was passing through the x-ray department, when Dr. Ed Keratew, the head of our radiology department at the Royal Columbian, asked me to look at an x-ray hanging up on the big viewing box.

It was a flat plate of the abdomen, and I assumed that someone, as a joke, had placed a beer bottle on top of this lady's abdomen before taking the x-ray. He assured me it was real and showed me the lateral view, which showed that same beer bottle. I said that someone could then have placed the beer bottle beside the person and just taken another picture.

Dr. Keratew looked a little insulted that I would even suggest something like this. Because he was a very straight guy, super conscientious, and really not into practical jokes like this, I believed him. If the tables had been reversed, it might have been a different story.

Ed then went on to explain what had happened. Apparently, there was a big drunken party in Coquitlam and this patient had passed out on the floor. One of her "friends" had stuck a narrow-necked beer bottle up her vagina and then another "friend" had given the base of the bottle what had to be a pretty good kick. It had ripped up through the back wall of her vagina and entered her abdominal cavity. She was already up in the operating room when Ed was speaking to me.

Ed was always quite serious and therefore, naturally, I tried to bug him from time to time. So I asked him who would get the return on the bottle, the patient or the surgeon operating upstairs?

This lady made a full recovery but, of course, now had a big new abdominal scar resulting from her surgery. No doubt, she is a little more careful now where she goes to party.

One day, I was telling Harry some of this bizarre sexual stuff that I had seen in the Emerg, and the various contortions that people go through to satisfy their urges. Of course, Harry too had seen more than his share of the same problems that we all experience working in a place like Emerg.

Right out of the blue, Harry said, "Tom, do you know why dogs lick their balls?"

"Harry, what kind of a question is that? Do I have to answer it?"

Harry seemed serious, and I knew if I wanted to see what was on his mind, I had better play his game.

I volunteered, "Well, I suppose it's a form of a sponge bath for them."

"No," he said, "it's because they can!"

"You mean if man could, he would?"

He replied, "You got the idea. You're not just another pretty face!"

CHAPTER 6

Psychiatry and Mind Games

WHEN WE WERE YOUNG — AND GAY?

In 1948, my friend and I were both eleven years old and our parents had enrolled us in an all-boys private school. David was quieter than I was, and perhaps a little small for his age, but we got on famously and he was really a friend of the family; his father and my father were both in a reserve unit of the Queen's Own Rifles. Besides, David lived just down the street. We had played together since my earliest memories.

When I look back, I can see that besides being quiet, he was particularly gentle, and tended to avoid the rough and tumble activities favoured by most of my other friends. I remember that on one occasion, he wanted me to play "house" with him. I probably thought that was girl stuff and too tame for my personality, and I don't remember actually playing that game.

During our time at Upper Canada College, the lower school — the "Prep" — was pretty good. There were lots of sports and we went swimming once a week. I don't remember much emphasis on religion, apart from the Lord's Prayer every morning. However, the atmosphere was somewhat constricting, discipline was strict, and the only woman that I can remember was what amounted to the grade two teacher. The school didn't enrol pupils until grade two.

We were supposed to be tough, and minor injuries were basically ignored. I remember being somewhat surprised when the captain of our team refused to get up immediately after what seemed a pretty innocuous tackle, and thinking, "Is he a "wimp" or what?"

It turned out that he had broken his tibia just above his ankle.

I guess when we found out what had happened, we all felt a little guilty — for about thirty seconds — and perhaps we were a little jealous later that nobody made a big fuss over us; and, of course, didn't get to wear that big cast with all the signatures on it. Duff was pretty good, however, in letting us try out his neat crutches.

David and I, unfortunately, weren't put in the same class, the school being big enough to have two classes of about twenty-five boys for every grade. We continued to see a lot of each other, however, and continued to play together at his house or mine. David was into arts and music at school and my father, by contrast, put my older brother and me into special boxing.

Each year, the school put on a very special performance of one of the Gilbert and Sullivan musicals. Naturally, my brother and I would not be seen dead in one of these things, and besides we both had a wooden ear. My mother was a little bit musical, but my father didn't have time for that sort of nonsense.

This is where David shone. Not only did he apparently have a good voice, he could also act. Each year, the production would have a final dress rehearsal in the afternoon, and the parents would come to watch the show that night. Our entire school would be marched into the gymnasium in the afternoon and we would be seated cross-legged, jammed together, on the hardwood floor. It wasn't all that bad, and besides we missed two classes in the afternoon. It was almost a festive occasion, and all the less artistic boys like myself would hoot and holler, as much as we could get away with, during the production.

On this particular occasion, it was *The Pirates of Penzance*. Of course, since we were an all boys' school, the authorities had to dress some individuals as girls.

When David appeared on stage there was a palpable silence. He was now twelve years old and gorgeous! His eyes were very skilfully made up (he had dark eyes anyway) and he sported a very stylish and sexy wig. Somehow, the make-up people had pushed him up from below and it appeared that he had a full bosom.

I was just sitting there and I couldn't take my eyes off him. I even imagined that I was getting a little bit of an erection! In my mind, I immediately changed the subject, and everything settled down.

However, after that I couldn't look on David in quite the same way. At school the next day, he didn't look any different than he had before. His eyes were pretty ordinary and his beautiful bosom was gone. We continued to see each other, but with advancing time, less frequently. As so often happens, I lost track of him completely by the end of high school.

Forty years later, on one of my trips to Toronto, I ran into one of my classmates from our old school. He told me that he had run into our mutual friend David who had said, "If you ever see Tom again, say hi." He apparently remembered me as always having been nice to him.

I said I would be very happy to see him again after so many years. "Do you have his number?"

My acquaintance said he couldn't give it to me because David was dead. "Yes," he said, "he died of AIDS."

I was saddened and also dumbfounded. How could I have been so stupid? It was as if a light bulb had gone off in my head. It hadn't even occurred to me he was gay. It would probably be pretty obvious to most people nowadays, but back then we didn't even think that way.

When I was a teenager, we thought that homosexuality was a joke. Nobody would actually commit sodomy would they? Too disgusting to even contemplate! Getting into bed with another man? For that matter, we often wondered why any woman would want to get into bed with a man, we are so ugly. We have patches of hair here and there, and often we don't have hair where we should. And if there ever was something that was truly ugly it had to be our external genitalia.

In those days, homosexuality was thought to be truly evil, and most people thought this belief was supported by their religion. As kids, David and I were dutifully marched off to church each Sunday morning, and to Sunday school the same afternoon, where we had to recite some passage from the Bible that we had to memorize the Saturday night before. Our religious upbringing ruined half our precious weekends!

My father and David's father were so right wing that their red necks would probably shine in the dark. My father, for example, wouldn't talk to Germans or to Japanese for years after the war; and when I started to date the girl I eventually married, he was upset because she had a very German last name.

Fortunately, for the sake of our family dynamics, my brothers and I weren't gay. Our parents weren't bad people, in fact, quite the opposite. They were just the product of their times. I have subsequently wondered if David ever came "out of the closet" while his parents were still alive. Knowing the mentality of my parents' times, I would doubt it.

In David's case, I believe he was gay from a very early time. I can remember him even before kindergarten and he was always "different;" that may have been one of the reasons I liked him. Certainly, I would not be competing with him and he would never be a threat in any way.

When I got back to work at the hospital, I ran into my philosopher sage, Harry.

"What do you think of this 'homo stuff'?" I asked, "Do we make a choice, or are we born that way?"

Harry replied in his usual direct way, "The churches are crazy. Nobody makes that choice. Do you remember making the heterosexual choice? And besides, do you think you would be able to turn someone from one to the other?"

Harry continued, "I have asked a lot of my patients who are gay when they first realized that they were different, and universally they have told me that they were very young. In all cases their realization was well before puberty."

"So, Harry, something goes wrong very early on and is likely beyond the patient's control?"

Harry told me that he didn't like the word "wrong" but felt that "this gay thing" must be genetic, or somehow influenced in the uterus. He said that there was now very little evidence that even the most bizarre early upbringing influenced one's sexual orientation.

Certainly, Sigmund Freud's idea of a domineering mother and a submissive father to be a cause has not been borne out. Personally, I never liked that Freudian stuff anyway that we had to learn in our psychology course. (Harry had long expressed the view that psychology was basically common sense, and when it didn't make sense, it was nonsense.) There was, however, one exception; I thought the Freudian idea of a church steeple being conceived as an upright penis might have some truth in it.

Another interesting finding that would seem to refute Freud is the fact that a small number of children who were followed after they had a special form of surgery did not lose their heterosexual tendencies. This was a group of boys that were genetically males, but due to various circumstances, had either been born with poorly formed external genitalia or had theirs severely damaged at an early age. Cosmetically it was always easier to form a rudimentary vagina than to try to make a penis and scrotum, and consequently, these little boys were "turned" into girls and raised as girls. But, as they got older, they didn't lose their attraction for women. (I think Freud may have been one of those "scientists" who come up with an interesting theory and then force the facts to suit the theories.)

Harry wondered if a hormone or antibody change during uterine life could affect one's sexual orientation. He was quite perceptive back then, as a recent study has shown that a child born with numerous older blood brothers has a greater chance of being gay and, in fact, the greater the number of older brothers, the greater the chance of being gay. These older brothers have to be biological brothers; adopted brothers have no effect on the next brother's gay orientation.

This study sounds similar to the Rh problem, whereby a mother who is Rh negative and has an Rh-positive mate and then has an Rh-positive foetus, may produce antibodies to the child's Rh antigen and damage the foetus's blood cells. The more Rh-positive children she has, the worse the damage to the next Rh-positive child's blood cells. Perhaps, then, in some cases, the mother may start producing antibodies to the maleness of her child, and the more male children she has, the higher the antibody level.

What about a gay gene? Identical twins are supposed to have the same genetic makeup. If one twin is gay, why is the other twin gay only 50 percent of the time and not 100 percent of the time? (It is thought that this may be due to "switches" being turned on and off activating certain segments of the genetic code, something to do with "methylation.")

> Methylation is a biochemical term for adding a methyl group ($—CH_3$) to a larger molecule, changing the properties of that molecule.

Recent studies of the male gay brain with PET scanning and at autopsy suggest that structurally a portion of this type of male brain is similar to a heterosexual woman's brain and the lesbian brain is similar to the straight male brain. These findings occur very early and likely in the uterus. The brain changes may be hormone induced and if so likely occur during the first three months of pregnancy. Who then can say we made the choice to be gay or straight? Sexuality is obviously extremely complicated. (I think most of us knew this even in high school!)

Could there be other traits that go along with being gay?

Those who work in a hospital environment day in and day out have often noticed that the gay male nurse appears to be more nurturing than his heterosexual counterpart. A straight male is less likely to walk up to a patient's bed and say, "Sir, can I fluff up your pillow for you?" It wouldn't even cross our dull minds. I also suspect that gay males may have other inherent traits, such as creativity, artistic ability, labile emotions, and a huge and bizarre sense of humour.

As an aside, an example of this humour comes to mind. On one occasion, Paul, one of my favourite male nurses, was practically doubled over trying to open the stupid safe in the cardiac intensive care unit. It contained narcotics and had some sort of lock on it that was difficult to open.

I said to Paul, "If you stay there any longer, I'm going to jump you!"

He stood up and whirled around and I thought, "Geez! I guess I have gone too far this time!"

He merely said, "Promises, promises!" and then bent over and continued working on this stubborn lock.

These traits are, among other things, behavioural, and may be passed along in your genes. If you can raise Canadian beavers in captivity without access to dam building materials for several generations, and then put them back in the wilds and they start to build dams and lodges again, this must mean that some of these behavioural traits are passed along in their DNA.

An even more interesting case is our Monarch butterfly. It flies down into the Deep South every winter, but takes several generations to make the round trip. That information had to be encoded somewhere; the butterfly couldn't have learned where to go from its parents.

Harry didn't like my choice of the word "wrong" when I mentioned that something had gone wrong, perhaps during early development of a gay individual. He told me being gay was in fact "normal."

"Okay Harry, what possible biological advantage could being gay be to the organism? And besides, wouldn't it be self-eliminating?" Harry, always the reader and sage, had read what he termed a wonderful article in *Discover* magazine. To paraphrase it, he began:

You have to stop thinking of the single organism, man, and start thinking of the entity, mankind. Mother Nature thinks of us as a sort of beehive, or perhaps more realistically a termite nest. We aren't all designed to be Rhodes Scholars. Some of us have to do the pick and shovel work. Some of us have to be good soldiers. Others are long and thin and become endurance athletes and hence can cover great distances, an attribute which may benefit the group. Others are big and strong and can lift heavy weights. Termites have their structures too. Some are workers, some are soldiers, and some are drones. And there are probably many sub-groups. Each individual usually benefits the group.

Go back 30,000 years and anatomically, man was little different than he is now. A kingdom or a tribe might have consisted of, for argument's sake, 1,000 or more individuals. Perhaps on the other side of the river there was another tribe of roughly the same number of people. Let us suppose the group on the west side of the river had a spontaneous mutant that determined that a small percentage of the male population of the group would end up being gay, perhaps 2–5 percent.

This group would not be a serious impediment to the group as a whole because there would be plenty of sperm to go around, and with numbers anywhere near 1,000 there would not be a major problem with genetic diversity. (That is, there would be sufficient numbers to prevent problems of inbreeding.) As we know, this group of gay men would probably not be into the rough and tumble as much as their heterosexual counterparts, and would not be out showing off in front of the girls.

When the woolly mammoth comes into town, one of the big strong heterosexual males ties a rock to the end of a stick and tries to bonk the beast over the head, and of course gets stomped into the ground. When the sabre tooth tiger comes to pay a visit, one of our heroes takes a sharpened stick and pokes the tiger in the ribs and the tiger gores him in front of the entire group.

The gay guys see all this, notice that there are a lot of rabbits running around and think they just might be good to eat, and they devise a trap or snare to provide meat for the kingdom. They also notice that those woolly mammoths are awkward and clumsy and dig a big pit, put branches over it with a favourite food on top, perhaps bananas, and then when the beast falls in they can work him over without getting stomped on.

Also, if they could launch a sharpened stick at the tiger from a distance, with a bow, they could injure him without getting gored every time. They may also notice that the very young children are always wet and cold, and they stay home and help the women repair the roofs on their thatched houses, perhaps preventing the kids from further hazards.

Then, when the two kingdoms go to war, which always seems inevitable, the group on the west side of the river has healthier fighters and better weapons, and inevitably wins. The gay men had made their improvements from a nurturing standpoint, likely not realizing the military spin-offs.

Genocide is probably not a new thing, and west wipes out east (they probably keep a few of the good-looking girls, but otherwise wipe out east completely) and takes over the other side of the river.

So, that spontaneous mutant in the context of mankind is a biological advantage, and it gets passed on. If all this seems a reasonable scenario, then one might consider that being gay is a normal variant!

"So that's it?" I asked.

"More or less," Harry replied.

I shook my head. "Harry, you make life so complicated. When I was in high school I thought gayness was a joke; and then I thought it was evil. When I got to medical school I thought it was a medical problem, and now, you tell me it's normal!"

CONVEYOR BELT GENETICS

I ran into Harry a week later and he said, "Do you remember all that stuff we talked about? Heredity, genes, DNA coding, behavioural traits, switches turning on and off?"

I answered "Yes," although I didn't remember any discussion

about switches being turned on and off. I knew that Harry's mind was boiling over again, and there was no way of stopping him.

"Well," he said, "that is all BS! None of that stuff is true. In fact, the way we are made is that Mother Nature (that woman again!) is sitting there and as we are being made we are actually on a big conveyor belt, passing in front of her. The top of our skull is off, exposing the top of our brains, and, as we go by, she inserts computer chips."

I decide that my friend was really "off his rocker" this time, and I expressed this sentiment, but he ignored me and went on as if I hadn't even spoken a word.

"As the brains go by, she puts these chips in, sometimes in a seemingly random fashion.

"As we discussed previously, 2–5 percent of brains get the gay chip, some get the music chip, some get the language chip, the math chip, and perhaps one in a hundred get the psychopath chip and so on. If your mother and father are both musicians, you are more likely to get one of those too, but not necessarily. You could even end up with a chip that is unique. Those are the random chips, that spontaneous mutant thing, and you could become world famous, or it could be a lethal chip and you could be extinguished."

A cheerful thought. I certainly didn't get a language or a music chip, but at least I didn't get one of those "lethal chips."

"Harry," I asked, "what about a good luck chip? Some people seem to be much luckier than others, as if they had a horseshoe in their pocket."

"Tom, you've got it wrong; you have to get that horseshoe up your ass. After you get all your brain chips, you then have to go into the knee–chest position on Mother Nature's conveyor belt and, if you are lucky, Mother Nature's helper, Lady Luck, will put a horseshoe up your ass!"

Anyway, Harry was off to the lab and I had had my lesson for the day.

Harry was pulling my leg, of course, but his concept of computer chips being put into our brains is perhaps a little easier to visualize than all the DNA coding stuff that we had to memorize for our exams. The interaction of all these genes and the role of our upbringing will likely never be completely understood.

I know I have over-simplified these gay traits, and not even

Harry's conveyer belt, a simpler version of that DNA stuff
we learned before our exams.

mentioned some of the obvious sub-groups such as the "man's
man" gay person, perhaps the Rock Hudson type, who appears
more manly than most of us heterosexual types.

There seems to be a genetic cause to gayness, as the twin study
mentioned above seems to show. In some families there also appears to be a mild hereditary component when the number of
gay individuals runs above the average occurring in the broad
population. It all seems very complicated and there are probably
a whole host of causes.

But, perhaps, the big lesson in of all this should be that the
gay individual should not consider himself "guilty." He has not
"sinned" any more than a small child who grew up with red hair
instead of brown hair. Society in general seems pretty afraid of
the unknown. Until we get to know some of our inherent differences, we will have these unfortunate reservations about other
groups.

Pedophiles are another interesting and totally different group, and statistically are less frequently seen, percentage-wise, in the gay community than in the straight community.

And the person with the "psychopath chip" doesn't care and just doesn't understand all the terrible grief he is causing. He has no humanity, and worse, usually has no insight into his problem.

Fortunately, the "pedophile chip" and the "psychopath chip" are individually fairly uncommon, and the chance of them both occurring in the same individual is even much less common.

When they do co-exist in the same person, however, they make an explosive combination that can cause widespread damage in any community.

I suspect many of those people caught with "kiddie" pornographic material are pedophiles, but fortunately have not, in most cases, been given the "psychopath chip." Hence they have the good sense and enough humanity not to act on their impulses in the real world. They can rationalize that their behaviour is "not hurting anyone," as after all, it's all out in cyber space. However, they conveniently forget that some poor kid has undergone unspeakable horrors on the other side of the world, in places like Thailand, to make this video.

Some of these sub-groups are likely not beneficial to either the termites' nest or to human society, and may possess a random and very unfortunate trait exposed by a combination of bad genes.

Enough of all this, but Harry really gets me thinking!

Pet Chip

A short time after my conversation with Harry, I had had one of those awful days in Emerg. We had had a heavy snowfall and, at the best of times, Vancouver just isn't prepared. The streets aren't ploughed until the second or third day when the authorities finally realize that the snow just isn't going to go away. Everybody has summer tires or those so-called "all-weather tires" and, of course, we don't know how to drive on icy streets.

On this particular day, our Emerg was even more packed than usual. There were the usual broken hips and Colles' fractures (a very common type of wrist fracture) caused by falls on the icy pavement.

But also there were lots of severe cardiac problems. Older people, out pushing their cars and/or shovelling snow, were getting unaccustomed exercise, and frustration and anxiety were likely playing a role. Also, the cold weather and accompanying vasoconstriction of their blood vessels were likely raising their already elevated blood pressure.

In any case, we had way more than our usual five or so cases of heart attacks, unstable anginas, or heart failure, in our Emerg.

One nice lady, well into her seventies, had been admitted with a massive heart attack. Her vital signs were still quite stable and the pain had largely settled because of the intravenous morphine we had given her.

Her ECG, however, showed she had a very severe problem. The whole front of her heart was in the process of dying.

When I explained that we had to admit her to hospital, and had found a bed for her in the coronary care unit, she said she couldn't come in; she just had to go home. She was very nice about it, and I remember her telling us how much she had appreciated all the good care, but she just couldn't stay in hospital.

I tried to explain to her, in layman's language, what had happened to her and the dangers she might encounter if we didn't try to dissolve or "flatten" the clot by angioplasty in her artery, or if there was no one around to treat her arrhythmias, if they occurred.

She just wouldn't tell us why going home was so important.

I think, in retrospect, she was just too darned embarrassed to tell us why she had to go home. It crossed my mind that I could give her a little more morphine to make her a little groggy and perhaps less ambitious to go home. Even though staying in hospital would be in the patient's best interest, we don't use morphine in that way, although it's tempting. I was soon "whisked away" to see other very seriously ill patients in the Emerg.

Suddenly, I was called back to my original patient who had collapsed on her stretcher from a long run of ventricular tachycardia. (For those who don't watch medical shows on TV, ventricular tachycardia is a very dangerous heart rhythm that may lead to loss of consciousness or to cardiac arrest.) This nice lady then agreed to stay in hospital, as she was really shaken when she collapsed. I don't know if she had watched the appropriate medical program on her TV, but, at least, she didn't need any more convincing.

It turned out that the reason that she couldn't stay in hospital was the fact that she had a cat at home and there was nobody to feed it. She had only come to hospital because she didn't think she would be there that long.

The Emerg nursing staff contacted social services, and arrangements were made to feed her cat throughout our patient's stay in hospital.

This lady actually underwent emergency angioplasty, and both she and the cat were eventually reunited, only a little worse for wear.

The next time I saw Harry I told him I had another chip, called the pet chip and I told him about our nice little old lady in the Emerg.

He finally agreed that it was a pretty dominant chip in some people, and there were probably some sub-groups as well. Some people are gaga over cats and couldn't care less about dogs that were always chasing their beloved felines. Some love all animals, even creepy reptiles. Others are real connoisseurs, preferring big dogs rather than those little yappy ankle-biters, and some take it one step further, preferring only certain breeds of their favourite animal.

"Harry," I said, "while we are at it I've thought of another chip as well."

"Good grief, now what?"

"Harry, I am going to call it, for lack of a better word, the "shit-disturber" chip; and Harry, you've got it in spades!"

Shit-disturber Chip

I then laid out what had been going through my mind about this particular chip. "Actually, Harry, it's perhaps a little bit complimentary, but this chip will get you into a lot of trouble. Let me describe it to you. And, Harry, I don't mean shit disturber in the sense that you just like to stir up trouble for no good reason. You have to have a good reason to try to stir this stuff up. It's the equivalent of the square peg in the round hole."

So I told Harry to go back to his kingdom of 30,000 years ago and Mother Nature putting these chips into our brains.

Most of us get the 'follower chip.' (I knew Harry would be thinking, "Not another chip!") But the follower chip is merely the opposite of the shit-disturber one. Most of us are born with the follower chip or variations of it. It makes us all, or most of us, good soldiers. When the leader says, 'Do this!' we all follow him and form a cohesive unit. There's no serious questioning — maybe a little bitching perhaps — but we get on with the job that we are supposed to do and the army or society hums along.

If you belong perhaps, to the unfortunate 5 percent of the population that gets the shit-disturber chip, you may be in for a rough ride. You are always questioning things and, particularly if you are persistent, you become an irritant to others.

In our society, you may be ostracized, or have few friends who can put up with you. Most of these square pegs, fortunately, don't have it as a dominant gene, and when they see the "writing on the wall," or the unreasonableness of their pet project, they realize that they are wrong, occasionally apologize, and perhaps take up a new crusade.

While some leaders got to their positions of power by "kissing butt," most got there through their own revolutionary ideas. None of them, however, would have become beacons if they hadn't had a bunch of devoted followers.

Shaka Zulu had the simplest of ideas that rocketed him to stardom and, as so often happens, to an early death. (Did I mention that life for a shit disturber might be rough?)

Shaka was a Zulu warrior who eventually fought against the British. His rise to power really started when he questioned their current method of warfare. Apparently the two sides of warring Zulu tribes in battle would line up and toss their three spears at each other and then move up to use their swords. The spear tossing rarely resulted in any injury; it was the swordplay that really counted.

Shaka came up with the then revolutionary idea of keeping one spear in reserve, by only tossing two spears. When the opposing warrior got really close, the final spear became a very deadly weapon. Perhaps not rocket science, but Shaka, who was a shit disturber, ran into a lot of trouble with his current chief. He prevailed, and eventually became the supreme leader of the Zulu Nation.

Going back to our kingdom of 30,000 years ago, if there were no square pegs, and the current chieftain got his position only by kissing butt, presumably society might not change very much. Of course, there was the thinking gay group, but to be effective these thinkers also had to be pushy and many would be reluctant to stick their necks out. The real shit disturbers in both the straight and gay group are likely to be more direct, more likely to take a risk and challenge their present leader. Their ideas are also more likely to be directly related to power and military applications. If there were no shit disturbers, a society would not progress so quickly and other kingdoms would get ahead of them. So, you see, we need these diverse thinkers, or shit disturbers, if our particular society is to stay ahead.

However, some shit disturbers can be really dangerous, particularly if they also have the psychopath chip, charisma, and a number of radical followers. They can literally turn society completely upside down. In the 1930s, the majority of Germans didn't want to have anything to do with Hitler and a lot thought of him as some kind of a joke. However, a small percentage of the population; Hitler's followers, forced their way into power, and look what happened.

Harry interjected that the percentage of Nazis in Germany in the 1930s may not have been much different from the percentage of radical Islamists in the present-day moderate Muslim states. It is to be hoped that these guys won't force their way into power, but don't place any bets.

I told Harry that the root of all evil, however, might be the "follower chip."

Follower Chip

Despite all the information out there, the majority of the world's population believes in some sort of dogma, or at least say they do. If you live in a Christian country, you'll likely be a Christian, and if you take the message literally, you'll believe that the only way to salvation is through the Christian Messiah.

In my case, before they tried to enrol me in those infernal confirmation classes, I was actually told that the only real way to get into the Kingdom of God was through the *Presbyterian* Jesus!

This may sound funny now, but when I questioned Mr. Douglas, our confirmation instructor, "Do you mean that unless I go to the Presbyterian Church, I can't go to Heaven?" his answer was,

"That's about it." I was only twelve at the time, but I remember it well.

The Muslim masses are told basically the same thing, that the rest of us are infidels. Like their Christian counterparts, however, Muslins are also split into their various factions, who sometimes war against each other for what some would call hair-splitting technical differences.

Historically, Christian nations have nothing to boast about in being kind to their neighbours. Indeed, aggressive Christian behaviour experienced perhaps its peak expression during the Crusades. The unfortunate Muslims, who by no means meekly submitted, were subjected to the Crusaders' zeal.

In some ways, it was perhaps fortunate for the Christians that Jesus never tried to run a government or an army. Maybe, therefore, it was easier for Christian nations to separate religion from government, to become secular.

Mohammed, on the other hand, *was* the government, and he was the head of a large and successful army. Having a secular government, separate from their religion, is thus not acceptable for many of the Muslim faith.

But is there not a price? If national governments completely follow a dogma that is out of date for modern times, are they not less flexible and less innovative? When was the last time that any of today's oil-rich Arab nations — devout adherents to the Muslim faith — added anything to our scientific knowledge?

Why do we continue slavishly to "follow" when we can clearly see the all-too-often alarming result? Is it because of that terrible follower chip, a chip that doesn't listen to reason or common sense? Hitler, Stalin, the Khmer Rouge, the Taliban, and many others have become powerful and able to gather others to their cause only because of the follower chip that most of us carry.

The follower chip may have been useful for the past 30,000 years; however, in modern times it may be our undoing.

Perhaps there is another chip that one might call the "war chip."

War Chip

If we have our two tribes, or kingdoms, living side by side and there is a spontaneous mutant that makes some individuals particularly cunning, ferocious and cruel, could that not be an advantage if that individual, or group of individuals, goes to war against a more passive or moderate group?

If the more aggressive group wins, then will not that trait be passed along?

May not the follower chip and the war chip be closely related or complementary?

Is it not possible that all of this suggests we may *not*, in fact, be made in God's image?

Harry said he had seen a recent letter to the editor that suggested we couldn't be made in God's image (Mother Nature, if you prefer) because, "Why would God/Mother Nature put a big brain in a killer ape?"

The worst combination might be the shit-disturber chip combined with the psychopath chip. If you have different ideas that seem to make sense to some at the time, if you are absolutely ruthless and have no conscience, those qualities may make you successful at least for a time.

Hitler rose to power by having a number of ideas that seemed good initially. Unemployment was virtually eliminated. He gave pride back to a nation that had, at least in their view, suffered from humiliating terms under the post World War One (1919) Versailles Treaty armistice agreement.

Unfortunately he also brought forth a number of ideas that, when implemented, were simply disastrous for the world. His idea of the Master Race, at the expense of everyone else, was probably not thought to be serious by many of his supporters.

Being a psychopath, however, he was deadly serious, and not having a conscience made it easy for him to implement his plans. He was able ruthlessly to crush any opposition, and eventually surround himself with a lot of fellow psychopaths.

When he finally got into the "driver's seat," there was nothing to control his evil actions, but this fortunately led to his many military mistakes, which in turn led to his downfall.

Stalin also had the psychopath chip and had already brutalized his nation before Hitler came to call. He had the advantage, however, of huge manpower and material resources, and allied help and, hence, survived the war and remained a tremendous problem in the subsequent years.

A demonstration of his irrational and psychopathic behaviour is the fact that he would not accept returning prisoners of war, his own countrymen, because he felt they might have been contaminated by Western ideas. He sent them off to Siberia to their ultimate deaths.

Iraq's Saddam Hussein sprayed poison gas on the Kurds, again his own countrymen, probably without losing much sleep over it. He didn't mind running some of his opposition, or per-ceived opposition, through buzz saws, probably, in some cases, just for the fun of it.

The moral of all this? Stay away from anybody with the unfor-tunate combo of the psychopath chip and the shit-disturber chip.

HIRSUTISM

At this point in our discussion, Big John Graham came into the doctors' coffee shop. (Big John is discussed more fully in chap-ter 9). We called him "Big John," I think, not because of his size, which was pretty ordinary, but because of his loud and deep voice and his habit of finishing every third or so sentence with a loud chuckle or belly laugh. He had heard the tail end of Harry's and my musings.

In his booming voice, he said that to be a successful politician, not necessarily a good one, you had to have charisma — that is, the ability to "fool all the people some of the time" — and have a thick skin. If you are a psychopath, you don't even need a thick skin, because you don't listen or feel someone else's anguish.

But he said that Harry and I lacked the real essential thing. We were apparently a little low on the charm and charisma thing, but, he said, accompanied by his large belly laugh, we made up for it pretty well on the "psychopath thing."

With that, he walked over and with one hand on each of our heads he gave both of us a brief but vigorous scalp massage. He said we lacked that essential ingredient — hair! Yes, hair. This comment was accompanied by another belly laugh. Both Harry and I had at an early age become involuntary "skinheads," and hence could never become important political leaders.

"Jeez," I thought, "he might just be right." Fortunately for our now bruised egos, I don't think either of us had thought seriously of trying to become a politician.

At this point, we both tried to think of a chrome-dome who had become an important politician. Big John said that Gerald

Ford didn't count because he wasn't supposed to be president; he just had to fill in for Richard Nixon. Harry came up with Jack Layton, now leader of the Canadian Federal NDP (New Democratic Party), but Big John said he didn't count because he had such a pretty moustache, that you couldn't take your eyes off it and didn't notice that he was as bald as a billiard ball. And besides, he wasn't important anyway, running a fringe, far-left-of-centre party that had no chance of winning. He was a spoiler, siphoning off votes from the centre-left party, letting the centre right and the far rights get in. He was like Ralph Nader of American politics, who siphoned off votes from Al Gore and let in Mr. Bush, who talks to God. Hence, Jack didn't count. Poor Jack. I kind of identified with him.

Trudeau didn't count because he had hair when he first went into politics, he was born with a silver spoon in his mouth, and he appealed to the intellectual fringe that had absolutely no common sense. Big John was gone, but we could still hear his big laugh down the hall.

The four bases of DNA (deoxyribonucleic acid) are:

Adenine (A)
Cytosine (C)
Guanine (G)
Thymine (T)

Sugars and phosphates added to the four bases forms nucleotides. It is the sequencing of the nucleotides that determines much of our hereditary components. The nucleotides form the two base pairs: A with T, and C with G. Mother Nature uses a molecular structure, while Bill Gates uses a mechanical structure, such as sheets of silicon and printed circuits.

BILL GATES HAS A LONG WAY TO GO

Harry's idea, however, of Mother Nature putting these computer chips in our brains may not be completely crazy after all. After all, didn't Bill Gates plagiarize Mother Nature in the first place? He used the binary system of numbers 0 and 1. All that information that we get off the computer is encoded in 0 or 1; that's it.

Mother Nature is better. She uses four bases that we identify with letters, and these determine a lot of our biological traits. It's the combinations of these four letters that represent bases that encode our biology. (I'm not saying that there are not other things in there that we don't understand, but these combinations are certainly a basic block in our genetic make up.)

Efforts are now being made to use a biological basis to computer models. We are extremely proud of how compact our computer chips have become, but the biological chips are a whole quantum smaller, much more efficient, and in many cases self-repairing. What do we do when someone puts a scratch in our computer hard drive? It's wrecked and we toss it. In the biological world, even devastating illnesses such as stroke are often followed by a useful or sometimes a complete recovery.

When we go back to our Monarch butterfly, we see that it can work all its body functions. It can fly, navigate, mate, find one of its favourite plants — the milkweed — and lay its eggs for the next generation. The computer in the Monarch doesn't have the luxury of a dry office and a steady supply of energy (electricity). It has to contend with all sorts of weather and an interrupted energy supply. Some might argue that it has too many moving parts in its support system (its body) and hence, for these reasons, a short life span. However, it compensates for this by reproducing itself thousands of times.

When the next generation of Monarch is ready to continue, it takes on the next part of its journey, eventually to Mexico. And then after several generations have passed, its descendant flies all those many thousands of miles back to Ontario.

All this information had to be passed from one generation to the next for this race of butterflies to continue.

By contrast, the American military was only able to make their flying wing, essential for their stealth technology, when their computers were advanced enough to make the fine aileron and elevator adjustments both individually and cooperatively at twenty times a second that allowed controlled flight in these contraptions. Not even Chuck Yeager (the famed US test pilot) could fly it without computer assistance.

The butterfly does all of this, plus all its aforementioned functions, with a brain about the size of the proverbial "head of a pin."

So, you see, Bill has a long way to go.

He has to go biological and he has to move to at least a four-letter code.

MIND GAMES

Napoleon

In medical school, we had to "do" a little psychiatry, with emphasis on the word "little." Harry called it, perhaps not entirely respectfully, "mind games." And large groups from our class in 1959 were marched off to visit 999 Queen Street, a huge mental hospital in Toronto.

We thought the address was a little peculiar, implying that the institution was "one brick short of a full load." In those days, I think we were a little too cavalier with some of our practices with the mentally ill.

At the time there were two patients in this institution claiming to be the reincarnation of Napoleon. One of them in particular was a bit of a showman, and classes from several years before had told us about him.

He was dutifully placed in front of us, the psychiatrist introduced him and asked him some questions to set the stage, and then the floor was thrown open and any of us could ask him questions.

My friend Harry, who was always very knowledgeable on just about any question when it came to history or philosophy, put up his hand and was soon peppering the patient with innumerable questions concerning the life of Napoleon.

It was soon apparent that the patient and Harry had been reading the same books. The rest of the class and, I think, even the psychiatrist, were soon sitting back and enjoying the question and answer period.

Apparently, poor old Napoleon had had a terrible time with hemorrhoids and his loss at the Battle of Waterloo has even been attributed to this painful affliction. Harry zeroed in on this and was soon asking "Napoleon" how he was making out with his hemorrhoids. "Napoleon" confirmed his problem with them, and said that they were just so painful that he had been unable to come out to the battlefield to make the necessary troop deployments and, hence, he lost the battle.

Afterwards, I asked Harry how he thought that "Napoleon" had made out and Harry said, with the straightest face that he could muster, that the patient wasn't schizophrenic or crazy at all.

It was the psychiatrist who was crazy; the patient was, in fact, the reincarnation of Napoleon!

Later that day, we were all farmed out to various patients we were supposed to interview. As bad luck would have it, I ended up with the other Napoleon. I guess they were having a special on Napoleons at 999 Queen Street. (I heard later that in the history of the institution they had housed six residents who claimed to be Napoleon.)

This guy was certainly not a showman, didn't speak French, and didn't have hemorrhoids. (Because of Harry I now knew, of course, what questions to ask him.) So when later one of our teachers asked what I thought his diagnosis might be, I volunteered that he was a fake and obviously schizophrenic.

This was one of the few times that a psychiatrist and I partially agreed, although he didn't seem to like the word "fake." In fact, the psychiatrist was right again because in fairness to the patient, being completely delusional, he truly thought he *was* Napoleon and hence he wasn't faking it at all.

Psychosomatics

One of the things that really bugged me about psychiatry was that, in my opinion, its practitioners read far too much into a person's family dynamics and previous life experiences.

Although things have changed greatly for the better, in my student days some illnesses were blamed in part or completely on what I considered to be "airy fairy" ideas.

Inflammatory bowel disease, and in particular, ulcerative colitis, was a very sore point with me. After I was "let loose on the wards" in 1959 and seeing real patients, I became totally at odds with this psychiatric viewpoint. Psychiatrists at that time felt that these patients were turning inwards and had a bowel fixation that actually caused or greatly aggravated their illness.

Although I wouldn't disagree that a person's personality could make their symptoms and clinical course much worse, it was not the *primary* cause, and no matter how hard one might try to bring on this disease, it would be hard to do so by mind alone.

In my senior year of residency (1965–66) at the "The Great Mecca," the Toronto General Hospital, we were looking after a beautiful patient with ulcerative colitis. She was twenty-eight years old and engaged to be married shortly. The psychiatrists were always called in, as was the routine in those days, for a whole number of diagnoses, including ulcerative colitis. We were told these patients had "turned inward," and if that could be cured, then the disease would go away.

This gorgeous young lady had a simply beautiful personality. However, she looked very pale and was absolutely exhausted, and at one point I thought we were going to lose her. She was on IV therapy, lots of antibiotics, steroids and sedation, and with time she rallied somewhat and was transferred off our ward.

Enter my friend, Harry. "What do you think, Harry? Is ulcerative colitis related to a patient's personality in any way?"

"You know, Tom, you ask the stupidest questions sometimes. Oh sure, after you have been chained to a toilet bowl for the last two months, for twelve hours or more each day, with up to twenty or more bowel movements a day, pooping out blood and mucus and with no end in sight, you would be a little crazy too, especially you, Tom."

Harry always had a nice way of making his points.

"There's something wrong inside all right, but it has nothing to do with a person's head."

In retrospect, I think the thing that threw off the medical establishment was the fact that all these diseases that we now call autoimmune had no obvious cause, and hence must be psychosomatic in some way.

Calling in the psychiatry department with all their funny ideas, I think in some cases only aggravated things, and it certainly didn't help the patients to be told that the problem was all in their heads. (Translated: "You're crazy!")

Although rheumatoid arthritis is now considered one of the autoimmune disorders, as far as I can remember it was rarely thought of as some sort of psychiatric illness. Perhaps the disease was so obvious — especially in its severe forms —nobody could argue that it was "all in your head." If we wore our colons on the outside of our bodies, then even the psychiatrists in those days, seeing the ravages of ulcerative colitis, might have concluded that it was not related to "bowel fixation" or, as in our patient's case, the "anxiety" of getting married.

ECT (electro-convulsive therapy)

There was no Medicare in the early 1960s in Ontario. Poor patients were considered "indigent," and didn't have to pay. But most of their care and day-to-day management in the downtown teaching hospitals were provided by the intern service, and third-year nursing students, with nursing instructors overseeing their performance, with staff doctors keeping an eye on things.

One of the additional services that we provided as residents at the Wellesley Hospital was anaesthetizing the psychiatric patients before their ECT (electro-convulsive therapy). This treatment was very common at that time, although it has become more controversial in recent times.

There were three of us who took on this responsibility each year, and my day was Tuesday mornings. We didn't particularly like doing this, as we were already too busy, but it was apparently part of the job. We didn't know the patients, didn't usually know why they were being done and, apart from introducing ourselves and asking the routine questions — Do you have any allergies? Have you had this done before? Do you have any heart problems, chest problems? and so on — we would just "get on with it."

"It" basically consisted of starting an IV that we were sure was going to be reliable and then drawing up a muscle relax-

The Toronto Wellesley Hospital, in my day (1963–64), was basically an extension of the Toronto General Hospital. I was assigned there as a Senior Intern, but again, there were no Junior Interns at the Wellesley, and we were basically at the very bottom of the pile; as usual, as Harry would say, somewhere between the wall washers and the floor cleaners. The pay was slightly better as a senior, I think about $3,000 for the entire year. (Two years earlier, as a junior at the Toronto General Hospital, I had made a total of $1,800.)

I thought however that the training was pretty good in all these hospitals and the staff persons went out of their way to teach us, even though doing so was mostly voluntary on their part. The downtown teaching hospitals, at that time, all had their attached nursing schools and the nursing students actually lived in residence until their third year when they were allowed to live outside their complex. These nursing schools we all thought were excellent, and their products became excellent nurses.

ant called "Anectine" in a syringe. Calling this stuff a "muscle relaxant" was a euphemism. In fact, it absolutely paralysed the patients, so that they couldn't even breathe on their own. Fortunately, it was very short acting, so that if we "bagged" the patients for a short time they would start breathing on their own again. In the same syringe, we would also draw up the approved amount of "Pentothal" and mix the two ingredients by inverting the syringe several times. "Pentothal," again for those who don't watch TV medical shows, is a very rapidly acting anesthetic, and just before your operation, if the anesthetist asks you to count to ten and you only get to six or seven before you find yourself waking up in the recovery room, it may have been "Pentothal" that was shot into your IV.

Over the year, each of us probably averaged about five cases on our particular day each week. Some of these patients would receive twenty or more "treatments" over a course of several weeks. A few of the psychiatrists seemed pretty weird, but we all began to just accept weirdness as coming with the territory. I guess they thought some of us were pretty weird too, but with their training, they likely thought they could put an accurate psychiatric label on us. At least in those days they still came to the Emerg when called.

At the appointed time, "the psychiatrist of the day" would come in and, usually without saying much, would check to see that the patient was truly asleep and "relaxed." The patient would be relaxed all right. By this time, he would have his mouth guard in and would be ventilated by the ever-present Ambu bag.

The psychiatrist would put the paddles, covered in some sort of "goop," on the patient's temples, shout, "all clear," and then step on the foot switch.

The poor patients would usually grimace a little, but show no other sign of abuse. We would continue bagging them for a short time and when the patients started breathing on their own, the psych nurse would take over and we would turn to the next patient. Over a period of time, we got to know some of the psychiatrists a little better, and a few of them seemed almost reasonable.

Bipolar Disorders

Then one day while I was still at the Wellesley I was on call for Emerg — as I was every third day — when a very beautiful and young airline stewardess came in (they were all like that in those days; it was obviously part of the hiring routine) in the manic phase of her "bipolar affective disorder" or what used to be called "manic depressive disorder." I don't know why they keep changing the names of these things. (I do agree, however, that changing the name of "Mongolian Idiot" to "Down Syndrome," does sound better.)

This young lady was still in good shape physically, but if left too long these patients can absolutely exhaust themselves. As so often happens during the manic phase, her behaviour was very promiscuous and she propositioned a couple of the younger men in the Emerg.

As medical interns, we had to see these psych patients and, if necessary, refer them to the psychiatry department. I was never sure whether this was to give us more general experience or, more likely, to give the psych intern an easier time. In any case, it was an easy referral. I could refer her, write a short note and get on with the next patient.

She was duly admitted upstairs and lost somewhere in the depths of the psychiatric department. After being put on a big dose of chlorpromazine, which heavily sedated her, she rested in bed, the idea being that this manic phase would eventually "run its course" and then she could be rehabilitated. Then, with proper monitoring and perhaps maintenance drugs, she could return to her job as an airline stewardess.

Unbelievably and tragically, she developed a rare reaction — called cholestatic jaundice — to this drug. She became deeply jaundiced, went into liver failure and ultimately died. It was a shock for the whole hospital, and I'm sure the psychiatry department felt particularly upset.

The things that doctors say to each other might scare the lay public, but most of the time these insults are meant in fun, or to make a point. Sometimes, what we say is strictly gallows humour to relieve tension, particularly after a tragedy.

Cholestatic jaundice is caused by inflammation of the small bile ducts resulting in plugging up of these tubules, causing scarring and ultimately liver failure. The drug chlorpromazine has occasionally been implicated as a cause of this disaster. For some reason, it is more common in women than in men.

Traditionally doctors are divided into two main groups, physicians and surgeons. The GP spans these two groups, but if one decides to go into a specialty program, he or she then becomes either a physician or a surgeon. Both groups still work together, of course, but there is also some friendly rivalry. The surgical group thinks of us physicians as the group that orders too many tests and does nothing but talk. One of my rivals said that physicians were just a bunch of "mental masturbators." On the other hand, we physicians think of the surgeons as "knife-happy Neanderthals." Psychiatrists are functionally in a class by themselves.

After what had happened with the lovely airline stewardess, one of the more boisterous surgical interns became aware of this story.

He said in his loud voice in the interns' residence. "Tom, isn't Tuesday your day in the 'psychotic' department?" (His word for the psychiatric department.)

"Well, you just give them hell and tell them that they killed a beautiful woman. I was in the Emerg when you referred her to the 'psychotics.' I was in seeing a young boy and his mother in the very next bed. I had just examined this young kid and was in the process of assuring them both that it wasn't an appendix, when your patient hopped out of her bed and came over and propositioned me on the spot, in very direct terms and at the top of her voice. So you sent her to the psychotics department and they killed her. You are responsible. The least you can do is give all those guys up there proper hell on Tuesday. All they had to do was just admit her here, to the interns' residence, and we would have been glad to look after her. No, I'm serious! And you are just chicken if you don't tell them off."

I replied, "She propositioned you, did she? She didn't proposition me!"

"It figures," he said. "She was just showing some taste. You're too damned ugly."

He was not on call, and stomped off. Probably, he was off to the nearest bar. I must say I don't blame him.

EXAMINING A HAMMER WITH A HAMMER

The next time I saw Harry we compared the crazy things we had seen since our last meeting, and I asked Harry, "You don't think much of psychiatry or for that matter, of religion, do you?"

"Nope, psychiatry has a big problem — a brain examining a brain. That's pretty difficult. It's like asking a hammer to examine another hammer.

"We have it pretty easy. I look down the microscope, and I can see the bad cells in there; and if I look at a resected specimen, I can feel its sometimes-gritty texture. You can look at a blocked artery with an angiogram, or in the OR you can actually touch and feel it, and in your case, Tom, you can even taste it if you like. I think a plumber could do your job, and probably better too."

Harry always had to get in his digs, and I know they were probably character- building, as my mother would have said.

"Psychiatry has a big, and possibly a fatal, problem. Oh, I know they can always give pills and that other thing — what's it called, ECT? But that other weapon in their arsenal, a brain examining another brain, psychoanalysis, you've got to be kidding!"

Religion

"Oh, and, Tom, that other thing you mentioned, religion. That's even more difficult.

"A spirit examining another spirit, albeit, perhaps, 'the Great Spirit'? Pretty difficult. We don't even know what our own spirit is. We can't see our own personal spirit in black and white terms. When it comes to the Great Spirit, lots say they can feel it, see it, hear it (but it's not something that *everyone* can examine); and those that *do*, have in some cases completely different experiences to other religious folks.

"All the really big-time prophets came a long time ago and we haven't heard a peep out of them since. Apparently, you have to die or perhaps go backward in a time-warp machine — 1,400 years for Mohammed, 2,000 years for Christ, or in the case of Buddha, 3,000 years — before you can strike up a meaningful conversation with them.

"Even though we are told that this spirit is everywhere, I suspect that these few people who *may* actually be genuine, and who tell you that they have actually talked with or seen their respective religious leaders, have been tricked or, more likely, have hallucinated. Examining a spirit with a spirit? I don't think so!"

"But Harry, you believed that the patient we both saw in medical school was the reincarnation of Napoleon, didn't you?"

"You *would* hold that against me, wouldn't you?"

"You know, Harry, you really have that shit-disturber gene in you. In spades. Just like I said!"

CHAPTER 7

At first I wanted to be a veterinarian

Most teenagers don't really know what they want to do when they grow up, and I guess I was no exception. My dad had bought a small farm and my brothers and I generally had a good time, and we didn't really mind the routine chores that every kid has to do. I had always liked animals and when I was fifteen, during the summer of 1952, I thought that among the many career options, veterinary medicine would be pretty interesting.

Even in those days, there seemed to be two types of vets, the big animal ones and the small animal ones. Big animal work appealed to me more than sitting in a building all day ministering to small animals. The big animal vets got out into the country, saw the farms, and from time to time had to use their muscle.

Our local vet was an older man, very sensible and always practical, and definitely a big-animal vet. My dad asked him if I might accompany him on his rounds. He was a genial man, and I think he just enjoyed having the company. I gradually realized that his job was more about economics than anything else. If the cow didn't produce, you just got rid of it.

My dad had a cow on our farm; she was about eight years old and, for some reason, she had gone off her food. She would drink, but not eat anything. This had gone on for about three days. She just stood there looking like a cow and wouldn't even eat the grain that we offered her. Our vet and my father walked around her a couple of times, and the vet put his fist between her last rib and her hip bone on her left side and gave several short jabs. Sometimes, if the cow has swallowed some hard object the vet can feel it hit his fist on this manoeuvre. He also did a "full length" rectal exam listened to her heart and lungs, and took a

153

rectal temperature. He didn't do any blood work that I can remember.

The vet felt that she likely had "hardware disease," which implied that some where along the way she had swallowed something like a piece of barbed wire, or perhaps, a bunch of fence staples. He said he could "open her up," but that cows aren't as good afterwards, and it was fairly expensive. In other words, it wasn't worth it. His final words were "you'd better ship her." (How many times did I hear those words during that summer?) This meant that she would go off to the abattoir and we really would never know what was wrong with her, no diagnosis. There were no fast-food outlets in those days, and hamburger meat was relatively cheap; hence, our cow was not worth much, one way or the other. It was all about money.

Another problem was that at some of these farms there was no organization. The animals would often be getting sub-optimal care, and you knew nothing was going to change. Also, several times, we would see our patients thundering off into the bush. How were we supposed to examine them if we couldn't even get close to them? I would guess that only one beef farm in three had a proper cattle squeeze. Usually we had to make do with a steel gate swung against the side of the barn; the farmer would slip a couple of 2 by 6's across the back of the gate to prevent the animal from backing up. We got stepped on, squashed, kicked and rained on.

My biggest reservations were, however, that no diagnosis was made and all decisions were based on economics.

My school marks were, for some reason, always good and I thought about applying to Guelph Veterinary College in Ontario when I was old enough. But by the time I was seventeen, I had opted for premeds, and I withdrew my application from Guelph. My experience with the two "Dr. Bills," described in chapter 1, easily clinched my decision.

I always remained interested, however, in veterinary medicine and I found the correlation between the two sciences amazing. Though veterinary medicine was relegated to a hobby, I retained a strong interest in this hobby. Can doctors be good veterinarians? A good question, the answer to which is "not likely." Veterinary medicine is far too broad a science for us poor MDs to handle. And people like me, who eventually specialized within human medicine, tried to avoid that broad science even further.

154

"ALVIN"

My wife had a young niece who was completely devoted to her pet, which happened to be a white rat. I had met her pet on one previous occasion, and the rat was very well behaved. It didn't seem to mind being handled, and most important, didn't bite.

I noticed that it had a small lump on one of its elbows; otherwise, it seemed very healthy. I didn't say anything to this young girl, because I didn't want to upset her, and anyway, I didn't have the foggiest idea what this lump represented.

Several months later, my wife informed me that this lump had become very big; the poor rat couldn't walk properly, and in fact, couldn't even bend its elbow. Why didn't she take it to a real doctor? That is, to see a veterinarian. Apparently, she didn't have any money. Then, before I knew what happened, this cousin was back in our apartment with Alvin.

The young lady very quickly talked me into "doing something." Being the only doctor in the family can have its drawbacks. We — or more correctly, she — decided that I should have Alvin admitted to the Emerg at the Toronto Wellesley Hospital where I was now a senior intern, and cut off whatever this lump was. That shouldn't be too hard; after all, it was just a lump. I looked at this lump with new interest.

The only problem that I could see was that I didn't know if, after we got the lump off, there would be enough skin to repair the defect. Oh, I thought we could stretch it a fair way, and if worse came to worst, I could probably turn a flap from its upper arm. I knew that the nurses wouldn't say anything, as they loved animals — even a white rat, if they were properly introduced.

I picked a very quiet time in the Emerg, the Monday morning on a long weekend. I had carefully primed the nurses beforehand, and they were game, and even looking forward to the venture. There were never nasty supervisors around on long weekends, only the younger, more adventurous types. Accordingly, I called my wife's niece and she brought Alvin down for his early morning surgery. We needed a small surgical tray and we therefore admitted Alvin under his own name and "of no fixed address."

I found the surgery quite difficult. No wonder the vets charge so much! I had made sure that I used lots of local freezing. I had another reason, besides not wanting to hurt Alvin. The little finger of my right hand was alongside his mouth.

Our patient was excellent and stayed still throughout the procedure. I did have a tough time trying to close the wound, but managed, after a fashion.

Everything, to this point, had gone well. I was much relieved to have gotten away with all this without getting bitten, and the patient seemed just fine and now could walk normally. Also, everybody seemed so supportive. I didn't think I would ever hear from administration about this one. Then, one of the very helpful nurses suggested that I send this lump to pathology for a "diagnosis." That seemed like the right thing to do, and I agreed.

A few days later, I ran into one of my former classmates and close friend, Dr. Allan Hart, in the hallway, and he said, "What on earth were you trying to do the other day?" Temporarily, I had forgotten about the specimen that we had sent to pathology. Apparently, all the pathology specimens went from the Wellesley to Princess Margaret Hospital for analysis including, of course, Alvin's lump.

My classmate was doing his stint in pathology, specializing to become an internist and gastro-enterologist. He immediately recognized that something was very unusual about this specimen, and he saw my name on the bottom of the requisition. I asked him what was unusual about this lump. He told me I should have known that it was a granuloma (a benign lump that often appears when an area of the body is constantly irritated) — and it was on a piece of *rodent* skin!

I was quite surprised that he knew it was from a rodent and not a human. He explained that they work with rats all the time at the Princess Margaret, and if he couldn't recognize rodent skin by now, there was no hope for him.

He told me he had quickly examined the lump, and then destroyed the specimen and the requisition so that I wouldn't get into trouble. Apparently, some of the older doctors at Princess Margaret just have no sense of humour. I was fortunate to have friends like Dr. Allan Hart.

Actually, I should have learned from my mistakes, because I had tried to pass some apple juice off as a urine specimen when I was an extern in Orillia. I had worked with a wonderful man, Dr. Philpott, who wasn't, in fact, a medical doctor, but had his PhD in some form of laboratory medicine and probably knew more clinical medicine than most of the doctors who sent him specimens.

He patiently helped me do the various lab chores that were mandatory at the time. In the morning, I usually drew blood from the in-patients and collected blood from any outpatients sent to the hospital. When I was finished these chores, I was then assigned to the urine section of the lab and, although it was a small hospital, we often had to go through fifty or more specimens. Dr. Philpot would come to help out if I had a problem with one of the analyses.

On one particular morning when I had to help in the OR, I heard that Dr. Philpot was going to be doing all the urines that morning. That wasn't a problem for him, because he was very fast and thorough. I decided to play a trick on him, and sent a sample of apple juice down from the ward, attributed to a patient who had already left the hospital.

I had just stepped out of the OR when I got a very vigorous call from the laboratory that I was to come down right away. I actually had forgotten what I had done early that morning, and confidently thought that they needed my help, and hence the urgent call. Perhaps I was getting to be a "somebody" after all.

When I arrived, Dr. Philpot was red in the face and asked me why I had sent him a specimen of apple juice. I asked him how he knew it was me. He said nobody else would do that to him!

When I asked him how he knew it was apple juice, he in turn asked me what colour sugar (glucose) in urine should turn when exposed to the reagent. (A reagent is a group of chemicals used in analysis of various substances.) When I answered "red," he said, "Precisely! And what colour should fruit sugar (fructose) turn?" I said I didn't know. He then shoved a specimen bottle in my face and said, "Brown — see?"

He still wasn't in a very good mood.

He then asked me what the specific gravity of apple juice was. Again, I didn't know, and he almost shouted "forty-two!" He sent the hydrometer spinning in the specimen to demonstrate. Then he asked me what was the highest specific gravity I had seen in the laboratory. That I knew. It was perhaps thirty-six.

I finally got up the nerve to ask him how he had known it was apple juice, and not something else. He then thrust the specimen under my nose. I thought, initially, he was going to ask me to drink it. But instead, he asked me to smell it and, indeed, it did smell like apple juice. He then gave out a big laugh and smiled, and I knew I was going to survive another day.

I never sent another bogus specimen to the laboratory — except for my second run-in later on with Alvin's lump. I guess some people are just slower learners than others.

PREGNANCY CHECKS.
(RECTUM? IT DAMN NEAR KILLED HIM!)

We moved to the West Coast in 1968, and my wife and I bought a farm in Surrey the following year. It was close to the Royal Columbian Hospital, and the bridge traffic was relatively light at that time — something that is hard to believe now.

Also by this time we had acquired four little "urchins," boys each about a year apart in age. I thought a farm would keep them busy and, hence, out of reform school. My grandmother had always said, "An idle mind is the devil's work shop."

Before long, we ended up with about a hundred head of beef cattle, the same number of pigs, broilers and laying chickens, and New Zealand White meat rabbits, and produced about 10,000 bale equivalents of hay. Just another one of my hobbies gone completely out of control! (See chapter 8 for the complete hobby story.)

Among the many chores that we had to do were the inevitable pregnancy checks.

Pregnancy checks in cattle have been a long-respected "pseudo-science," since the information gained was sometimes difficult to obtain and not always precise. Our farm was no different from the average Canadian farm. Each fall, usually in November, all the cows and bred heifers were run through the cattle squeeze in single file, and the vet and I were supposed to do this obscene task. Sometimes, I had to do it on my own.

A long plastic glove was put on, extending from the fingertips to well over the shoulder and down the side of the chest. Then I would move timidly behind the large frightened beast, moisten my glove with loose feces that was ubiquitous, and cautiously extend my fingers, and then my hand and eventually wrist, forearm and elbow up the animal's rectum, usually stopping at the mid biceps. But sometimes, when necessary, I would have to flatten the side of my chest against the cow's rear, to get as much length as possible of my arm into the cow's innards.

I know this may sound bizarre, but what a fabulous wealth of information lies therein!

David learning the "shit falls" of the big rectal.

Usually, the ovaries can be palpated very easily between the thumb and several fingers, and the pit from the departed ovum can be felt. The uterine wall can be readily palpated, and there is a manoeuvre called "slipping the membranes" that I was never very good at. If the calf in utero is six months old, its body parts can be felt and identified. In fact, if the calf is over seven months, you can easily poke your finger into his nose or anus depending on his foetal position. A cow's pregnancy is about forty weeks, the same as that of *Homo sapiens*.

Every minute or so, a peristaltic wave (pressure wave action) passes down the cow's colon and rectum, and during these times you feel as though your hand, then forearm, and then elbow are in a moving vise, and all thought of getting further information ceases. When the peristaltic wave reaches the rectum, a big fart and/or an explosion of feces results, and lands on your boot.

After a while, one could judge how long it was going to be before the cow was going to calve. (In our herd there was always at least one animal that, for some reason, hadn't become pregnant, and these animals were always shipped. "Frigidity" was not tolerated on Canadian beef farms!)

All this information was dutifully written down in a notebook opposite the cow's tag number by my "secretary," usually my wife, one of our sons, or a neighbour. If the glove was in pretty good shape, you moved up to the next cow that had been brought to the squeeze.

We would run through perhaps thirty-five cows and bred heifers in a morning. All the animals' annual injections and worm medications were given at this time. Sometimes delays would occur because an ear tag had to be replaced, tails docked, or some minor surgery performed. I always thought this a unique experience and in a very short time got very valuable information about our beef herd. Naturally, our children, when they were in their teens, were encouraged to share this experience, including giving the animals their injections and doing a few rectals.

One time, as we were walking back from the barn for lunch I asked our son David, who had just done his first three preg checks (rectal examinations), what he had learned that morning. Well, he said, next time he would remember to take off his wristwatch before he put on the glove and would make sure he put his pant leg outside his rubber boot. I looked at him; he had lost

odwin family 1946, left to right: parents Helen and Ernest, Thomas, Stuart, and Bruce.

aster 1958. Beer drinking was a family tradition. I am flanked by my father Ernie and mother elen; on the far left is my younger brother Bruce, and my older brother Stu (now deceased) on the far right of the photo.

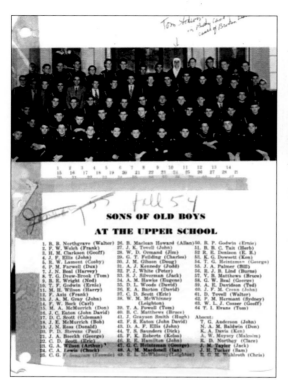

Sons of the old boys at the upper school, class photo 1954. I am very obvious in my body cast in the back row.

Pictured with my dear and la[te] coach, Tony Canzano. Boxing prob[ably] wasn't good for my brain an[d] was, as I later found out, very bad f[or] my sinuses. 1958.

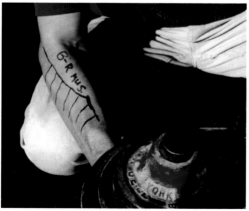

Photo of the infamous brachio-radialis muscle, described in chapter one.

The perpetual student. Graduation from medical school in 1961, and now six and a half more years of post-graduate training (intern and fellow).

oto of the Royal Columbian Hospital, circa 1968. The old 1912 building (where the two ctors had a fistfight in 1967) can be seen in the front of the photo.

rial view of Royal Columbian Hospital, May 6, 2008, taken from my homebuilt airplane h permission from Pitt Meadows tower. Note the only original building still standing is nurses' former residence at the upper portion of the photo.

Royal Columbian Hospital cardio staff, circa 1984.

My best buddy and my successor as chief of cardiology, Dr. Dave Hilton, circa 1992.

. Mark Henderson, human
namo and chief of cardi-
ogy at Royal Columbian
ospital, succeeding Dave
ton, circa 1996.

arjorie McKnight, my surrogate mother
nd former chief cardio tech. 1996. (Ch. 2)

Kristin Warburton, my "inspiration" lady in
the heart cath lab. 1996. (Ch. 9)

Unveiling my retirement plaque at RCH on Friday, October 4, 1996. On the right with me is Mark Henderson and my wife, Elaine.

Retirement article in hospital newsletter.

Receiving the Coady Award in 1998. Left to right: Dr. Arun Garg, Elaine Godwin, Tom Godwin.

"Heart" of RCH's Cardiology retires after 28 years

"*I'm just a pig farmer.*"

Fran Kuhn, patient care manager, Coronary Care Unit (CCU) at Royal Columbian Hospital, laughs and shakes her head. "Dr. Godwin often said that. It seems to sum him up – a down-to-earth guy who made no bones about anything. He called a spade, a spade."

But while Dr. Tom Godwin is indeed, as he is fond of describing himself, a "pig farmer" (he and his wife Elaine live on an 85-acre farm complete with livestock), he has also been a well-respected and highly valued head of Cardiology at RCH for the past 28 years.

"Tom played a large part in supporting the hospital board's decision in raising the medical standards of Royal Columbian from that of a community hospital to a tertiary care referral and teaching hospital," recalls Dr. Tony Nolan, chief of medicine, RCH. "He encouraged specialists with more advanced training and qualifications to consider re-locating to New Westminster rather than thinking only in terms of working in downtown Vancouver."

Jim Fair, president and CEO of the Simon Fraser Health Region, agrees that Dr. Godwin made significant contributions to the Cardiology department at RCH. "Tom is known far and wide as an excellent clinician," says Mr. Fair. "He was completely dedicated to

And that dedication is appreciated by his colleagues. "He worked tirelessly," recalls Dr. Bob Hayden, cardiac surgeon. "Dr. Godwin is a premier contributor to the Cardiology department – those of us who practice in cardiology

today truly appreciate his years of efforts."

Dr. Godwin, who recently retired due to health reasons, came to RCH 28 years ago after training in cardiology at Toronto General Hospital. "I was offered a contract to organize a heart cath lab at RCH," he explains. "The P.A. Woodward Foundation gave us $200,000 to start it, which was quite a lot of money in those days."

He was more than simply the head of the ever-expanding Cardiology department. He treated the staff and his patients with respect, often peppering it with his wry

miss him. He was always approachable."

Dr. Godwin treated the cardiac services team as if they were members of an extended family. "Every year," Fran recalls, "he would have an annual dinner at his home to thank the interns; it was a big function for the staff. He was thanking us, when really, we should have been thanking him."

But Dr. Godwin is simply that kind of person. "He is the kind of friend you are proud to have," says Mr. Fair.

And his patients have always appreciated that he was honest and straightforward with them, believing that they should be treated with dignity. Jan Rulon, manager of Cardiology, RCH, says, "His patients always came first."

Dr. Hayden agrees, "Tom was always professional. He put his patients first – he looked at the whole person and who that person was."

The positive impact he could have on people is the very reason Dr. Godwin chose cardiology as his specialty. "It's a fascinating specialty, and it's changing so much," he says. "There is so much you can do for a patient. That's rewarding."

Perhaps Jan sums up the feelings of staff at RCH when she says, "Dr. Godwin's name is, and always will be, synonymous with the 'heart' of Cardiology."

166

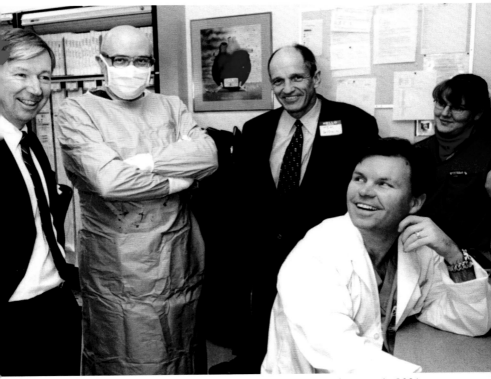

ave Hilton (left) and Mark Henderson (with mask), the two human dynamos in 2001.
uthor is centre with two staff members on the right.

wo of my 500 "girlfriends" at the RCH annual
ardio department party February 15, 2001, five
ears after I retired. Karen Bevin Pritchard is on
ne left and Maureen Jennings is on the right.

My esteemed partner, Dr. Bob Brown (son
of Dr. K.W.G. Brown) "following in Dad's
footsteps" — having a late lunch. (Ch. 2)

My wife, Elaine, took this ph\
to in 1973. My father-in-law\
sitting by our hay wagon; o\
four little urchins are sitting\
standing on the wagon, w\
Stephen, our "baby," ridi\
our 180-pound Irish wolfhoun\
(This is the same dog that Co\
Brown refused to allow me\
sigmoidoscope in one of t\
treatment rooms of the Colur\
bian Emerg, described in chapt\
seven). I am standing, keeping\
hand out to steady Stephen.

This photo, taken in 2007, is a\
re-enactment of the one taker\
in 1973. Same hay wagon, same\
urchins (only bigger), differen\
dog (Old English mastiff). The\
mother to these urchins is sit\
ting where my father-in-law\
(since deceased) was sitting.

Two aerial views of our farm.

inbow over our cattle rd, 1993.

The boys and friends working the farm.

Marching our herd off for their annual preg check, circa 1990.

Scuba diving in the Georgia Strait, August 1979.

Our old converted fish trawler.

Parachuting, circa 1984, using army surplus WWII chutes. Note my good form until I hit the ground and went flat on my face. Below, after landing — a big smile on my face, but limping. *(Dave Hilton photos)*

Michael building the Lazair (the near-death machine), circa 1984, described in chapter eight. He is leaning over the wing and his two friends are helping, Tom Sawyer style.

The same machine with Dave Hilton. Note the two nine-horsepower engines lying on the ground ready to be installed.

Camping on "just anoth
virgin lake" in beautiful B
in our good old homebu
aircraft.

Landing on the beach.

Phantom Lake, BC (behind Powell River), August 200

ytime sleeping buddy, Judge, circa 2002. Judge was twelve in this photo, very old for a stiff.

mily photo December 2008 with our dear immediate family. You can't see my "two horse-
oes," described in chapter fourteen, because I'm sitting on them!

Tom and Nubi, 2008. At 202 pounds, Nubi is not exactly your average "little yappy ankle-biter." (Ch. 6)

the crystal from his watch, and his boot was almost full of that ubiquitous feces.

PARTY TIME!

Each year, we used to have a party for the intern staff at the Royal Columbian Hospital. They would bring out their spouses and, predictably, get into the beer. On one of these occasions, an old classmate of mine, Dr. Don Hughes, came out to give the intern staff instructions on how to do a "real" rectal examination. Don had been a real doctor (a veterinarian) before he decided to "slum" and become a doctor for the human species. I had met him in first-year medical school and we have been fast friends ever since.

On his instructions, I had haltered six fairly docile cows in various stages of pregnancies, and tied them to a series of poles spread along our big feed trough. Don, always the showman and always in good humour, gave instructions on how to perform this diagnostic pregnancy test.

I was surprised how reluctant these interns were to do this "little test." (I still find it amazing how few people, nowadays, have had any farm experience.) We finally persuaded one of the more adventurous types to give it a try. Don stood close by and gave him detailed instructions on what he should feel. Don had chosen a cow that was likely eight months pregnant at the time, and our intern was soon putting his finger into the calf's nose. He got very excited about all the things he could feel and Don showed him how he could feel coarse hay in one of her stomachs. The other interns were soon crowding around, and listening with keen interest. We had no more trouble persuading the other interns to follow suit. About ten interns were given instructions that evening. We released the cows and went back to the house to continue the party.

After a few more beers, some of the other interns who had not wanted to walk over to the barn earlier because "they weren't properly dressed," were now quite interested in trying out this new procedure. Some of the original interns, who felt they now were "experienced," were even volunteering to give instructions.

Fortunately, I had taken the halters off the cows and released them into the general barnyard population. I could see things getting completely out of hand with a bunch of inebriated interns giving instructions to another bunch similarly indisposed.

Many years later when I would meet some of these old interns, they would remind me of the "big rectal."

IRISH WOLFHOUND

Our dog Shawn was always a crowd-pleaser! He was huge, very friendly, and had the appearance of a particularly large Great Dane with long shaggy fur. He weighed 180 pounds, a good size, even for a wolfhound.

When people first saw him they were usually intimidated, especially when they would drive up in their car and find this beast peering down on them as they were turning off the ignition. He never smiled; I don't think he could. His tail wagging was very subtle, and when he was excited to see a new person, his mouth would be half open. People who hadn't met him would stay in their car, honking their horn until my wife, or one of our kids, would go out and rescue them.

Fortunately, Shawn didn't have a mean streak in his body. He was never really rambunctious, and it was a rare event if someone got bowled over. On the odd occasion that it did happen, he was sure to give his victim a big wet kiss right across their lips.

One snowy wet December day, I noticed Shawn straining at stool. He would squat, obviously strain, and then on the snow was bright red blood. Over a period of several hours, there were fifteen or twenty patches of blood on the fresh snow. It began to look like an abattoir around our house. The poor dog, and very embarrassing too! I tried to examine him, but it was very difficult, and I saw no abnormality around the anus.

So, that same snowy morning Shawn and I went off to see a real doctor — our local veterinarian. He was very nice, but when he pulled out an auroscope (that's the thing that a doctor uses to look in ears) to examine Shawn's rectum, I knew Shawn and I were in trouble. As soon as the vet put it in Shawn's rectum, it was full of stool and visibility was zero.

I asked him if he had a sigmoidoscope (that's the long steel pipe that a doctor uses to examine the lower part of the colon; it's not used as much now with the advent of the flexible colonoscope) and he told me rectal bleeding was a rare problem and they had very little need for one of those "things." He said, however, to bring Shawn back if he continued to bleed, but he thought the bleeding would likely stop on its own. I vaguely wondered, as I wandered out the door, what was the point of bringing him back if he continued to bleed.

Predictably, he not only continued to bleed but it got worse, and with that fall of new snow his condition looked really bad.

By this time, it was Saturday night, so I decided to take him down to The Royal Columbian emergency department early the next morning. I arrived at 7:00 a.m. Sunday morning. It's usually a good time to go, as the Saturday night rush is over and, apart from the usual "mopping up," is fairly quiet before the next on-slaught of patients arrives in the morning. Also, I hoped the Casualty Officer would be too tired to refuse my request.

Unfortunately, the Casualty Officer, Doctor Cory Brown, was still awake enough to argue with me, and told me if I brought Shawn into the treatment room for sigmoidoscopy and Admin ever found out, "the shit would hit the fan," I guess literally.

Cory was a very sympathetic man and could see the obvious disappointment on my face. He suggested that rather than bringing Shawn into the Emerg, I could take a sigmoidoscopy tray home with me, and bring it back Monday morning. What a good idea!

At home, I tried to be very professional, of course, and pretty soon had my poor wife enrolled as my nurse. There were two pairs of rubber gloves on the tray, and I was soon trying to perform a rectal on our dog. The rectal examination went very smoothly, but for some reason he seemed to be in a great deal of pain when I inserted the sigmoidoscopy tube. Our dog always seemed to be a bit of a stoic, and never complained when he fell off a log, or otherwise hurt himself. But on this occasion, he let out a low-pitched sound as the tube entered his rectum.

After that initial complaint, he seemed to be in no more distress and sigmoidoscoping our dog was surprisingly easy, and in fact, much easier than doing the same thing in *Homo sapiens*. His rectum and his sigmoid (that is the short piece of bowel immediately above the rectal area) seemed to be in a straight line. In a human, it is often difficult to get out of the rectum into the sigmoid. There is a sharp curve between the two, and one has to wait and sometimes insert air with a hand pump to negotiate this bend.

On the way in, apart from this low-pitched moan, every thing seemed absolutely normal. The wall was smooth, pink and glistening, just as in a human. I advanced the instrument the full length, approximately eighteen inches. There just didn't seem to be any pathology, no obvious source of bleeding. I was very puzzled.

I withdrew the instrument, and didn't scratch my head, of course, until after I had removed my gloves. I vaguely remembered reading somewhere, a long time ago, that in some cases of ulcerative colitis in humans, the bowel wall can look normal, but if it is wiped with a piece of gauze, it will start to bleed. Ulcerative colitis is seen in dogs, and so I thought, to be absolutely sure, I should put the scope back in and wipe the bowel with some gauze.

Accordingly, I repositioned my wife and the poor dog, and re-inserted the scope. We both expected the dog to give the same low-pitched sound he had initiated on the previous occasion the tube had passed the rectal sphincter. This time, however, he seemed absolutely unperturbed. I advanced the scope again, as easily as before, picked a spot, and wiped the bowel with the gauze. The bowel wall seemed no worse for wear, and I withdrew the scope more puzzled than before. The fact that he didn't seem at all perturbed the second time we inserted the instrument was also puzzling, as he had been quite upset the first time.

Amazingly, he stopped bleeding completely. It seemed to be an instant cure. There was still fresh snow on the ground but no additional red blotches! Somehow, the problem had gone away and there was no explanation.

About two weeks later, I was explaining my confusion to one of my buddies, the late Dr. Roy McNeill (a very talented general and vascular surgeon). He was like Sherlock Holmes. He said the problem was obvious. Shawn had a "fissure in ano" and when I put the scope in the first time, I had stretched it, tearing the fissure wide open so it could heal. He had done this many times in humans and it was indeed quite painful, but stretching was all that was needed.

Roy explained that Shawn had complained the first time because of the initial stretch; the second time the scope was inserted, the fissure was basically gone and there should, in fact, be no pain. Also, he said, these fissures were very difficult to see, as

As "fissure in ano" is not usually discussed too often in the average doctor show on TV, an explanation is probably justified here. A fissure is basically a crack in the ring of tissue that forms the rectal sphincter. Sometimes these things can be quite deep, dirt gets in the bottom of this crack and aggravates it, and the stupid thing never heals, and it can be very painful. If this crack is stretched wide open, it becomes a shallow depression and it then heals very rapidly.

they were just inside the rectal margin. Shawn may have eaten a bone and passed a sharp spicule (fragment) that had cut the delicate margin of his rectal mucosa.

BOAR BITS

One fine day in the late 1970s my wife and I decided to have a party, and we thought we would invite the doctors that had trained in Toronto and had come to practice in Vancouver. They were basically contemporaries, classmates, or had been a year ahead or behind me, in medical school. We called ourselves "the Toronto Rejects." They were a really nice bunch of guys. Probably fifteen of them showed up. As events unravelled, it turned out to be unfortunate that their wives had accompanied them.

A few weeks earlier, we had gone through the gruesome task of castrating our young male pigs. At that time, we had a lot of pigs in our pig barn right along side our cattle barn. Consequently, we had to do this job quite often and ended up with a large amount of "material."

Up until this moment, we had always disposed of it, usually by burying it in the manure pile. I always thought it was a shame just to waste it. If they eat this stuff from cattle and called it "prairie oysters," why couldn't we just call it "pen oysters," short for pigpen oysters, or, perhaps, "boar oysters"?

So I started collecting this material, dutifully putting it in our freezer, correctly labelled, of course. My poor wife just shook her head.

Well, we had to have a taste test, didn't we? And with this upcoming party, what could be a better time?

So, I took the specimens out of the freezer the night before and the next morning I announced, much to my wife's horror, I was going to serve them that night at our party. She said that she would have nothing to do with the idea and that if I was going to serve them, then I was going to have to cook them. I think she thought that would put a stop to the project, because I rarely cooked anything.

However, I was determined, and before the guests arrived I took out our brand-new Teflon frying pan. I thought with this Teflon stuff I would have less of a chance of screwing up. I put in a little olive oil (supposed to be healthy you know) and of course some breadcrumbs, which can disguise anything. I gently fried the "oysters" up and then got out a very fancy stainless steel tray that we had been given for a wedding gift. I put a fancy toothpick in each morsel, and then around the dish sprinkled a little parsley.

Everything up to this point had gone, at least from my point of view, as planned. Then, when the guests started arriving, one of these "compulsive hostesses" (every party has at least one) came along to see if she could help. She spied my "work of art" sitting on the back of the stove, took it, and left the kitchen.

I had been temporarily distracted at the time, and at first didn't realize what had happened. I had planned to make the eating of these things quite voluntary. I was going to tell the assembled guests what was at the other end of these fancy toothpicks.

I knew that the Toronto Rejects shouldn't have brought their wives.

As happens at a lot of parties, the husbands were off on one side of the room discussing, in our case, medicine, and the wives were off somewhere else, discussing kids. Naturally, my "compulsive hostess" went straight to the women's side of the room and started passing the appetizers out. It was definitely too late to say anything. They went very fast; some of these wives took two or three morsels, and not all of the men got to have even one.

I wondered at this point, whether I should ever say anything. My dilemma was soon solved, because Dr. Tom Gibson came over and asked what these "things" were. He asked if they were kidney, and I said no, but I foolishly added the rider that he had the right "system" (the genital urinary system). Tom was no dummy and immediately figured it out. I knew that I shouldn't have asked a shit disturber to the party.

He said, "You bastard!" and then went off and announced to everybody what they had just consumed. As the reader may imagine, I was a little concerned what the reaction might be. To my surprise and relief, nobody seemed particularly upset. Indeed, Tom was soon back and he said, "Tom, let's go back to the barn, as the little piggies won't have any use for their penises now and we can organize a wiener roast!"

A PIG'S CHEWY

I often used to tell the staff that I was really just a pig farmer and that I came to the hospital every once in a while to pay for the losses on my pig farm. (That itself was a joke, because at that time I practically lived at the hospital.) But, from time to time, some of the referring doctors would simply ask one of the nurses to put in a referral to the "pig farmer," when they wanted me to see a patient. It was all a big joke, and the nurses got a lot of mileage out of it.

Also, I think that, partly as a joke and partly because my friends in Emerg had genuine concerns for my welfare, I got called down to Emerg on two occasions when pig bite victims came in. One of these victims, a man in his late thirties, had been in a pen with young pigs running around and the sow just charged him, knocking him down "on his ass" with his back to the side of the pen. The sow kept charging him and biting whatever part was available to her. He tried to fend her off with his fists but it was becoming a losing battle.

Very fortunately, his wife was in the barn and heard all the commotion. By beating on the side of the pen away from her husband, she was able to distract the beast long enough for her husband, despite his now rather grievous injuries, to get out of the pen.

A few hours before a sow "farrows" (gives birth) she undergoes a huge personality change and this lasts for four to six weeks, depending on the proximity of her litter. This particular sow had a young brood about four weeks old and, therefore, she was well in the danger zone. During this period, she will charge like "a freight train" any perceived threat. She has, in effect, PMS big time!

I know, too, that sows are in some ways quite athletic. When we were small kids, my older brother and I would throw winter turnips at a sow, and if our aim were good, the turnip would hit the side of the pig, fall to the ground and the sow would sometimes pick it up on the first bounce. These winter turnips were grown in Southern Ontario for animal feed and were about the size of a small grapefruit. They seemed nearly as hard as a piece of wood. Before being fed to cattle, the turnips would be put through a dicer. A large sow would easily fit the whole turnip into her mouth and we would watch, in awe, as her jaws closed down on it, the juices flowing out of the sides of her great maw. These sows obviously didn't need a dicer.

AUNT JEMIMA

We were amateur pig farmers, but we always made money, or at worst, broke even with every litter that we eventually sold. When we had a particularly good sow with good maternal instincts, we hated to part with her, even though she just got bigger and bigger with passing years. But our favourite was a Hampshire pig. She was almost completely black and, between litters, very friendly. She eventually acquired the name Aunt Jemima. Reliably over the ten years we had her, she produced two litters of between eight and ten healthy piglets approximately twice a year.

We didn't really notice how big she was because she was kept separately, and by this time was much too big to fit into a "farrowing crate." Sows always walk with their heads down; I think they are afraid that if they look up even for a second they might miss something good to eat lying on the ground. It's only when they do lift their heads up that you realize how big they are.

One day, perhaps about four weeks after Auntie J had had her last litter, I was in her pen cleaning out the last of the debris. She was lying in her usual corner, facing away from me; her little piggies were contentedly suckling on her. She suddenly flipped over and came straight at me, her brood flying in every direction. Fortunately, I had my large curved steel snow shovel, and as she charged I was able to get it into that huge open maw. I held on for dear life and when I hit the side of the pen I was flipped out over the top, landing in the alley; she still had the shovel in her mouth.

One of my neighbours, who saw the whole thing, said after-

Auntie J. was not in a good mood.

wards that he thought I was done for. I had been stupid enough to think that Aunt Jemima and I had become good friends. Most people don't think that these big, somewhat ponderous animals could be fast and athletic.

That was her last litter, and Auntie J was shipped. She was the largest sow that they had ever butchered at El Rancho Meats. I can't recall her exact weight, but she was well over a thousand pounds.

And that's how I escaped becoming a pig's chewy!

CALF BED

My wife has a dear cousin, Vic Williams, who was a long practicing beef farmer in Armstrong, BC. Although now retired, he was well known in the area for his "polled" Hereford cattle. (Polled means that the species has a mutation that results in their not having horns). Each year during spring break, after skiing for a week in the Okanagan, it became our family custom to visit him and his wife. We would arrive with our four kids, stay overnight, enjoy their cooking, and continue on the next day. It was always a pleasure to visit them, walk around their farm, see their animals, and hear about various problems on the farm.

At the lower elevations at that time of year it was often raining and generally cold and miserable. This particular night was typical — cold and rainy. At about ten o'clock, Uncle Vic was worried about an older cow that had not yet calved, and before going to bed we put on our raincoats and went out to the pasture to see how she was making out. We could see her in the distance lying down, and her calf was standing beside her. There was water everywhere, and the calf looked bedraggled and, of course, completely soaked. As we got closer, we could see a large pink mass protruding from the cow's vagina. It measured about 18 inches in diameter and was covered in dirt. Farmers call this mass the "calf bed."

It is actually the uterus or womb of the cow that has literally turned itself inside out during the birth of the calf, and slid down the vagina and is either hanging down, if the cow is standing, or out on the ground if the cow is lying on her side. And it is usually a disaster for the cow, and a big problem for the farmer. The cow stood up, and we were able to lead her to an area where there at least weren't any large puddles of water on the ground. At this point, the cow lay down again, and refused to cooperate any further. The calf dutifully had walked behind and we were able to herd her into a dry building.

Vic told me it was an old cow and he intended to ship her in the morning and put the calf on another cow who had just lost her calf the day before. But an MD doesn't like to give up so easily on a patient, even if it is an old cow. So I offered, stupidly, to try to stuff this big mess back into the cow.

There was no vet on call in this part of the country, and economically it probably wasn't worth it anyway. I should digress a moment to say that I had enough strictly amateur experience to know that we should have something to sew up the cervix (the mouth of the womb) afterwards, if I intended to stuff this mess back in where it belonged. This is to prevent the uterus from turning itself inside out again, and sliding back out of the vagina. Vic didn't have anything that we could improvise.

In veterinary medicine, they have a very large curved needle with some suture material attached to the blunt end that is used to sew up the cervix temporarily. This suture material looks about as thick as a lace for a pair of hockey skates. The farmer is then instructed to sneak up on the cow about three days later and grab the end of this big suture hanging out of the vagina and give it a sharp pull. If it is put in correctly, the slip type knot gives way and the suture comes sliding out. By this time, the uterus has had long enough to heal and doesn't come sliding back out. Surprisingly, the cow can get pregnant again, and usually the uterus behaves itself in subsequent pregnancies. That's the theory anyway.

Well, I had opened my big mouth. We lifted the big gooey mass onto some newspaper and poured water all over it in an effort to try to clean it off. I stripped down to the waist; no sense turning my shirt and sweater into an unrecognizable slimy mess similar to this confounded calf bed. I then found myself flattened on my chest with my right arm stuffed well up into the cow, trying to get this slimy mass back where I thought it belonged. I got it all back in, and tried to make sure I hadn't got it twisted. I think I was lying on the ground for about five minutes — although it felt a lot longer — trying to be sure I had it correctly positioned.

I stood up, cold and wet, and before I even had a chance to take two breaths, the old cow gave the gentlest sigh, and the whole mass was back on the newspaper. I told Vic that we had to get a big needle somewhere and as big a cord that we could thread through the eye of the needle, stuff the infernal thing back in again, pull down the cervix, and try to sew that stupid calf bed shut.

By this time, I think poor old Vic had totally lost confidence in my veterinarian skills and said, "Let's ship her in the morning." We went back to the house. I was cold and very wet and glad to get warm again.

The next morning, Vic made the necessary arrangements to have her shipped, or so I thought, and our family was on its way.

I felt that, if I had had a tail, I would have had it stuffed well between my legs.

The following year, we were back skiing again and dutifully dropped in at Uncle Vic's on our way back home. We did the usual tour of the farm and the animals. We were slightly later that year, and, mercifully, the calving season had been over for more than a week.

We had the usual supper of fine cooking: soup, wine, and a delicious stew with lots of vegetables, buns, jam, and most of the trimmings. Half way through the meal, Vic asked me if I liked the stew. I naturally said it was delicious, which, of course, it was.

He said he thought I would like it, because, after all, "It's your old patient."

Indeed, Uncle Vic had had that cow slaughtered on the farm and had put it in his freezer. The poor cow was close to ten years old and never had any grain in her life. He said the roasts were also excellent. A lot can be said for organically grown grass-fed beef.

I guess it was a consolation prize for me, although I hadn't earned it.

I also noted another meaning to the term "ship her." It also could mean that you didn't actually move her off the farm, but you phoned the man with the truck to come out to your farm. For a fee, he will kill your cow, string it up and dress it on the spot.

HOW FAST CAN DR. FRED RUN?

Our family doctor had just bought a few acres near our farm in Surrey. I think, in retrospect, he was part of that "back to earth movement" that was quite popular at the time in the late 70s. He asked me if he could buy two weaner pigs from us that he planned to fatten over the summer and have butchered in the fall. He was going to give one to a friend and keep the other for his family. (A weaner is a piglet about five to six weeks old and about twenty-five pounds that has been transferred off its mother and is now eating on its own.)

Ordinarily we didn't sell weaners because I felt by the time we had got them up to the weaner stage we might as well keep them until they were "butchers," usually at about five to six months of age. We had a special feeding program that our customers liked, as the pigs were leaner, a little older, and the bacon wasn't laden with fat, ours looking like real English bacon.

The customer who bought a "butcher" from us received all this freezer meat in nice neatly wrapped parcels and didn't get bags of fat with his pig that he would just throw away. Besides, we always had more customers than we had product, and we seemed to have to disappoint some of our customers with every butcher sale.

But what could I say when Fred only wanted two measly weaners and he was, after all, our family doctor. We sold him his two weaners, and off they went to his brand new pigpen. Every thing went well for the first two months, and then, wouldn't you know it, one of his charges got sick.

I went over to have a look and found it had simple "gastro." The poor pig was quite listless and the pen was full of loose stools. The other pig, its littermate, was apparently quite healthy. Fortunately, the treatment is pretty easy — just a course of "fix-all." This is an antibiotic combination that seems to fix most of these ailments. It is a combination of Penicillin G and dihydrostreptomycin that is pre-mixed in the same vial, one millilitre for every one hundred pounds, and given by intramuscular injection.

Fred gave the first dose, with me looking over the wall of his shiny new pen. After that, Fred was on his own. About four days later, Fred phoned me to say that he had a big problem now, because he couldn't catch his pig any more. It ran too fast and was so manoeuvrable that he couldn't tackle it. I told him that he had obviously cured his pig and that he could stop injecting it. But Fred, being a human doctor, always knew that we were supposed to give a complete course of antibiotics, usually lasting seven to ten days.

This "fix-all" is great stuff, but watch out! It can be hazardous to your health, as an English farmer found out the hard way. He felt a cold coming on, and as this stuff seemed to work so well with his animals, he decided to give himself an intramuscular injection. The dihydro type of streptomycin had been known previously to make some humans go permanently stone deaf, and that's what happened to the farmer.

The label says "for veterinarian use only" for a reason.

PACEMAKERS IN DOGS

Dr. Michael Dear, a veterinarian in Richmond, BC, phoned to ask if I could provide him with discarded permanent pacemakers that he could put in dogs. He ran a very successful animal hospital and I always found him to be progressive and very up to date. He made particular mention of an older lady who had a small yellow Labrador retriever that had gone into complete heart block. The dog was relatively young, as I recall, about six years old.

This lady had recently lost her husband, her children had long ago left home, and she was living alone. This dog was now her constant companion, and probably her best friend. What could I say?

Dutifully, I phoned the pacemaker salesman I knew quite well and explained the situation to him. He was quite receptive, and did have available some "second hand" pacemakers. These units came from patients who had had a pacer that had only been in for about two years or less, and who had died, usually from a progression in their underlying heart disease.

If a patient is going to be cremated, the undertaker has to "explant" these units anyway, as described in chapter two, because the lithium units, in particular, are completely sealed in a metal "can" and are virtually guaranteed to explode in the crematorium process. The pacer company usually retrieves these explanted units and hence they could be available for our canines.

If a pacer has six to eight years left on it and the dog's normal life expectancy, by the time it goes into heart block, is shorter than that, it makes sense to use one of these units. Our pacer representative, who even took the time to assist Dr. Dear in the initial operations, didn't charge for these pacer units.

I found it interesting to note that heart block does occur in dogs, in much the same way as in humans. It seems to be related, however, to a cardiomyopathy (heart muscle disease) rather than to coronary artery disease, as seen so commonly in humans. Surprisingly, some dogs tolerate heart block quite well and despite a low heart rate, get around, although with less energy. A friend of mine had a very friendly retriever called Tessa, and she had heart block for several years. It may have slowed her down a bit, but she was otherwise asymptomatic. However, a lot of dogs with complete heart block get into serious trouble.

BUT THE GOAT ATE MY NECKTIE!

It was my birthday again, not a special number; I was going to be thirty-seven, but my wife, Elaine, felt that I should get an Alpine goat for a birthday present. And so, on a Saturday right after I got home from the hospital my wife told me to get into our Econoline van. There was apparently no time to change into my old clothes. Accompanied by our four urchins, off we went to a small farm in South Surrey.

These particular farmers were basically hippies and had converted their house into a partial barn. The "kids" basically had the run of the place — there were young children and goats everywhere. Shortly after we arrived one of the older children yelled, "Agnes has gone 'bombers'!" which meant that these goats were certainly not house trained. The lady of the house simply got a dustpan and small broom and swept up these things that basically looked like a larger edition of rabbit droppings and dumped them into a wastebasket in the living room.

The house smelled like an overripe barn, but nobody seemed to notice except Elaine and our kids. For once, nobody said anything until we got back into our van. We paid twenty dollars for my birthday present, collected a four-month-old Billy goat, and gratefully got out of this house.

The goat, which our kids of course promptly named Billy, seemed quite docile and I easily lifted him into the van. The poor goat had never had a ride in a vehicle before, however, and seemed to become quite upset, so I sat beside him and tried to comfort him on the trip back to our farm.

When we finally got to our barn the goat refused to get out of the van. Repeated gentle coaxing was to no avail. Eventually I grabbed him by the horns and hauled him out to make the two-foot drop to the ground. I felt kind of embarrassed being so rough with our new animal, particularly so early in our relationship, so, holding him by his horns with one hand, I bent over to give him a reassuring pat and discovered that he couldn't have been that upset because he had been quietly chewing on my tie! It was one of my few remaining ties that my wife said were still "decent," but there were now several large holes in it.

Because I had to get up so early in the morning, I never got inspected before I went to work, so I decided to continue to wear the tie as a "badge of honour." It was a great conversation piece at the hospital, and the nurses and the patients got a lot of mileage out of it.

Predictably, I ran into my friend Harry and of course told him my story. He seemed amused and said that he had heard that goats would chew on almost anything, and then said as he walked off, "It was a good thing that you hadn't left your fly open that day!"

CANARY

The next bit of history is "second hand" as told to me, with permission to include it, by my old buddy, Dr. Don Hughes (the same Hughes from the "big rectal" story). It's simply too good a story on the subject of veterinary medicine to leave out.

Don had just graduated from the veterinary college in Guelph, Ontario, and his very first job was covering a vet who was going away on a short holiday. It was a typically hot, extremely humid day in May or June in downtown Toronto — seasonal weather I have mentioned earlier. Predictably, all the blinds were down in the vet's consulting room, and the windows were opened only on the shaded side of the building (they all had screens on them because of the fly problems), and a large fan was doing its thing under the window sill, air conditioning being a rare commodity back then.

A nice middle-aged lady brought in her canary in a large birdcage that had a cover over it, and explained that her pet was "sick." Don told me that, in vet school, they didn't spend much time on birds, and he and most of his classmates weren't that interested in them anyway.

Feeling he had to go through the motions, however, Don lifted off the cover, and very cautiously opened the door of the birdcage. He reached in and gingerly grabbed the poor bird. He was afraid to hold it too tightly, yet on the other hand, he had to hold it tightly enough so that it wouldn't escape. He had just got it out of the cage when it, indeed, did escape and for some reason it flew directly into the spinning fan. The room was filled with yellow feathers and bird debris.

That was Don's first patient in private practice. No wonder he subsequently decided to go into human medicine.

❖ ❖ ❖

I sometimes wondered how the local vets would take to my amateur animal doctor practices. I only received encouragement, and I would often phone the appropriate one if I needed advice about some animal problems.

Though all were very busy, I think sometimes I provided them with amusement regarding the predicaments I would get myself into. They would readily come out to our farm if I needed to be bailed out.

I take my hat off to these vets. After all, was I not the one who was too "chicken" to go to vet school? And was I not the fellow who was *not* man enough to take the punishment of getting kicked, bitten, and flattened against the wall in some bullpen, or getting completely soaked?

CHAPTER 8

Hobbies

ALL WORK AND NO PLAY MAKE JACK A DULL BOY

Hobbies are often good for a patient's morale and were really important for me when I was sick, and on heavy chemotherapy. However, unlike farming, which is relatively safe and doesn't get you into a lot of trouble, some hobbies can be too much of a good thing.

THINGS THAT GO UP MUST COME DOWN AGAIN

Typically, the doctor goes to work early in the morning, is greeted by the nursing staff on the ward or in the operating room, gives instructions, sees his patients and he tells them the simplest of things, such as when they can finally walk to the washroom. He then goes back to the nursing station and writes a list of orders which are faithfully carried out. In the afternoon, he is greeted by his office staff, who are on his payroll and, of course, do exactly what they are told. The same thing applies to the office patients he sees in the afternoon. This routine goes on, day in and day out.

After a variable length of time the doctor believes that he is a "somebody," if not a god. He may begin to believe that he really knows the answers to a lot of things, perhaps not even in his field of so-called "expertise." Unfortunately, this belief has resulted in the premature deaths of many doctors.

On a particularly cold, miserable Saturday in October 1981, I was out rotovating a large field on our farm when a very strange-looking contraption — an ultralight aircraft — flew slowly across our field, perhaps twenty feet over my head. It had been only a cloudy day when I had started out, but now it began to drizzle. I was about a mile from home, and I decided to finish, although I was getting wetter and colder by the minute.

I was, however, enchanted by this aircraft. It flew very slowly and it made no noise above the noise of my tractor. It looked like a very large mosquito and was partly transparent. I had been trying to break up the sod before winter, and I wondered why I was doing this on my day off when I could be up there cruising around in that ultralight aircraft that I was now beginning to think was quite beautiful. The pilot looked so tranquil and contented just sitting in his little seat, looking around. What a wonderful view he must have! (I also noticed that he was sensibly dressed in a rain suit.)

As it turned out, it might have been better if I had never looked up on that day.

When I got home, I asked our oldest boy, Michael —one of those kids who seem to be born with a passionate interest in all things that could fly (he had Harry's "flying chip") — who the person was in that beautiful contraption. He knew immediately that the pilot was Bert Sanders, a man who was a 747 pilot in his real job, and flew these ultralight contraptions on his days off.

Michael soon had him on the phone, and on January 4, 1982, Bert Sanders and Vic Claire (the salesman) arrived on our field by our house, each in his own Lazair aircraft. The Lazair is an aluminum and clear plastic structure powered by two nine-horsepower water-pump (Rotax) engines. These engines were, of course, two cycle and not any more reliable than your average chainsaw motor of that vintage.

I was hooked. We probably all handle the mid-life crisis in different ways. I was well into my middle life and, I suppose, it might have been better if I had taken to the bottle or bought a sports car. However, I opted to buy this kit to make an ultralight aircraft. Dr. Dave Hilton, my partner, readily agreed to buy half of the kit. He was still too young to be suffering from the mid-life crisis; I think he joined up just for the excitement. We each paid three thousands dollars to the nice salesman, Mr. Vic Claire (who was also going to be our instructor), and we eventually were the proud owners of a lot of aluminum pipe, some sheet aluminum and several rolls of a clear plastic sheeting material. The kit also included two small gasoline engines about the size of chainsaw engines.

I don't think Dave or I really had a sufficiently high IQ to actually build the airplane ourselves, and so we duly commissioned my fifteen-year-old son, Michael, to build it for us. We paid him (less than the minimum wage at the time) and he immediately got to work with great enthusiasm. He sub-contracted some of the work to his friends, in much the same way that Tom Sawyer conned some of his friends into painting the famous white fence. In Michael's hands, the project progressed quickly and was completed in less than four months. When it was finished, the salesman told us that it was unusual to have it completed in less than six months.

The bad thing was that now Dave and I were going to have to fly this aircraft. There was no turning back. I started to half hope that there would be some unavoidable delay. Dave and I had started taking lessons from Vic while our aircraft was under construction. These had consisted of two evenings in his basement being told, apparently, everything you need to know about flying an airplane. The aircraft was a single-seater, so there was no room for an instructor on board. Also, Vic didn't have a radio at that time, so he couldn't yell at us from the ground when we were making mistakes.

Our practical "flying" lessons consisted of taxiing around a very large hay field in the salesman's airplane. When we could taxi in a straight line, we were allowed to "hop" off the ground for a few feet, then reduce power and come down again. I took at least a half-hour before I felt I could taxi even half properly. At slow speeds, one could turn by dragging one foot or the other on the ground, as the aircraft had no brakes other than, in my case, the heels of my rubber boots. At faster speeds, one could use differential power, pushing one lawn mower handle or the other forward, which opened the throttle to either engine. (I think the two throttle levers were, in fact, genuine lawn mower parts!) Just before take-off speed, the stick finally worked, and pushing it left or right made the aircraft turn left or right on the ground. This stick was a "mixer stick;" the rudder and the ailerons were connected in some sort of a coordinated fashion, which I never did fully understand.

The real problem was that to make it turn properly, you had

to give it a fair amount of power, and while I was trying all this out the aircraft "hopped" off the ground, long before I was ready. I was not really psyched up to land yet, and so I decided to leave the ground completely. In fact, I'm not really sure if I decided or the airplane decided for me. In any case, I was soon too far off the ground to know what to do, and I was too far down the field to land straight ahead.

I had only been in a small fixed-wing airplane once before in my life. I had been in a helicopter a number of times before when I had trained with the American Marines near Norfolk, Virginia — this on "summer exercises" during my student years in the Canadian Navy (RCN) Reserve. On those occasions, we all sat in the belly of the aircraft surrounded by ammunition and small-calibre machine guns, and never got near the pilot. These earlier experiences had not prepared me for my present situation.

I felt cold and very sweaty, and I knew that the salesman was going to be very angry if I wrecked his airplane. A week before, we had been told all we needed to know to fly a circuit. I just hoped that I had paid sufficient attention. I had not gone over my notes, as I hadn't expected to be in this predicament so soon.

I flew straight ahead, gaining altitude, figuring, I guess, that the further I was above the ground the more time I had to think what to do. I eventually started a very gentle turn to the left and pretty soon was well away from the landing strip, and now three or four hundred feet above the ground. I was afraid that I might lose my bearings. I always had a crappy sense of direction, Mother Nature not giving me the necessary chip. I continued to circle very gradually until I was behind the large hay field from which I had just departed. To get back to the field, I now had to cross the King George highway and, of even more concern, there was a fairly high hydro line running parallel to this road.

I started to descend slowly, but the lower I got, the more the hydro line threatened, and I ended coming in apparently far too high. My instructor and owner of the ultralight, was madly waving his arms on the centre of the runway. I knew he was trying to tell me something, but didn't know what. He hadn't taught us hand signalling in the two nights in his basement, and I found his wildly waving arms were making me even more nervous. Consequently, I decided not even to look at him anymore and just came in to land, too steeply. He ran out of the way as I pulled the power back, only when I was absolutely sure I wasn't going to hit the power lines.

The poor ultralight bounced quite severely, but fortunately I didn't do any damage. I was informed that I had had enough "training" for the day, and I gratefully went home. I did reluctantly agree, however, to come back the next weekend for another lesson.

The next weekend when I arrived, with considerable trepidation, I was told the lesson was scrubbed; the student immediately before me had run into trouble, and landed in one of the local sloughs and nearly drowned. Hence, I was allowed to go home. Vic Claire's airplane was out of action for about a month for repairs. I must confess that I wasn't all that sad that I had missed my lesson and that there would obviously be a further delay while the aircraft was refurbished.

I had had a brief chat several weeks earlier with this student, and I assumed from his thick accent that he was probably from an Eastern European country. He didn't seem overly alert, and although he was probably only five years older than I was, I wondered if he might be a little too doddery to be taking up this sport. I certainly had doubts about myself.

Anyhow, when I talked to him about a month later, he did nothing to help my confidence. Apparently he had taken off, and shortly after he had become airborne he noticed that his airplane was losing altitude, and he could see he was soon going to land, whether he liked it or not. The only flat place he could see was a slough of calm water and so he headed for it and crash landed on the surface. Fortunately, the aircraft did not flip over, but he found himself sitting about four feet under the surface of the slough.

The seat on the Lazair was more like a lawn chair than a typical aircraft seat. It had a single lap-type seat belt. The wing was covered with a type of clear plastic material both top and bottom and, fortunately, contained a lot of air; hence it floated. He tried to get out of his seat, realized he still had his seat belt on and tried to undo it, but could not, because he was still wearing thick gloves. He remembered trying to take off his gloves and then nothing else until he found himself lying on the top of the wing, "breathing like a steam engine." Luckily, the slough was fairly small and he was close to shore.

It turned out that the throttle levers had a tendency gradually to back off due to the vibration of the engines. He was unaware of this problem, and assumed that something had gone wrong with the engines. I don't remember being told about this throttle problem in our two evening classes. In any case, I don't think I ever took my hand off these lawn mower throttles for more than a few seconds after hearing that story!

Four weeks later, when the aircraft had been repaired, I was called back for my next lesson. I was told to take it up to 1,000 feet. When I expressed some surprise, the nice salesman asked if I was scared. I foolishly stated that I wasn't. After all, anything over forty feet was probably fatal, and I had been up three to four hundred feet on my one previous flight — remember? In truth, I was pretty scared, but I felt I had to learn somehow.

Everything started pretty well, at first. I took off and climbed straight ahead as I had done before, and then started a gradual climbing turn. I was watching the altimeter closely. I wanted to know when I got to the magic 1,000 feet so I could come back down and get on *terra firma* again.

However, at some point, I must have tightened my turn too much and/or raised the nose of the aircraft too much, because suddenly, without any warning, I was violently thrown forward and was staring straight down at the ground. I had a lap belt, but no shoulder straps, and my chest was sitting on my knees.

A most peculiar feeling came over me. I wasn't sure if I was going to shit my pants, or get sick at my stomach, or perhaps do both simultaneously. At this point, I was about 600 feet above the ground. The ultralight was gathering speed, and I vaguely wondered if I pulled the stick back if it would make any difference. With some trepidation I did.

What a relief! The aircraft levelled out. I was no longer looking at the ground and could sit up without any effort again. I had lost about 300 feet, and so started my climb again, round and round. Finally I got up to 1,000 feet, gratefully descended again, and made another bouncy landing.

My instructor had told me to stick to the area over the hay field so he could keep an eye on me. He obviously hadn't been watching, and when I told him what had happened he said a gust of wind had probably gotten under my tail. In retrospect, I don't remember having been told about stalls or spins.

I was now apparently ready to fly my own ultralight. After

all, I'd had two nights of ground school, been up to 1,000 feet, and had completed two circuits. Most importantly, Michael had finished his work, and had run up the engines. What were we waiting for? The airplane actually looked beautiful — if you knew someone else was going to fly it. The big day came when both Dave Hilton and I had a day off, July 10, 1982.

When I arrived, Dave was already "chomping at the bit." I was late and he was ready to go. He did consent, however, somewhat reluctantly, to flip a coin to see who would be the first to fly this "thing." I won the toss and, almost immediately, was taxiing out for takeoff. The aircraft seemed to hold a pretty straight line considering who was driving, and I was airborne long before it got to the dreaded barbed wire fence at the end of our field.

However, just as soon as I was airborne, something went wrong with both engines, and they soon had dropped their rpm's to something just over idle. When I looked down, I realized I was over the top of a very large cottonwood tree. Because I had lost airspeed, the controls were suddenly very "mushy" and, although I really had no idea what was wrong, I wondered if something had gone amiss with the controls.

I probably did everything wrong, and soon I really was merely a helpless passenger trying to miss a television aerial and then another large tree. One engine kicked in with increased power for a very short moment and then died back to very low power again.

Aghast, I realized I was now heading toward the top line between two hydro poles. By this time, I seemed to have no control at all over the aircraft. It didn't matter what I did with the stick. I found out later that I was in a "full stall" and didn't even know it. It crossed my mind that this might be the end.

I hit the wire full on (18,000 volts). My neighbours, who had come out to watch this maiden flight, saw a big flash several poles down from where I hit. It turned out that the wire had broken at this point at a connector, and the short piece had touched the wire below and shorted out, causing a big flash and blowing a breaker somewhere. My right engine, which was still turning over, gathered in some of this slack hydro wire around the propeller. The left engine had apparently stopped completely.

My poor airplane was flung violently around, doing a 180-degree turn, and the wings were roughly parallel to the three wires below. The momentum carried me a little further forward, and I missed these three wires in my hasty descent to the ground. I missed the flash from the short circuit; my eyes may have been closed, or I may have been facing the wrong way at that time.

When I hit the ground, I experienced no pain and couldn't believe my good fortune. I then saw two young kids running toward me and I yelled at them to stay away, as the wires "might be hot." However, I then noticed that the wire was wrapped around the right propeller and was in fact across my legs as I was still sitting in the cockpit. There was no sparking and I climbed out.

I had landed in my neighbour's front yard and he came out immediately. He kindly lent me his phone, and I called my wife, who was still within earshot of our home telephone where she had been standing to see my maiden flight. When I came out of our neighbour's house, our kids, including Michael and several neighbours who lived close to the crash site, were already at the scene.

My poor partner, Dave, who had run at top speed the whole distance of the flight, about a third of a mile, arrived a few moments later. He was pale and sweaty, and I thought he might faint. He subsequently told me that when he mounted the small hill on his run over, he saw a white object swinging back and forth and he thought it was my head. Just before takeoff he had lent me his hockey helmet, complete with a wire facemask (we were supposed to wear a helmet in these airplanes). As it turned out, what he had seen was the gas tank, which had jumped out of its harness and was still attached to the gas line, and that was causing it to swing. I was still wearing the helmet but I was in my neighbour's house making the phone call, and that was why he hadn't seen me.

On the other hand I, unlike David, had a peculiar feeling of euphoria. I even wondered if I had, in fact, died and was now in some kind of a dream state.

Dave quickly brought me back to reality and said, "Let's get this plane out of here before the authorities arrive!" By this time, a good crowd of neighbours had gathered and the aircraft, including some pieces, were bodily picked up and taken down the street and up my driveway and put out of sight behind our barn.

My buddy, Mr. Simon Kurtenacher, from the next farm, reminded me that perhaps I should phone BC Hydro. Besides, all my neighbours on the street were without electrical power. When I called BC Hydro, the person on the phone asked me how I had broken the line, and when I told him I was flying "one of those stupid airplanes," he just laughed. I never even received a bill.

I really dreaded phoning Vic Claire, and when I did later that afternoon, he bawled me out and said I could have given his business a bad reputation. As it turned out, the Ministry of Transport had no jurisdiction at that time over ultralights. There were no serial numbers on the aircraft, no formal instructions, and in fact, no regulations of any kind. I went on to fly about 200 hours on this aircraft, but I had eighteen further engine failures. We eventually sold it, "before somebody got killed."

Vic told me that he thought my original engine failure, affecting both engines, was likely due to the initial breaking-in of the engines. We had run both engines at varying throttle speeds, as had been recommended by the manufacturer. But, with the airplane tied down, the props could only get up to about 3,000 rpm, turning in stagnant air. When the airplane got airborne, the air was rushing past the propeller and the prop could now go much faster, perhaps up to about 5,000 rpm. Carbon had likely built up on the cylinder walls, and when suddenly, and for the first time, the engines had achieved this speed, the deposited carbon started flying around inside the cylinder and ended up fouling both spark plugs. That was Vic's theory, anyway.

All my subsequent engine failures were likely related to using the wrong type of gas. When one engine failed, we had to throttle back on the other engine, because otherwise the "mixer stick" arrangement made the airplane fly in circles. The "mixer" could only offset a small amount of thrust from a single engine. Consequently, we could not maintain altitude on a single engine, and would lose about 200 feet per minute. This slow rate of descent allowed us, however, to find more places to land or crash land.

Fortunately, I ran into Reg, of Reg Motors, and he got me off the cheap farm gas that we were using onto a high-octane gas. This made a tremendous difference. Reg also got me onto a schedule of regular maintenance. I would unbolt the two engines every twenty-five hours, put them into the back of my car and drive over to his place in Port Kells. After this, we had no further engine failures.

Of course, the ultralights now are much better, have reliable engines and better airframes. Moreover, the Ministry of Transport is fully involved, and some might think it is now even over-regulated.

Sometimes it's more prudent to just keep working and stay out of trouble. As I mentioned earlier, it might have been better if I had ignored Bert Sanders when he flew overhead on that cold October day.

Maybe I might have handled my mid-life crisis better if I *had* turned to the bottle. But, then again, think of the excitement I'd have missed. After these mishaps, I decided to try to get my private pilot's license. I started with a proper ground school, and did that open my eyes! I then did my practical and during the training for the simulated engine failure, my instructor was quite impressed how well I did this procedure. I then confessed that I should be pretty good at it because, after all, I had had eighteen real ones in my ultralight.

I found that I really enjoyed this flying business, and took a course in mountain flying and aerobatics and obtained my night and float endorsements. I eventually bought a "home built" aircraft on floats.

> Bert Sanders died several years later in a rare ultralight accident. He was always a very generous person and would give me tips on how to fly our ultralight. Sometimes he would literally drop into our hayfield while we were haying and give us a break from our work by giving each of us rides in his aircraft. He flew a different type of ultralight plane called a "Spectrum Beaver." The accident occurred because one of the wing struts had not been properly bolted back into position after it had been transported.

THINGS THAT GO DOWN MAY NOT COME BACK UP

In 1962, Vancouver's Shaughnessy Hospital was considered "the rest home" for tired "migrant" Toronto General Hospital interns. When my wife and I arrived there, on Saturday, July 1st of that year, it was a holiday weekend and I was told to report back on Tuesday morning, "around 9 o'clock."

It was a shock to the system to be able actually to have time do something else other than medicine. Normally, at a big Toronto teaching hospital you would start work on the first day of a long weekend and be in full swing by 7:00 a.m. The contrast was amazing, and it continued to be amazing because we were never really overloaded with work at Shaughnessy, and we had time to read around our more interesting cases.

Perhaps even more importantly, we had time for some recreation. One of the first activities that we got involved in was scuba diving.

I'd had an introduction to scuba diving when I was in the University Navy program. It had caught my interest, and now I had an opportunity to take this interest forward. I was keen to become proficient as a diver. After a little research, I found there were only two possible places to get the proper training, and one of them offered a good group rate.

Pretty soon, we had signed up eight interns and some wives and girl friends, including my wife, to make a total of twelve people. Apparently, that was enough to get a really good rate with that particular company. Recreational scuba diving was still in its infancy, and a few well-publicized accidents and relatively poor and uncomfortable equipment had slowed its development. However, we were aided by being young, enthusiastic and, best of all, too trusting and stupid.

Fortunately, the diving store was safety oriented, and we were assured that every thing had been thoroughly tested. Soon, we were enrolled in a course that consisted of two weekends of classes, some work in a small pool, and then a deep-water dive. The deep-water dive took place at Britannia Beach, just outside Vancouver. The water was very clear that day, the beach had a gentle slope, and we experienced no unusual problems.

Two people had to go down really slowly because their ears had to equalize with the increased pressure that we had not noticed in the shallow pool training. The rest of us got on without any difficulty and became fairly enthusiastic. During that fall, after we got our little card that said we were "divers," about half a dozen interns would go out on most weekends for half a day at different sites along Howe Sound.

We quickly found that the steep shores were better, because we could find interesting plant life, lingcod, and other fish that were interesting to watch. The gently sloping beaches were soon abandoned for rocky outcrops. The weather became less of a problem, and it didn't matter if it was windy or raining; once we were down twenty feet or more, we didn't notice what was going on at the surface. We started going further afield, and when we could afford it, hired dive boats and rented spear guns.

Our enthusiasm, predictably, of course, outstripped our common sense (that doctor thing); and the "buddy" system soon went by the wayside, because it was very difficult to keep the other partner in sight, particularly if the water wasn't very clear. As we went further, we started dealing with currents and very poor visibility.

I found I was blessed with two features of physical health that helped me in this endeavour, another feature that was probably neutral, and yet another feature that was a constant problem for me.

My two helpful features were that I possessed eustachian tubes (those little tubes that connect our middle ear to the back of our throat) that allowed me to "sink like a stone," with no ear pain; and I was an excellent breath holder, and could free dive to 65 feet and still have enough breath left to cruise around.

My "neutral" feature was my relative lack of subcutaneous fat. I found I got cold faster than others in the same water, and the deeper we went the greater compression of our "wet" neoprene suits ensued, hence the less insulation there was and the colder I got. On the other hand it is said that skinny people do not suffer nitrogen narcosis ("the rapture of the deep") as quickly as their more padded colleagues.

> Nitrogen narcosis is a reversible alteration in consciousness producing a state similar to alcohol intoxication in scuba divers at depth. It becomes more noticeable at great depths, but is also a function of time. It appears to be a direct effect of nitrogen under pressure dissolving in nerve membranes and causing temporary disruption in nerve transmission.

My big negative feature is that I have no sense of direction, and regularly get lost in a department store. In fact, I am so bad that I can go into a building, sit down in a chair, try on a pair of shoes and then get up and turn the wrong way. Then, when I leave the store, I inevitably turn the wrong way again, sometimes not even remembering what door I came in. I get very annoyed with myself. It has become a family joke that I got married to a geographer, not for the sex, but so I wouldn't get lost as often.

Although I could never describe myself even as an experienced diver, I did try to partake in a lot of activities including cave diving and going under ice. During my time of active diving, I ran into several potentially fatal diving-related problems.

FROM PENIS TO ZUCCHINI

One day, early in my scuba career, I looked up and thought I saw one of my friends floating on the surface. We had just started our dive, and I thought everybody had gone down. Because of my lack of eustachian tube problems, I was usually the first one down.

I swam back up and took out my mouthpiece to talk to my friend on the surface. He said he had a slight pain in his chest. He was a little anxious and the surface water was rough, so I suggested that he just sit on some nearby rocks to get out of the swell, and we would come to pick him up when our tanks had run out. I remember that we had a particularly interesting dive that day, and when our tanks were finished we collected our friend and headed to shore. He still had that "little" pain in his chest.

We got into our cars and headed back to Shaughnessy Hospital, where we had planned yet another beer fest for that evening (part of our recovery program from the previous year of purgatory that we had experienced at the Toronto General as juniors). Our poor friend looked okay, and we advised him that he would probably feel better if he had a few beers.

I feel bad to this day, and the only thing that makes me feel better about subsequent events is that as he was a doctor — and all of the divers that day were doctors, and we were all aware of his "little" pain — perhaps I could spread the blame around a little bit. During the party that night, most of the interns were there and we all checked up on him and encouraged him to "have another beer." He was not a particularly strong swimmer and the weather had certainly not been ideal. I thought he had become a little frightened, and we all just jollied him along. Besides, we didn't want him to quit diving, as he was a good guy and we all enjoyed his company on these outings. Just before midnight, he said that he still had a little pain in his chest and he thought he would go to bed early.

The unmarried interns stayed in residence in the hospital in those days, as it was free and interns' salaries were very poor. I was married and my wife had a good teaching job, so we could afford to stay in an apartment. This poor doctor then wandered off and went to bed just down the hall. The party broke up sometime after midnight and I went home.

Around 3:00 a.m. our friend awakened, and now he thought he was a little short of breath. He walked into the hall and woke up his next-door neighbour who was sound asleep. His neighbour reached out his hand to see who was disturbing him and touched the man leaning over his bed.

Although the light hadn't been turned on yet, he realized that whomever he had just touched had "surgical emphysema." Any medical student could recognize this, because of a very peculiar and almost spectacular feeling of "egg shells" breaking under the skin. He turned on his bed light, and standing before him was our friend, who was now almost unrecognizable, being completely puffed up, one eye completely closed, and the other nearly closed.

As it turned out, the poor fellow had likely burst a small area in one of his lungs, perhaps caused by coming to the surface too quickly without letting out sufficient air. The air had tracked up through the soft tissues in his neck and then spread out under his skin. This subcutaneous air had gone everywhere from his neck to the top of his face and down to his knees. His penis was so swollen that he could not void and he had to be catheterized.

He ended up with two chest tubes, and spent a week in the intensive care unit. We all visited him every day in the hospital, and of course made the crude jokes that only doctors can make to each other when one of their colleagues is suffering. We watched, with obvious disappointment, as his overly enlarged penis shrank down from day to day.

Fortunately, he made a complete recovery. But we had all learned a lesson, I hope.

Our little diving group had gradually become smaller, and only the die-hards like me had started gradually to buy second-hand equipment to cut down on the rental fees. I bought an old wet suit and had to lengthen the arms and legs before it fit. I got a refurbished regulator and a pair of oversized fins. Eventually, I got an air tank that everybody told me looked as if it had come out of Noah's Ark. I also purchased a depth gauge and a pressure gauge for my air tank.

These latter items were supposed to have been refurbished, but they soon ceased to function, and I had found that I could roughly tell when my tank was running out as the pitch of sound coming from my regulator kept rising as my tank pressure fell. Also, I could guess my approximate depth by looking at the thickness of my wet suit. By the time I was down to about one hundred feet, my wet suit was less than half as thick as it was on the surface, and of course had much less insulating value. My lack of subcutaneous fat probably contributed to my coldness and was a good reminder to check my depth. I did eventually replace these items after persistent badgering by my associates who felt the extra equipment would lower my risk potential.

Often, I would end up diving alone, as I would be away with my wife or some other people who didn't quite share my enthusiasm for diving. I carried my scuba gear in our old van in case I found a good place to go swimming. I eventually bought a second tank and made a particularly powerful spear gun. In subsequent years my wife and I took holidays to go scuba diving as we both found it all very interesting.

MEETING THE FERRY

In the spring of 1963 I often went to Horseshoe Bay, just north of Vancouver, to get Dungeness crabs. These creatures are real garbage hounds, and in those days there was always lots of garbage in this bay.

I entered the water at the north end of the bay, well away from the ferry terminal. Cruising along the beach in about thirty feet of water, keeping the rising shore line to my left, I started picking up crabs and sticking them into my "goodie bag" that was specially designed for this purpose.

Unfortunately for the "directionally challenged," the bottom of the bay in its mid-point is pretty flat, and I no longer could use the gently rising shoreline to keep my direction. Somehow, I got myself completely turned around and I thought I was heading back to my starting point. I was doing well, getting my bag full of nice crabs. It was a common practice to exchange the smaller crabs for the bigger crabs as they came along. I had my bag full of big crabs and thought I was probably pretty near my starting point when I came across a large pole the size of a telephone pole stuck in the sand. I wondered why anybody would put a post out there and thought I should investigate. The visibility in the bay was usually less than fifteen feet, and today was no exception.

In these harbours there is a constant noise level as the many boats go about their business overhead. After a short time, we ignored these sounds and would come to the surface as close as possible to the shore or come up by a buoy, usually with our hands over our heads to reduce the unlikely possibility that we might be hit on the head by a passing outboard.

As I rose towards the surface, I knew that I would not be in any danger as long as I stuck close to the post. But when I got near the surface, I found that a large dark "ceiling" blocked my way. I assumed that I must have become disorientated again and gone further than I thought, and had now come up under the ferry dock, as it was the only large structure in the bay at that time.

I thought if I went slowly along this structure, I would come to the end of the dock. I did notice there were grooves running parallel to each other, but I assumed that they were spaces between the boards on the dock, so I headed in their general direction.

Suddenly, without any warning, I was pitched head over heels and there was a simultaneous roaring sound in my ears. I dropped my goodie bag and headed for the bottom, but I had trouble because I was being pitched around so much. Soon, to my relief, the turbulence was less and relative tranquility was restored.

I came across another post, and then another, and I thought I would try again to come up to get my bearings.

This time I had no problems, and when I came up I found myself in the slip for the Horseshoe Bay ferry. When I turned around, and faced seaward I could see the ferry about four hundred yards out, just starting to turn around.

I had apparently come up under the ferry on my first attempt, and what I thought was the decking on the dock was actually the flat bottom of the ferry. The captain chose this time to start the engines! Fortunately, he was backing out, so I was ejected by the wash from the propeller and not sucked into it.

I found my goodie bag and headed north, none the worse for wear.

After that experience, I bought a compass and practiced using it. If I ever have occasion to find a telephone pole sticking down in the water again I think I will be a little more circumspect.

NITROGEN NARCOSIS — ONE MARTINI PER ATMOSPHERE

In the summer of 1965 my wife and I went on a diving holiday to Andros Island in the Bahamas. We stayed briefly at Small Hope Bay Lodge and found the owners, who were originally from Toronto, to be extremely hospitable.

The first morning, the diving guide asked me if I wanted to go down to the top of a ledge, apparently 185 feet down. He said there were a lot of big fish down there, and he had done it many times. There was another tourist who was keen to go, but the guide wanted me to go too in case something went wrong, because I had had more experience.

I remember that in a Navy course in 1958, we were told not to go down more than 100 feet, unless in an extreme emergency. (The Royal Navy Diving Tables were the "Bible" in those days.) I don't know why I didn't follow my better judgment, but the diving guide was obviously very experienced and seemed to know what he was doing. Who was I to argue? And besides, he said there were lots of big fish to see and when was I ever going to get a chance like this again?

The guide was probably in his mid thirties and the other tourist was in his late twenties, about my age, and he seemed like a pretty nice fellow and was very enthusiastic. I noticed that they both had extra body fat, which I had read somewhere could be a risk for deeper dives. I somewhat guiltily reasoned that I had two "barometers" with me who would probably run into trouble before I did. I decided to keep a very close eye on them, not just for their sake, but also for my own protection.

We went to the assigned spot. I don't remember if we had an anchor down, but we probably did, and there were three extra scuba tanks hanging down on a rope for decompression before surfacing. We descended fairly rapidly, which I thought was good, so we would have lots of air in our tanks to get back up if there was a problem. I made sure that I had a functioning watch and that my depth gauge and pressure gauge, which belonged to the hotel, seemed to work. We got to the promised ledge, at about the 185-foot mark. We cruised along briefly and our guide indicated that we had to just go over the wall to see the bigger fish down below. At this point, the nice tourist suddenly started swimming erratically; we both rushed over and without much trouble assisted him upwards.

When we got up to about the fifty-foot mark he seemed to have become normal again, and we let him swim on his own and gave him a short decompression before we went all the way up to the surface. The water was as clear as it probably gets, and I just don't know what would have happened if we had lost sight of him in poor visibility.

Back in the boat, the tourist was very quiet and, despite my badgering, he didn't want to talk about what had gone wrong, so I never did find out what he had experienced in his head. In fact, he stayed by himself. Even the next day he still kept his distance, despite the fact that we might have saved his life.

Unfortunately, my wife and I had to leave and I lost track of him. Being a physician, I was naturally curious about the feeling that one was supposed to get with nitrogen narcosis, and I wanted to know how to detect the earliest signs if it occurred in me.

Subsequently, while I was working in the hyperbaric unit at the Toronto General Hospital, we had to be in the chamber with the patient in order to watch the IV and administer any necessary drugs. However, we only went "down" three atmospheres, or about sixty-six feet and I was never aware of any feelings of euphoria. I think we were always chronically fatigued, and of course had the responsibility of looking after the patient in the hyperbaric unit, so perhaps the euphoria escaped most of us. We had been told that we were supposed to experience "one martini per atmosphere." But it never seemed to materialize. Most disappointing. I really could have used a martini in that confined space.

Many years later, however, one of our sons, Stephen, provided me with a very bizarre description of an episode that happened

The hyperbaric unit at the Toronto General Hospital was basically a large air pressurized chamber in which patients and one or two attendants could be placed and pressured to an equivalent of sixty-six feet under water. This chamber had a number of clinical applications discussed later in this chapter.

211

Doesn't everybody want to bury themselves in dead fish?

to him while he was working on a fish farm on the west coast of Canada. A type of algae had apparently clogged the gills of the Chinook salmon (Atlantic salmon were not at this time raised on these farms), and they had a large number of "morts" (that is the name they use for dead fish that accumulate on the bottom of the fish pens).

The fish pens are normally sixty-five feet deep, but with a large fish kill, the bottom of the netting material is stretched down in a funnel shape to about eighty-five feet. His job was to get these fish out of the pen as soon as possible, as they were still marketable for a short time. He sat on the top of this pile of dead fish and a large basket was lowered to him. He would fill this basket with the dead fish and then jerk the rope three times and the crew on top would haul it up.

He was on his second tank of air when he began to wonder what it would be like to just bury himself in all these dead fish. He had about three minutes between the time the basket was hauled up and it was returned to him. During this time, he decided to carry out this bizarre behaviour. He was up to his mid-chest in dead fish when he saw that the basket had become tangled in the side of the fish pen and he had to swim up to about the 50-foot level to free it up. Just as soon as he got to this level, he suddenly realized what he had been doing, and recognized his bizarre mental state.

He went towards the surface, decompressed, and called it a day.

Stephen's experience caused me to wonder whether our tourist, all those years before, had experienced some thoughts that perhaps he felt were just too bizarre to relate to anyone.

Within a few years after we had been on Andros Island, the American Navy built a large submarine base there. It was very suitable for them because this beautiful paradise provided a long trench that was a mile deep and totally protected by surrounding coral reef, away from prying Russian eyes. I doubt the place will, unfortunately, ever be the same. It was aptly named "Tongue of the Ocean."

BUBBLES AND MORE BUBBLES (THE BENDS)

In 1966, when I was back at the Toronto General for more training before my fellowship exams, I was asked again to work in the hyperbaric chamber, which was a popular treatment for some conditions in those days. It was found to be particularly useful for the treatment of gas gangrene and carbon monoxide poisoning.

While I was there, a study was in progress to determine if hyperbaric oxygen was useful in the treatment of ischemic limbs (that usually meant a leg that, due to arterial disease, had a poor blood supply, and hence was not getting enough oxygen to sustain itself). These patients were almost always elderly, often diabetic, frequently had a long history of smoking, and had bad chests and often a history of heart disease.

Any of these patients required lots of attention when in the hyperbaric unit, and in those days the patient had to be accompanied by an MD while in the chamber. Physicians willing to work in this unit were in short supply, and none of us was paid to work there, apart from our regular intern salary. Anyway, whenever we had a spare minute at that time we would use it to study for our approaching specialty exams. I found it a real imposition having to go to the hyperbaric unit whenever I was called. Also, for some reason I seemed to be very tired after I got out of the chamber, and it was hard to go back to the books.

I had just gotten into bed after a particularly bad night in the Emerg, when I was called by Dr. B. Fairley to report to the hyperbaric chamber. I was still half asleep when I arrived outside the unit.

Dr. K, one of the particularly popular anesthetists, was sitting in a wheelchair. He had noted central chest pain and found his left arm and left leg, in his words, "unreliable." He apparently had just left the chamber after attending one of the "ischemic" patients and had walked a distance of several hundred yards to attend patients in another building (Centre Block) connected to the Toronto General Hospital.

He suddenly experienced this pain and simultaneous clumsiness of his left arm and leg. Rapidly testing him, I found he also had a complete left visual field defect. But his speech had not been affected and he seemed totally "with it."

I assumed he had, for some reason, developed small bubbles (a case of the bends) in his cerebral and coronary circulation and was not getting enough blood to his brain or heart muscle. In essence, he had developed a small stroke and simultaneously was having severe angina.

It was therefore imperative that he be put right back in the chamber on 100 percent oxygen to remove these nitrogen bubbles that had formed.

In those days, the Navy ran the hyperbaric chamber. Navy personnel staffed the unit, ran the compressor, and turned the big valves. The anesthetic staff ran the medical component of the unit. When I arrived at the chamber only one Navy man had arrived, and one of the Navy orders was that nobody could go down until two Navy people were on hand outside the chamber. We had no idea how long it would be before the other "hand" would show up.

At this point I had to become very forceful, not my usual personality, and had to persuade this Navy robot that we had an emergency. I had been promoted to the rank of a full naval lieutenant on obtaining my MD in 1961. (Due to my four years in the reserve Navy, and having completed the required courses, I had already been given the rank of sub-lieutenant.) I told this petty officer that I would accept full responsibility, and there was no more argument.

I had always thought of my commission in the Navy as a bit of a joke, as I never thought I would actually have to use it. But the occasion had arrived. The petty officer then went right ahead with his job and within the next two minutes Dr. K and I were headed "down."

As soon as we got down to the equivalent of about sixty feet (so-called three atmospheres) all Dr. K's symptoms disappeared. The second Navy robot finally arrived, and Dr. Fairley came in on his heels. Dr. Fairley came immediately into the chamber through the compression door, and I was asked to leave to preserve my bottom time if I was needed again. I gratefully went back to bed.

Dr. K fortunately had no after effects, but after this event all personnel had to breathe 100 percent oxygen during the decompression phase. That didn't completely jibe with our Navy teaching, which specified that with the oxygen re-breathers we weren't allowed to go deeper than thirty feet. (The re-breathers were a military de-

> "Bottom time" is the time spent under pressure and is strictly regulated. As the amount of time and amount of pressure is increased, the risk of serious complications rises. Occasionally, even sticking very closely to the rules can still result in complications. It's strictly a case of playing the odds, trying to keep the risks within an acceptable limit.

A year later, when I was no longer involved in the hyperbaric unit, there was a rumour that the Navy staff had done some experiments whereby they had rendered the relief valve in the unit inoperative so that they could go down to greater depths in this chamber. It was alleged that during one of these experiments one of their senior personnel had suffered paraplegia (a lower body paralysis) and never made a complete recovery. It was likely that he had formed a bubble somewhere in his spinal cord circulation; he was left in a wheelchair and had a permanent indwelling catheter.

vice used in shallow dives because they didn't give off telltale bubbles, and would allow clandestine frog men to put "limpet" mines on the sides of ships in harbour or riding at anchor).

I continued to dive periodically along the west coast of BC, or occasionally when I was away on holiday. But after my experiences I think I became a little more cautious. After one very difficult dive, one of my friends once said, "I don't think Mother Nature ever intended us to be down there." Amen to that!

THE CIGARETTE MACHINE

In the 1940s and 50s everybody smoked. During World War II, my own mother was even told by our family doctor that she should *take up* smoking! Because my mother was having a lot of anxiety, he thought it would help settle her nerves. She was often alone, and had three little urchins running around raising hell. The doctor might have made a better choice if he had put us all on phenobarb. (Ritalin wasn't available back then.)

Sitting in the back of the car, my brothers and I would be "fumigated" by the adults smoking in the front seat. They weren't being bad; in those days nobody even thought that smoking might be unhealthy. And as far as I know, all my friends were being equally fumigated by their parents. In every movie, the hero and heroine smoked, and if somebody was badly wounded, the first thing he got was a drag off one of those infernal cigarettes. When I was in the university Navy, once a week we were issued a carton of cigarettes, containing ten packages of twenty cigarettes each. The total cost of each carton was one dollar, or ten cents per package. This was a bargain even in those days, because a package of twenty cigarettes cost thirty-seven cents at the store.

In 1961, when I graduated from medical school, I would estimate that at least a third of our class smoked cigarettes. Those of us who didn't smoke had tried it and didn't like it, or we felt we just couldn't afford it. My father was "hooked" but he discouraged us from starting, and said he would give each of us a gold watch or a hundred dollars if we had not started by age twenty-one. Naturally, we all went for the one hundred dollars — who needs a gold watch? Unfortunately, like so many of his friends, my father developed emphysema in his later years.

In 1961, the surgeon-general of the United States came out

with his definitive report that smoking was responsible for a whole list of maladies. It was the first report of this kind and, of course, was soon followed by so many other reports that there could really be no serious argument that this stuff was harmless. Not surprisingly, the cigarette companies still contested this information, and did many manoeuvres to try to mitigate all this adverse publicity.

Well into the 70s, hospital personnel, particularly doctors, continued to smoke, even a lot of the younger ones who really, in my opinion, had no excuse because all the information was available before they got hooked. At medical meetings we continued to get fumigated. What an example we were setting! The Royal Columbian Hospital was still selling cigarettes, the Woman's Auxiliary gift shop, the blind man's shop (a feature in many Canadian hospitals at that time) and, of course, the cigarette machines.

I often noticed that many adults, and even teenagers, would come in to the hospital at night when the outside stores had closed to buy cigarettes from the cigarette machines; and young kids were sometimes seen coming into the entrance of the Emerg to use the cigarette machine.

The doctors on staff would have to attend three out of the four general staff meetings each year, if they wanted to maintain their hospital admitting privileges. These meetings were well attended, with seldom less than 150 doctors present; it was often standing room only. Sometimes these meetings were quite turbulent.

In those days the GP's virtually ran the hospital, and most were still active in obstetrics. Specialists were almost invitees; because we seldom admitted our own patients, there had to be a GP assigned to each patient's case. Also, though it is perhaps unbelievable now, the administration back then even *listened to the medical staff*, and where possible, implemented our suggestions.

Every year I would, like clockwork, introduce a motion to the effect that the hospital should not be in the business of selling cigarettes. Apparently, twelve months had to elapse before someone could reintroduce the same motion. Each year, I would introduce the same motion, and each year, the medical staff would soundly vote me down!

As the years passed, however, the vote was getting "closer," and some of the doctors were beginning to think that I was going to win within a year or two. The women's auxiliary, to their credit, voluntarily stopped selling cigarettes, but the blind man persisted and, of course, the cigarette machine still did a thriving business.

At one of these public spectacles, when I spoke to my motion I said, in frustration, "I can't even go up and poke out that blind man's eyes because someone has already done it for me!" This was, fortunately, taken as a joke and I got a lot of laughs, but a lot of boos too.

However, although the cigarette machine didn't have eyes that I could poke out, it was very particular about its diet. All it would accept was money. It didn't even accept those cheap Italian liras. Those large bent paper clips definitely were not on its recommended diet, and if inadvertently, it was offered one of these, the result was a "bowel obstruction."

Sometimes, I noticed that some vandal had rendered the machine "out of order" by spreading one of those large paperclips and then putting it in the cigarette machine's "mouth" (the coin slot). At other times, someone had taken a pair of side cutters and cut off the machine's "tail" (the electrical plug). Mysteriously, a whole shoebox of these plugs appeared in our office.

Because of my job, I was often in the Emerg at very odd hours, and around the entrance it often seemed to be just the poor cigarette machine and me. Sometimes, I would have to wait around for lab results before I could go on to the next thing, or I wanted to see what effect a certain anti-arrhythmic drug had on a patient before leaving the area. Often I couldn't go to bed because an ambulance had called in to say that they had a cardiac arrest in progress on the way to our Emerg. On occasion, the nurses would find a stretcher in the back of the Emerg, where I could "crash."

As I mentioned before, my Baptist grandmother said, "An idle mind is the devil's workshop." There is a rider to this; the idle mind has to have some toys in order to get into trouble. A prisoner in solitary would have an idle mind, but without his toys, such as knives, guns, and, or, drugs, he can't get into trouble. My toy might be the cigarette machine, and I was still on "the outside."

On one occasion, a rather pretty young nurse (she was still quite young, hence her face had not yet become wrinkled from her cigarette habit) had put her money in the coin mechanism,

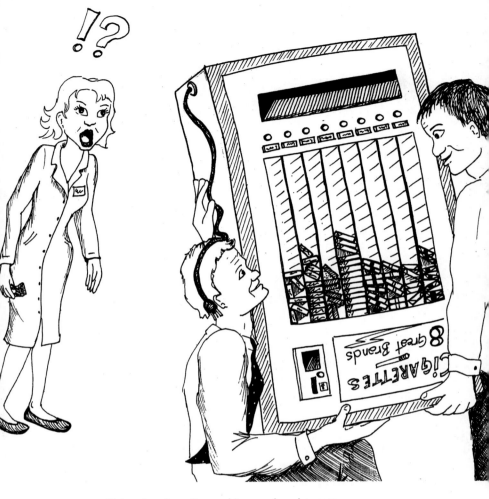

Giving the cigarette machine a colossal enema.

and I guess somebody had screwed up the machine again, because she didn't get her cigarettes.

Dr. Cory Brown and I just happened by, and we decided that if we turned the machine upside down we might be able to shake her money back out of that coin slot. Cory would do anything for a damsel in distress, and he also hated smoking. Fortunately, Cory was a pretty big guy, because the machine was surprisingly heavy. When we got it upside down, no money came out of the coin slot, but about twelve packages of cigarettes came down when we righted the machine. I guess we had given the machine what amounted to a colossal enema.

Just at that moment, an orderly appeared and asked what we were doing. I thought we were sunk, but Cory suggested that if he took half of the "free" cigarettes, he would be an accomplice and hence he could be relied on to keep his mouth shut. He rapidly agreed, took half, our nurse took the package that she had paid for, and Cory destroyed the rest by crushing them up and throwing them into the garbage.

Despite all these travails, the machine manager persisted. But, one day someone left one of those construction dollies right beside the cigarette machine. Once again it was late at night, or more likely early in the morning, my mind was idle and, of course, I had my toy in view and there was nobody around.

I decided to lift this heavy machine onto the trolley. I got one end on and was struggling to get the other end on, but the trolley wasn't co-operating because it wanted to roll away every time I went to lift the other end. I was cursing under my breath when Dr. Don MacDonald, the big orthopod, came along and said, "Tom, let me help you."

I was shocked. I didn't think he would get involved in anything like this. He was an older man, and definitely of "the old school." But pretty soon, we had the machine on the trolley and took it for a ride into a nearby building that was under construction. We found a nice "cosy" place for it, put a drop sheet that was lying close by over it, and then put some old building material on top for good measure. Our "patient" now had what amounted to a private room, and with all this stuff on top of it, would get a good rest.

The next day, it was announced that the machine had been stolen, and it took two weeks before it was discovered that the machine had merely been "misplaced."

Amazingly, the cigarette machine was again back in business; it was like post-nasal drip, and just wouldn't go away. Fortunately, the next vote of the medical staff banished the machine from the hospital.

I kind of missed it though. What was I going to do for entertainment in the middle of the night while I was waiting for some lab results?

I had lost one of my favourite hobbies.

CHAPTER 9

Medical Buddies

Medicine, unlike a lot of other professions, is largely a co-operative venture. It is not adversarial, as with lawyers against other lawyers, or some company outbidding or under-cutting another for a contract. Rather, it is us medics working to-gether to defeat "the enemy" — the disease.

The GP ideally heads the pack. He refers the patient to the specialist. But radiology, the laboratory, the surgical unit, etc, may be involved. The process represents a lot of people — dif-ferent types of technicians, of doctors, of nursing staff, and ulti-mately administration.

During any doctor's career, he has to rely on his large num-ber of "buddies." I, like everyone else in medicine, relied on a huge number of medical buddies that I needed to help me, and when necessary, bail me out of trouble, and I greatly cherished them.

Below, I have very briefly attempted to describe a small num-ber of these people, as representative samples of the people with whom I worked. Fortunately, like-minded people are common to most hospitals, and the reader may recognize similar individuals in his place of work, be it a hospital, manufacturing plant, or a business organization.

DR. HARRY LEWIS

Harry was a classmate and became a very close friend. He was also one of the men who kept me thinking during my training and subsequent practice at the Royal Columbian. Both his sen-sible, and sometimes bizarre, comments on many aspects of life have already appeared many times in this book as part of the ruminations of the composite "Harry."

He was originally three years ahead of us in school but he had apparently got fed up in second pre-med, and halfway through the year he left classes and went on a trip to England. He ended up staying there for three years and even got married. I don't know how he ever persuaded the dean of medicine to allow him back into pre-med, because once "out" was usually the end. But Harry was always a good talker. When he arrived in our class in second pre-med, he was more experienced than most of the rest of us, and just more worldly. He got on famously with everyone, however, and we all enjoyed his bizarre sense of humour. I suspect he also had a superior IQ.

Whether or not he liked it, he was thrown in with our little clinical group of about ten guys. We did, in fact, have some choice with whom we worked. But often it was just who you ended up with; or sometimes, there was no choice because of scheduling. In any case, Harry was a great asset to our group and would be welcomed in any group. He could keep us laughing by telling little anecdotes from his life, and he was a great philosopher. I would even say that by this point in his life he was a thorough-going atheist. Certainly, at that time, medicine was not the main point of his life, and his marks reflected this. However, he always managed to pass; and he always said he was the last to pass each year without a "supp" (that is, a "supplemental" exam, the one you wrote if you did not make a passing grade on the regular end-of-year exam).

When we graduated from medical school, we all went our different ways, and Harry ended up practicing in a small town on Vancouver Island. He was busy and had started a family but, after several years, he went back to academic life and began a residency at the Vancouver General Hospital. He did very well. He was very bright and probably had never seriously applied himself before. I think that finding there was a "live patient" at the end of his studying, and knowing that if he didn't do his homework the patient could really be injured, was a great motivator — probably for all of us!

Indeed, over the years, Harry became almost a walking medical encyclopedia. He always had journals in his briefcase, and he never let it out of his sight. There were always journals over his desk, in the coffee shop with his name on them, and on his bed at home. He had become a hematologist and oncologist, and was highly sought after for his opinion.

There was also a kindness about him in the way he handled patients, and he had lots of little jokes to lighten their anxiety. Fortunately, he didn't become completely divorced from general internal medicine since he had to take the "on-call" roster, as did the other medical specialists.

Every time that I was on-call for the cardiology department, I seemed to be jinxed by the number of cardiac arrest calls I would have to attend. Often they seemed to occur at the least opportune time, and lengthened an already long day. In my earlier days at the Royal Columbian, the cardiologist on call had to go to all these episodes. You soon figured out that most calls from one of the long-stay wards likely weren't going to be successful, and, in most cases, a waste of time.

On this particular day it was no different. The call had come from the modular units, a so-called "temporary" complex made up of eighteen Atco trailers or modular units piled two deep in a two-floored interconnected rambling arrangement. This area had been used for a period of about twenty years and was, to put it mildly, less than ideal. It accommodated chronic care patients, but during very busy times, which actually became the norm, over-flow patients from the Emerg would go there as well.

On this occasion, the cardiac arrest patient was a very elderly man with multiple myeloma.

When I arrived on the ward, somewhat breathless, a nurse ushered me to the patient. None of the rest of the arrest team had yet arrived. The patient had arrested in bed and, as assessed by the only nurse on duty at the time, was not breathing and had no detectable pulse.

I did what was standard procedure: there was no breathing

> This disease is caused by a malignancy of plasma cells that commonly reside in the bone marrow and, as a rule, spreads very rapidly. In those days the usual life expectancy, from diagnosis to death, was less than three years. The tumour metastasizes heavily to bone, and pathological fractures are very common, some of which are spontaneous (these fractures may occur without any trauma, for example, if the patient rolls over in bed and breaks his pelvis).

and no pulse as the nurse had already reported, I checked the airway and started immediate cardiac compressions. By this time in my career, I had probably attended several hundred cardiac arrests, but this one was strangely different; at the first compression, I felt as if I was falling into the chest. There was an accompanying sickening crunching sound. I felt that I was literally feeling the outline of his heart and the prominence of his spine. It was dreadful and I discontinued compressions immediately.

When I took my hands away I saw that I had left an oval-shaped depression in the middle of the front of his chest about one and a half inches deep and perhaps five inches in diameter. By this time, the rest of the team had arrived and the patient's chart was produced. One of the emergency doctors walked over, and looked at my patient's chest and said, "What did you do to this guy?" I told the team to wait, and very quickly perused the chart and called off the arrest procedure.

The chart revealed that the patient had multiple myeloma with extensive metastases everywhere including the ribs. The poor man had been intermittently in severe pain, his kidneys were failing and he required a great deal of sedation. What really disturbed me was, nobody had written a "No Code 21 " on the chart, which would have meant that no cardiac arrest routine should be carried out. It turned out that the family had, in fact, been asked, and had wanted "to think it over." They felt, somehow, as so often happens, that if the "No Code 21 " order was written, that they, and perhaps the staff, would be abandoning the patient.

Harry had seen this patient over the previous year or so. He had been given the usual chemo agents, but had recently failed to respond anymore and had been placed on palliative care. Harry had urged the family doctor to press the family about the man's "code status." But basic family resistance had prevented any action, and his multiple systems failures — kidneys, heart and general toxicity — had likely resulted in his cardiac arrest.

Well, my trip to the modular units wasn't entirely wasted because as I was leaving (I was the last to leave because I had to phone the family doctor and do the paper work), the nurse who had called asked me if I would have a quick look at another patient who had been admitted from Emerg the night before. She said her patient looked pretty bad, and after what she had just been through, she didn't want a repeat. Although I hadn't been requested to consult, I felt that I had no choice and that a quick anonymous look wouldn't get anybody into trouble.

To my surprise, I found a young woman in her early thirties among mostly geriatric patients. Indeed, she looked ghastly. She was pale, sweaty and terribly anxious. I thought, "Oh, no, not another arrest!" However, when I took her pulse, it was somewhat slower than I would have expected for someone who was in such obvious distress; by palpation at least, her pressure felt strong.

Contrary to what a lot of people might think clinical medicine can be very routine and even boring. Frequently it is endless physical examinations, asking the same questions over and over, usually knowing the answer even before the patient has had a chance to answer. The mind tends to wander, and one of the ways to avoid this is to play little games with one's self. One of my little games, on the physical examination, was to compress the brachial artery found at the elbow, while feeling the pulse at the wrist; and by assessing the amount of pressure needed at the brachial to obliterate the pulse at the wrist; I was usually able to get some idea of the systolic blood pressure. With enough practice how accurate could you be? I would make a mental note and then take the blood pressure and see how far off I was.

When the heart contracts, blood is ejected into the arterial system and the pressure rises. The top of this pressure, measured with a blood pressure cuff, is called the systolic pressure. When the heart relaxes prior to the next contraction, the blood pressure falls, and the lowest level it falls to is called the diastolic pressure. A normal pressure might be written 120/80. When the pressure cuff is inflated to a pressure higher than the systolic pressure, no blood pulse can be felt from the elbow to the wrist. Listening with the stethoscope at the brachial area, immediately below the cuff would reveal no pulse sound. As the cuff is gradually deflated below the systolic pressure, the blood can at last get through and a pulse can again be felt at the brachial artery and a tapping sound will be heard through the stethoscope placed on the brachial artery. As the cuff is deflated below the diastolic pressure, the tapping sound stops, as there is now a continuous flow. By using my finger to press on the brachial artery I can stop the pulse at the wrist. Guessing how much pressure it takes could give a very rough estimate of the systolic pressure.

I asked for a blood-pressure cuff, and when I tried to take her pressure something was very odd. I could hear a diastolic pressure but couldn't get a systolic pressure. Had I forgotten how to do even a simple procedure like this? Was it time to turn in my badge? I ripped the stethoscope out of my ears, felt for her brachial pulse, which was easy to feel, re-wrapped the cuff and tried again.

I then tried my little blood-pressure game; certainly she had a good pressure and, in fact, it was hard to obliterate that wrist pulse. It finally dawned on me that the problem was that I couldn't pump up the cuff high enough. Her blood pressure had somehow risen to over 300 Hg of mercury, which was higher than the cuff would measure!

She told me that she had been admitted the night before with a headache and had high blood pressure, but it had settled down quickly after she had been admitted. The concerned nurse then informed me that it initially had been thought she might have had a sub-arachnoid hemorrhage (a bleed into her brain), but as she had settled down quickly in Emerg, was admitted just for observation. Indeed, overnight she had no further symptoms until she heard all of the running around on the men's ward — where I had been at work — next to hers. It was then she started to feel bad again with the headache and sweating.

Pheos are tumours that are usually, but not always, located in the adrenal gland. The tumours may periodically excrete an inordinate amount of adrenalin and/or noradrenalin resulting in a sudden blood pressure rise causing so-called hypertensive crises that should be treated as an emergency. Left untreated, these very high pressures can result in brain hemorrhages, heart failure and other life-threatening disorders. Fortunately, these tumours are rare and usually benign.

Every medical student is told about hypertensive crises, and pheochromocytoma is always mentioned, although it is very rare.

Needless to say, when these rare things do arrive it is always a surprise.

I ordered a small dose of intravenous Rogitine initially, as I figured it was likely the safest thing to do under the circumstances. Her pressure fell almost immediately, her headache cleared and she stopped sweating. When I took her pressure again, it had at least got into a measurable range, and over the next hour or so completely normalized. I ordered the usual battery of tests, including the most important test, under the clinical circumstances, the VMA urine test. (If the urine collection is taken during one of these hypertensive crises, the test is usually positive. Because she had not voided since before this last episode we had a "valuable" urine collection.)

I phoned the family doctor and apologized for seeing his patient without any referral. He just laughed and said he was glad I was there, and to carry on the good work. We were able to get a bed for her in our now somewhat improved and enlarged Intensive Care Unit.

The next day her VMA urine test came back strongly positive; the other tests were essentially negative. I felt quite proud of myself. At least I hadn't screwed up on this one after destroying the last patient's chest. My friend Harry came along just after the ICU nurse had chased down the patient's lab data, and he needled me that pulverizing that last patient's ribs during a cardiac arrest was no way to cure his cancer.

So I told him about my patient with the high blood pressure, feeling a little smug, and hadn't even finished the story when he asked me if I had ordered a VMA. That guy really is a walking encyclopedia. What a difference from when he was a lowly medical student! He went on to tell me that there was a doctor in Vancouver, Dr. Ted Wilkins, who was doing a study on these things, which was fortunate, as these tumours are sometimes hard to find and may involve difficult exploratory surgery.

Our patient was duly sent off to St Paul's Hospital, had more tests, and then underwent successful surgery. Her tumour was benign and she soon returned to normal, except for a big scar on her torso.

Over the years, I continued to see a lot of my friend Harry; after all we had been classmates and were fellow slaves to medicine. I also eventually became one of his patients. It was always rewarding to see him and hear his latest philosophical pearl. He sincerely cared about his patients, and long after he knew there was nothing more that could be done to help them, he spent countless hours comforting his patients and their families.

When he was away from work, he was forever commanding our attention with his innumerable, weird and very interesting theories. He had a wonderful sense of humour and sometimes it was difficult to know if he was just pulling our legs with some of his theories. It was always enjoyable to sit beside him in the coffee shop or in the cafeteria and be thoroughly entertained. However, beneath this usually ebullient personality, I sensed a certain deep sadness. It was worrying. Yet, he would never admit to any problems and would skilfully change the subject, if anyone approached a sensitive area of his life. I am certain his sudden and very premature death was due largely to the profound sadness and deep personal distress caused by his chosen occupation.

Harry's personal life had become difficult. He had four kids and his marriage was beginning to unravel. He eventually moved out, but kept in close contact with his family. His wife then developed breast cancer and for a while was quite sick as a result of all the chemotherapy. It always seemed ironic that an oncologist should have to deal with these problems on a very personal basis. Harry moved back home when his wife was so sick and stayed there for about two years. When his wife had recovered quite well, however, he moved out again.

Eventually, he met a very nice nurse at the hospital and developed a very close relationship with her. She was worried about Harry, however, because he seemed very depressed. He also was smoking heavily, something he rarely did before, and several times when I caught him alone I would ask him how he was doing, and he would ask me in that loud voice of his, "Tom! How many people have you killed in the catheter lab today?" Then he would immediately change the subject, and tell me about his latest observation on mankind, which was always interesting, but beside the point. Many years later, his son told me that he would sit for long periods in front of the television, just staring at it. And when his son tried to strike up a conversation, he seemed to be in another world and would scarcely answer him.

Some time later, Harry was brought in dead. He apparently had died in his sleep and wasn't discovered until the next morning when his girl friend had called on him. He was only in his forties and had been very well loved at the hospital. His death was a great shock to everyone.

Of course an autopsy was mandated. When the post mortem was finished, the pathologist told me that Harry had a 50 percent block in his left anterior descending artery. That is the great big artery that runs down the front of the heart and in many cases supplies almost one-half the blood supply to the heart muscle. Spasm in this artery, possibly aggravated by irritation of this block, could lead to a sudden arrhythmia, and all that nicotine in Harry's system could have further aggravated his case.

I asked the pathologist if he had done any toxicology tests and he said it hadn't been necessary, as there was nothing in his stomach and nothing to suggest a poisoning. We were greatly relieved by this piece of news.

It was all very sad. I was a pallbearer at his funeral, and my wife and I kept in touch with his wife and kids. The family generally did very well, and his wife outlived him by many years, but eventually she developed cancer in the other breast, which metastasized widely. She remained active up until the very end.

I can still hear Harry's voice and remember many of his comments on the problems of the world. If there is a Heaven, I can see Harry, the confirmed atheist, walking up to God and saying, "You know, you must be part of my hallucination because you really don't exist!"

DR. JOHN GRAHAM

I first met him in March 1968. He was a tall, good-looking guy, and had longish wavy hair with a few streaks of grey. I think it was because of his loud voice that we often referred to him as "Big John." He wasn't fat, but he didn't look particularly athletic. I noticed that he usually appeared somewhat tired and a little dishevelled, which I liked to see. I just don't fancy, for some reason, doctors who look too prim and proper. Big John was openly friendly, and had a loud somewhat raspy laugh.

He was a general internist, a very common specialty in those days, but its practitioners were, unfortunately, under attack as the sub-specialties were just coming on-stream. Neurology had just arrived at the Royal Columbian Hospital about a year earlier, and I was to be the first cardiologist. (In larger centres, there were already sub-specialties in medicine, such as respirology, gastroenterology, endocrinology, nephrology and dermatology.) John got along well with his patients and openly empathized with them. And if any of the referring general practitioners wanted a good, solid opinion, he would unfailingly provide it.

Over the years, I got to know him a lot better, and I had great respect for his "sixth sense." When he saw a difficult case, somehow he often managed to figure it out when things just didn't seem to add up. He would phone one of his friends, perhaps discuss the problem over coffee and the ubiquitous cigarette, go back over the problem again, get a consultation from an un-related specialty, and not just write the patient off as "SKN" (some kind of a nut.) When a doctor is frustrated, and the case doesn't make any sense, it is always easy to think that the symptoms are "hysterical" or "psychological."

I always felt that no matter how many sub-specialties came to our hospital, there would always be a need for people like John. Calling a psychiatrist in to sort out all these sometimes very bizarre symptoms can be a disaster. Some of our psychiatrists, in my opinion, were themselves a little bit loony in the first place, and sometimes perhaps a bit overly zealous trying to establish that the patient's symptoms are related to childhood psychological problems or some other cause that "real doctors" tend to overlook.

John, however, had a good solid background in clinical medicine, had worked long hours on call in the Emerg, and could usually sort out the wheat from the chaff. He also had a full life outside of medicine, which I think tends to make a doctor better able to understand human nature. He had the usual wife, kids who were doing well, and a fancy car. But he also had another life. He liked to gamble, sometimes for pretty big stakes. He could indeed be flamboyant, in the true sense of the word.

I usually went to the hospital intern parties. These are parties organized by the intern staff, and pretty much anybody from the hospital who wanted to come did so. It was still the days when doctors knew "how to party," which just means we drank a lot.

I still have a picture of John in my head, dressed in his party clothes, which consisted of a dark suit, dark tie, a white shirt, a little obvious jewellery and long hair hanging down his forehead, looking like a Chicago gangster. He was leaning over a card table with dice and cards everywhere and a big pile of money in the centre of the table. These card games would go on into the early hours of the morning. I noticed there were a lot of one hundred dollar bills in the pile. Anxious and excited faces surrounded the table and John was making a critical move. I wondered where all the money came from.

Most of the interns were standing well back. The wealthier

surgeons and a few medical specialists had gradually upstaged them all. I basically don't play cards, and I would never be any good at bluffing anyway. However, I certainly didn't mind watching.

On one occasion, we all had the opportunity to read John's name in the paper because he and several others in the more "high flying" community had formed a syndicate (whatever that is!) and had bought a whole bunch of lottery tickets. They had apparently figured out that there was going to be more money in the lottery than the cost of the tickets to be sold, and apparently had cashed in big time.

One day during my first year at the Royal Columbian John asked me to see a difficult patient. She was a fifty-two-year-old Iranian lady who owned a high-end boutique. For some reason, she just couldn't seem to give a good history.

She was divorced and lived alone, but had a successful retail business and certainly didn't seem stupid. Actually she was quite likeable, and I enjoyed talking to her. However, asking her even the simplest questions about her health just went around in circles.

In medical school, there is a so-called "green book" that describes all the endless questions that the student is supposed to ask the patient to obtain a proper history. One of those questions is, "How many times do you get up at night to go to the bathroom?"

I asked this question and she told me immediately that she got up "many times," and she often had a recurring dream. She said that she dreamed that she was at a fancy house party, probably in New Westminster, and she had to go pee so urgently, but the washroom was locked. There was nobody in the dining room at the moment, so she got up on the dining room table with all the fine silver and delicate china, squatted on the punch bowl, just ready to let fly, when suddenly everybody at the party came back into the dining room and surrounded the table. At this point, she would wake up and go to her bathroom; but when she sat down it would feel like the punch bowl of her dreams, and she had trouble getting started.

She asked me if I thought that the dreams were causing her to get up at night, or if bladder symptoms were starting her dreams. I told her that this was getting away out of my field, and graciously suggested that she ask Dr. John. I knew that I was just "passing the buck," but I was curious as to what John would tell her.

She had been in hospital for two weeks by now, had undergone a huge number of tests, and was very emotional. Her anxiety and brittle emotional state, I felt, were well beyond the realm of what one might expect, even after a two-week stint of hospitalization and a series of fairly nasty tests.

She complained of virtually every symptom in the book. (As medical students, we used to joke, that patient so-and-so was "green book positive." In other words, every question was answered in the affirmative.) Among her symptoms, she complained of abdominal pain that would come and go, and that she was continuously nauseated. Yet she was "plump" and had not lost any weight since her admission. I was asked to see her because amongst her innumerable complaints, she had also complained of sudden flushing and palpitations. All her tests to date were normal.

This was in the days before CAT scans, MRIs, echo and colonoscopy. But John had done an upper GI (gastro-intestinal) series, a barium meal, and a barium enema, and the general surgeon who had been consulted had done a sigmoidoscopy. She'd had about every blood and urine test that was available at the time.

John had even ordered a urine test that I would never have thought of: 5HIAA. This is a test for a very rare small bowel tumour called argentaffinoma. I had only heard about this tumour during my residency, and had probably crammed for it before my fellowship exams. I never knowingly saw a case. It can apparently cause flushing. The urine test is also not very reliable, and may only be positive during an attack of flushing. When John duly got the test result back, it was negative.

From a cardiac standpoint, she had a normal chest x-ray and a normal resting ECG, and her complete physical examination was also normal. I remember going over her particularly carefully, as I was afraid that I might miss something. Everybody knows that these are the cases that you are likely to screw up. In fact, the only time she seemed to calm down was when I was examining her physically. Could she be having some sort of weird arrhythmia? In those days, we did not have any portable monitoring.

I agreed, however, that we could sacrifice one of our precious beds overnight in our so-called "intensive care unit." This was all hard-wire monitoring; the patient could sit in a chair but couldn't go for a walk on the ward. The patient had "palpitations" overnight and according to the nursing staff seemed very hysterical and was eventually settled with an extra sleeping pill. The monitor showed only a very slight tachycardia during this episode. I thought I was off the hook and she was transferred back to her ward on the surgery floor. During this "attack" in our ICU John had ordered another 5HIAA test, which was also negative.

John then called in the psychiatric department. Immediately, they found all sorts of pathology. Did we know that she had had a very difficult childhood and a long-term abusive relationship with her "ex"? She apparently had fixations on her abdomen, something to do with a previous abortion. They also found her to be depressed with "suicidal ideations."

Because of the lack of beds, she stayed for the next three weeks, unbelievably, on the surgical ward under the care of the psychiatry department. I was no longer on the case, but because her room was right beside the stairwell and she was not confined to bed, I would see her quite often and usually waved at her as I went by.

I hadn't seen her for several days and then one day as I was going by her room, I saw that she was lying on her back in bed and her abdomen was hugely distended. It was obvious right under the bed sheets. Although she was not technically my patient any more, I did an immediate examination of her abdomen and found the abdominal walls tight as a drum, and she had no bowel sounds; and although she was in distress, she was drowsy, in severe shock.

Despite heroic efforts she died within the next twenty-four hours.

What happened? As nobody was prepared to sign the death certificate, she automatically was slated to undergo a full autopsy.

In those days, most physicians were in fact prepared to sign the death certificate if they were sure of the cause of death, in general terms. In this case, it was obvious that we were far from having any confidence in our diagnosis, apart from the terminal events of bowel obstruction plus or minus peritonitis.

We were all pretty upset, and I know I didn't sleep very well the next few nights. I was seriously annoyed that the psych department hadn't called the "real" doctors back when our patient was obviously deteriorating.

The autopsy showed that she had a small, rare bowel tumour called — guess what? — argentaffinoma. This, of course, was the disease John's urine 5 HIAA test had not picked up. In fact, just to be on the safe side, he had two of these tests done. This is what had caused her bowel obstruction and perforation. It was a single tumour and had shown no evidence of local spread. In other words, even in the absence of a positive 5 HIAA urine test, if we had bitten the bullet and done an exploratory laparotomy early on in her admission, she would still have been alive.

In those days, without benefit of scans, these small bowel tumours were very difficult to diagnose; in fact, they still are. The "barium meal" is very difficult to read because of so much overlap of bowel. The 5 HIAA urine test, we knew, also had its drawbacks. The one test that hadn't been ordered was the laparotomy, despite the fact she had been seen in consultation by a general surgeon. The surgeon, of course, was being prudent. Opening up someone's abdomen is a pretty invasive test and numerous post-op complications are possible.

The day after the autopsy report was available, I ran into John again and he tried to reassure me, saying that we all had worked pretty hard on this case and, after all, "sometimes hysteria can be fatal."

From the patient's perspective, she did indeed have legitimate symptoms. But she had been able to function until her abdominal complaints, extreme anxiety, and perhaps her flushing and palpitations, just added to her huge pile of general complaints and made her seek medical attention.

Then, being in hospital, being poked and prodded, and finally having all of us suggesting or implying that her complaints weren't "real," and that she was "SKN" can only have added to her distress.

I will never feel right about this case. She died in our hospital under our care. Hers was a totally preventable death.

"Big John" — A Sad End

Over the years, I saw a lot of John professionally and he continued to sort the wheat from the chaff. As our department continued to expand, however, and the number of cardiologists increased, and the department of medicine added an increasing number of internists of various sub-specialty interests, I started to see less of him, and in his later years he gradually "pulled in his horns."

The last I saw of him, he had become a patient himself. He was admitted as a long-term patient with "ca" (cancer) of the prostate, which had metastasized to his spine and rendered him a paraplegic.

When I visited him, he was as alert as ever, but in mild discomfort and obviously frustrated. Still when we talked about the old times, he seemed to brighten up and even chuckled a few times. But we both knew that his time was nigh.

Mercifully, he died several weeks later.

KRISTIN WARBURTON

Kris was great. She ran the huge old American Optical machine in our catheter lab that measured all the pressures in our tubes that were connected to various chambers in the heart. When we crossed a valve, she would tell us an immediate "ball park figure" of the gradient, if the valve was narrowed.

She kept a total eye on the ECG monitor. I can still hear her voice behind me yelling, "Extra! Extra!" She wasn't trying to sell newspapers. She was trying to tell me that I was irritating the heart with one of my catheters and possibly risking the onset of more dangerous arrhythmias.

After the test, she would calculate the cardiac output, measure the gradients and the mean gradient, and basically put all the report together. She also had a background in calculus, which clearly helped. All I had to do was to look at the tracings, view the films, and dictate a letter.

This scenario went on day in and day out. On a bad day, Kris would suddenly yell, "Ventricular fibrillation!" Our scrub nurse would quickly pull down the sterile sheet over the patient's chest and Kris would magically appear with the "paddles" poised. She would dutifully shock the patient back to the previous rhythm, and just carry on very peacefully, completely unperturbed.

In the original lab, Kris always sat on a high stool wearing her lead apron backwards to protect her back, which was always facing the radiation coming from the image intensifier. The rest of us always faced the machine, and we wore the aprons protecting our fronts. Sometimes, our job trying to get these catheters into the mouth of the coronary arteries, or worse, into the mouth of one of the patient's new venous bypass grafts, was very frustrating. Sometimes, we might "fiddle" for a half-hour to get the end of our tube into the mouth of some pesky orifice. The experience was reminiscent of those frustrating little puzzles we used to get as kids at Christmas.

After trying several different tubes, I would tell Kris that I needed a little inspiration and would go over and rub my butt on the back of her lead apron. It was supposed to be just a joke, to relieve the tension, but sometimes it seemed to work. I think just walking over to the other side of the table tended to clear my mind a little and allowed me to try another approach.

Kris subsequently worked a lot in the pacemaker clinic and became very knowledgeable about the newer, more complicated programmable pacemakers. Before long, she knew far more about these things than I did, and I would bet, more than most of the other cardiologists as well. She also had a very good background in electricity and understood the principles behind what she was doing. One day I asked her how she was so smart and knew all this stuff. She laughed and just replied that she "went to school." (She was a graduate of BCIT, the British Columbia Institute of Technology, a large technical college in Vancouver.)

I went to school too, and even took university physics, one of my best subjects. But our course was pretty theoretical. We could solve monstrous equations in our electrical course, but I doubt there were very many guys in our class who even knew how to work an ohmmeter, much less do something practical like fix a toaster, or change the condenser on a small gas motor.

Kris was always cheerful and very kind to the patients. Fortunately, the hospital world has many dedicated people like her.

DR. NORM WIGNALL

My new boss and subsequent friend, Dr. Norman Wignall (Wiggy, for short), was there to greet me that day in 1962 when I showed up for my first day of work at Shaughnessy Hospital. When he told me to go home and not to show up until after the long weekend (I had expected to find some sort of a slave driver), I knew we would be friends. Indeed, Norm was a very caring man and everybody's friend. He was another Englishman, but he didn't have that fancy accent, or feel he was over in Canada to show the "colonials" how to do things.

He patiently explained to us how to recognize a lot of things under the microscope and how to conduct a full autopsy. He didn't mind stupid questions, and had all the patience in the world. He had to, as I was one of his pupils!

Towards the end of my six-month stint on pathology, the hospital was planning a Christmas party. Traditionally, our department's contribution was a donation of a couple of two-litre bottles of that awful ninety-five percent lab ethanol. (The liquor that we usually buy in the government liquor stores is just forty percent.)

Norm was a hard-working, busy man in those days, and on the Friday of the party, he had a meeting downtown, missed his lunch, and arrived after the hospital party was in full swing. The interns felt sorry for him, and he was handed a "stiff" drink by one of my compatriots.

I was on the other side of the room and didn't even know that he had arrived, when one of my friends came over and said, "I think you should look after your boss." I asked what had happened, and I was told that Wiggy had just made a toast, and then thrown his glass into the fireplace. When I arrived, he said, "Tom, I think I have to have a pee."

I led him off to the bathroom and tried to steady him, while he did his thing. Unfortunately, the bathroom was the old-fashioned hospital type, where the toilet faces the tub. Norm, for some reason, as he was finishing up, stepped back and suddenly we were both in the bathtub facing the ceiling! Fortunately for me, Norm had finished his business and I didn't get wet. By this time, happily, Norm was more of a friend than a boss.

Norm liked to go hiking. I was married, but at this point we had no children, and as the Shaughnessy schedule was light, I readily agreed to go with him. In those days, there were no particular gun laws, and Allan Rock's very expensive gun control measures were a long way off. (Allan Rock, a cabinet minister in the Liberal federal government, had banned most handguns and made it more difficult even for innocent duck and deer hunters to have a gun at home.) In the 1960s and early 70s, I often carried

How did we get in here?

my older brother's .22-caliber, 10-shot Beretta with me on hiking trips. It had a very short barrel and fitted easily into my back pocket. My brother had bought it for sixteen dollars many years earlier and had given it to me.

We did this hike in early June, and although I was by this time no longer on Norm's service, we had kept in touch and I saw him frequently at the hospital at the various hospital rounds. Norm is about twenty years older than I am, and when we finally got to the destination that he wanted, he was completely exhausted.

We had not counted on getting into snow, but we were in the Whistler Mountain area and during the last five hundred feet of elevation, we sloshed through about a foot of wet snow. There was a cabin, but there was so much garbage in it that I wanted to pitch the tent that we had laboriously carried up the hill. Norm was just too tired, and he persuaded me to just make a level spot in this cabin and we unrolled our bedrolls there.

We found a spot under a low overhang of this very filthy cabin, got into the booze, ate our meal and went to bed. Norm's bedroll was right beside mine. During the night, I soon realized that this cabin was absolutely full of pack rats. When one ran right across my chest, I had had enough. I turned on my flashlight and there, sitting on a small table about five feet away, was one of these little creatures. Norm was sound asleep, gently snoring on his back. The rat had come from my right and must have run across Norm's chest as well, but he was obviously unperturbed by it. I fished out my Beretta, and tried to get the muzzle parallel to the light beam (laser sights were still a long way off) and fired. The poor rat! But worse, I had fired the automatic right over poor Wiggy and he sat bolt upright and banged his head on the low overhang.

Norm went right back to sleep (I think just suffering from exhaustion rather than a concussion) but I think I stayed awake the rest of the night, because of all the rat noises that started up again right after the brief lull following the loud bang. The next morning, it was bright and sunny, and now we only had to look forward to the easier walk back down to the parking lot. We spent several hours trying to clean the place up. I could never get over how anyone could spread garbage in such pristine places. Unfortunately, it seems to be the rule rather than the exception.

Norm has just turned 90, but we still see each other periodically and he is as bright and kindly as ever. Most importantly he still has one hundred percent of his "marbles."

WENDY LITTLEWOOD

Wendy (now Wendy Scott) was a nurse whom I first ran into at St. Mary's Hospital. She was very outgoing and had eyes that could still give an old married guy like me shivers down my spine.

We soon persuaded her to transfer to the Royal Columbian, where all the action was. She worked in various areas, but usually in the Intensive Care Unit, or the Coronary Care Unit. Before long, she learned all the routines and was extremely competent. Occasionally, on her days off, she would come over and help my wife with our litter of four very active boys.

On one very busy day, when I had been up in the coronary unit and was in the process of checking out a temporary pacemaker in a patient, I was distracted by a big problem in the next bed. The next moment, I was in a big rush off to the Emerg downstairs to see a new patient who had just arrested. I had, inadvertently, left the pacer set at 40 beats per minutes.

Wendy waited until she heard that the crisis in Emerg was

over, and then phoned me and asked, "Did you want to leave that pacer set at 40?" I was horrified and was going to rush upstairs again, to put it back to somewhere around 70 beats per minute, but Wendy told me she already had done that right after I had left.

It was probably against the nursing rules at that time, but the patient comes first, and in cases like this the rules should come second. It's so gratifying to work with people who think for themselves, and are not just robots. Unfortunately, Wendy eventually left the Royal Columbian and went on to bigger and better things at St. Paul's Hospital.

Wendy is just a single representative of an amazingly dedicated nursing staff. They are, in fact, the cement of any hospital.

DR. DON GAIN

Dr. Don Gain was one of the "old school" GPs in our area. He had started a clinic in the catchment area of the Royal Columbian Hospital. All the GPs in the Gain Clinic were, to a person, hardworking, and the patients and their families always came first. In some ways, I found Don intimidating at first; he was certainly opinionated, even though he was usually right. I had the feeling he didn't suffer fools easily.

At the medical staff meetings, in the early days of my career there, he usually sat in the front row and smoked a big cigar. I am sure he initially voted against my motions about selling cigarettes in the hospital.

With time, I gradually got to like him and could see that his bark was far worse than his bite. He was always very supportive of me, and in my early days of practice, when it took a while for the majority of the medical staff to find out what a cardiologist did, he and his group referred many patients to me. His group also sent a referral letter or phoned me prior to me seeing any of their patients, making life much easier for the patient and also for me.

One night, just after midnight, I was called from home to see one of Don's patients, who had come into Emerg. He had very advanced coronary disease and died in congestive heart failure. By this time it was about 5:00 a.m. All the family was present in the Emerg and they were fully aware of what had happened. I dutifully phoned the Gain Clinic and my phone call was transferred to Dr. Barry Bentz. He checked to be sure that the family had been fully informed about the death of their loved one.

The next morning, probably before 8:00 a.m., Don, an early riser and very conscientious doctor, arrived at the Royal Columbian. One of this deceased patient's relatives, who was just leaving the hospital, told Don what had happened. Don was furious, for up to that point he was unaware of what had transpired during the night. When he saw me, he actually yelled at me for not informing him.

I was initially shocked and didn't say anything until he had said his piece. I think I delayed saying anything because I realized I needed to "cool it." I thought I had done everything that I should have done, and I had spent extra time explaining to the family what had happened. I was pretty tired too. Finally I got angry and yelled back at Don that his stupid office had been informed, and it was their fault, and he also owed me an apology.

I was a little surprised at myself, but I had had enough. I felt like punching him in the nose, but Don was too short and it wouldn't have been a fair fight. Don's face turned red and I think I surprised him with my own outburst, as I had never before yelled at anyone in the hospital. He settled down a bit and walked away.

Early the next morning, when I was in the doctors' lounge getting my mail, Don walked in and gave me a bottle of Scotch. My wife told me it was a very fancy Scotch, single malt or something, and I was only allowed to serve it to my friends and not drink it myself. I really admired Don for doing this. It's not easy to eat humble pie, and I think for Don it might have been even harder, because he tried to do everything right.

Very unfortunately, Don developed a cardiomyopathy. I looked after him for several years, and then after my forced retirement, Dave Hilton in Victoria continued his care. Dave kept me informed, and Don managed fairly well for a number of years.

He died a fighter all the way, and was always a real brick throughout his illness.

It was guys like Don who were the backbone of doctors in our area and kept specialists like me in line.

DR. DAVE HILTON

Probably most large organizations have at least one "human dynamo," and that was my friend and colleague, Dr. Dave. If he hadn't been so productive and focused, I would have thought that his mother should have put him on Ritalin shortly after birth and left him on it permanently. Sitting beside him, I always felt like one of those South American three-toed sloths.

He came to the Royal Columbian to head up our angioplasty service, the procedure whereby a balloon is put through a partially obstructed artery and inflated, flattening the obstruction against the walls of the artery. This procedure greatly enlarges the opening to allow the blood to get through, and often relieves the patient's symptoms completely. Before a hospital can have a cardiac angioplasty service, it has to have a well-functioning open-heart service. This is necessary as a backup in case something goes wrong during angioplasty.

With Dave, nothing was ever done in half-measures. He had to have the best possible results, and pretty soon he became the chief of our department, as well as running the angioplasty service.

I was relatively unfamiliar with angioplasties and had taken a trip to Atlanta, Georgia just to see the very famous Andreas Gruentzig perform this new procedure live on an oversized closed-circuit television. Subsequently, Dr. Dave and I had also gone to Victoria, BC to watch Gary McKenzie perform the procedure in his catheter lab at the Royal Jubilee Hospital. Our department managed at this time to persuade Dr. Mark Henderson, another dynamo, who was well trained in angioplasty, to come and work at our hospital and basically "hold the hands" of those using this new technique.

The big day arrived when we were going to have this service at the Royal Columbian; it was all very exciting for us. We now would be able to save some of these desperately ill patients who arrived in our emergency department.

About this time, I had just catheterized a helicopter instructor pilot. He was young, strong, and really the epitome of the "man's man," but he had been in my office complaining of the recent onset of exertional chest pain. He had failed his treadmill test miserably, getting chest pain within the first two minutes, and he showed the characteristic massive ECG changes that one would

242

expect to see with serious coronary artery disease. He obviously could not fly anymore.

When I subjected him to heart catheterization, he was, predictably, found to have pretty severe disease, but he looked as though he would be suitable for angioplasty, and hence we could avoid open heart surgery. I was very interested in angioplasty, and booked the time off to observe the procedure to be carried out by Dave Hilton. Some of these arterial obstructions are very fragile, and I often noticed, back when I was doing autopsies at Shaughnessy Hospital, that the obstructing material often had a fragile mushy texture somewhat akin to rotten cauliflower.

During this angioplasty attempt, the tip of the catheter got under one of these rotten cholesterol plaques and stripped up a flap that then folded over and blocked the artery completely. Our patient was now in the process of having a heart attack, right before our eyes!

Dr. Dave, predictably, was at his finest in the way he handled this emergency. A call went into the surgery department, and at the same time he got out the counter-pulsation balloon and ordered all the general supportive steps to minimize the damage to the heart muscle.

The counter-pulsation balloon is shaped like a big long sausage that is threaded up the femoral artery (described in chapter three), into the aorta just below the heart, and every time the heart contracts the balloon collapses and takes the load off the heart. When the heart relaxes, before the next beat, the balloon inflates and pushes the blood ahead. In this way, the circulation is maintained while the heart has much less work to do. Helium gas is used to inflate and deflate this balloon as it has a very low viscosity and hence goes rigid and then relaxes very quickly to keep in time with the patient's heartbeat.

Everything went like clockwork. Dave was almost like an orchestra leader, always calm and completely organized. Our patient was soon in the OR and underwent a three-vessel bypass. The surgery was very successful.

I did the next two treadmill tests on him and, in fact, his exercise capacity was soon well above the North American average for a patient in his age group without known heart disease. To the credit of the Ministry of Transport, within two years he was back flying and giving helicopter lessons. A few years previously, that department would never have allowed him even to fly again. (Even the Ministry of Transport was, from a medical point of view, coming out of the Stone Age.)

We were fortunate to have people like Dave who played a huge part in establishing our open-heart service, and then was one of the main instigators of our angioplasty service. However, he was but one of a number of very good cardiologists who worked hard to expand and improve our department. These cardiologists have now taken on the role of providing an angioplasty service around the clock, seven days a week — "24/7" in modern parlance. The Royal Columbian is one of the few hospitals in Canada to provide this standard of service.

SHARON BARCLAY

I think we often forget all about our office staff. This may also be true of industry, but it certainly applies to medical personnel. In cardiology, most of the real "excitement" takes place at the hospital, and the office is a quieter place by comparison. For the most part, in the office we are not doing cardiac massage or sticking tubes in someone's chest or groin. However, the office personnel are the ones who organize our day and often organize what we end up doing at the hospital as well.

Sharon was my first "real" secretary. To be honest, she was not actually "mine" but "belonged" to Dr. Jim Quayle, a plastic surgeon. I shared her for just two afternoons a week and the rest of the time, unfortunately, she worked for Jim. The fact that she was a "ten out of ten" and had been a former Miss Kelowna had, of course, no influence over me.

She was also an excellent secretary and was one of those ladies who could read a doctor's mind. She had me completely organized within the first afternoon I met her. Her real boss, Jim, had kindly volunteered to let me use his office space, as there was a shortage of space in our area. Also, because I was brand new in the area, it would be unlikely that these two afternoons would be very busy for Jim's staff.

In fact, Jim turned out to be totally a "people person," and really disliked all the paper work that went into running his office. He would put off dictating his letters until the last moment, and he was one of those doctors who drive the secretaries over at hospital medical records absolutely crazy. As a consequence, Sharon started typing my letters on my afternoons because she didn't have to type Jim's letters until he decided to dictate a whole bunch all at once. At that point, my free typing service would temporarily come to a halt.

As the weeks went by, I got to know Sharon better. The fact that she was married to a Golden Gloves boxing champion didn't go unnoticed either. My office business was not busy in those early days and, as mentioned in the last chapter, "an idle mind…" Consequently, one afternoon, I thought I would get a rise out of "my" new secretary.

Very innocently, or as innocently as I could fake it, I asked Sharon if her boss made little tits bigger? She immediately assured me that he did a lot of that type of surgery.

"Oh," I replied, "that's good. But there's a rumour going around that he also makes big tits smaller?"

"Oh yes," Sharon replied, "but in most of these cases the government pays for it."

I could see that I was making progress and Sharon was getting into stride.

"You mean that I, the taxpayer, have to pay your boss to make big tits smaller?"

Sharon seemed a little bit confused. I guess that she thought it was perfectly normal that the taxpayer should pay for what she regarded as necessary surgery. She had previously agreed that making little tits bigger should be paid for by the patient, and not by the taxpayer.

Then, trying to look very shocked, I said, "I think your boss is awful and, in fact, he should be taken out and shot! Making big tits smaller is terrible! Don't you know that there is no such thing as too big a tit?"

Before this, I didn't realize how loyal some of these office secretaries could be. I guess when you work with someone day in and day out the relationship changes. There must be some mysterious bonding that goes on. I have noticed over the years that this bonding will go on even with the grandmotherly-type secretary defending the young surgeon. It has very little, if anything, to do with sex, but may be more akin to the bonding that goes on in families. I realized, too late, that I had gone too far. It's surprising how strongly a secretary will defend her boss.

Sharon was now shouting at me. I had never heard her shout before.

"Sonny, you just sit in that chair, right there! ...No! Not that chair! The chair over there!"

She was pointing to a straight-backed wooden chair that I always associated with the chair my grade-four teacher used and frequently made me sit on in a corner in the class when I had over-stepped the line. I also think that the last time I had been called "Sonny" was in grade four. This chair was also the exact replica of the chair in the Emerg at Orillia to which they tied those overdose patients when the staff wanted to pump out their stomachs.

I humbly obeyed her instructions and sat in the chair, fidgeting, while she started rummaging around in a filing cabinet. Soon she pulled out a lot of photographs of young women sitting in the exact chair that I was now sitting in.

Jim and Sharon had, likely in part for legal purposes, photographs taken before their patient's reduction mammoplasty, and again several months after their surgery. Both frontal and lateral views were taken. I was frankly astounded. Some of these poor women, even those still in their teens, had breasts so large that when they sat straight upright in this chair, their breasts were sitting on their thighs. In many cases, their brassiere straps had cut deep dints into their shoulders. Only a very few of them were significantly overweight.

Talk about eating humble pie! I know that Sharon knew that I was, at least in part, trying to pull her leg. But what she had shown me was very instructive. Even though I was supposed to be a doctor, I had no idea of the extent of this problem. Of course the taxpayer should pay for this, if only to relieve these poor patients of this crippling burden and loss of self-esteem.

I continued to "share" Sharon and we had lots of laughs. But after about six months, my practice just became too busy and I had to find a place of my own. There was no chance that I could have taken Sharon with me.

By this time, Jim and I had become friends, and subsequently he became a patient of mine. When I first examined him, I noticed he had a lot of scars scattered around his body —not a good ad for a plastic surgeon, but these weren't surgical scars. They had resulted from shrapnel wounds caused by German mortars in

World War Two. He had been in the infantry both in Italy and in France, and had been wounded four times. Jim was a huge bear of a man. He was at least six foot, four inches tall and just as big to match, but definitely not over-weight. He would be the sort of guy you would not want to meet in any war if you were the enemy and Jim was coming at you at close quarters — with or without a Bren gun!

So, between Jim and Sharon's husband, I had two very good reasons not to try to steal Sharon!

HANK ERICKSON — "FEE SPLITTING" WITH THE HOSPITAL CHAPLAIN!

Because I was virtually the only cardiologist in my earlier days of practice at the Royal Columbian Hospital, I saw a lot of death. Fortunately, we had a very compassionate, hard-working hospital chaplain, Hank Erickson.

Many patients had their own minister, priest, rabbi, or imam who would willingly come into hospital to provide spiritual comfort for the patient and family. However, there were many patients who were lapsed in their religion, or whose spiritual leader was not available, and Hank would fill in. Often the circumstances were very sad and it would be a very difficult job for anyone to undertake; however, Hank filled this role admirably and provided tremendous support for the family.

Some of the family doctors were quite religious and on several occasions I saw a family doctor praying at the bedside with the family. Many times the family doctor would suggest that Hank get involved. If there was no family doctor, an increasingly common situation, I would suggest to the patient or family to consider calling in our local chaplain.

It was very interesting for me, the totally secular doctor, to see how Hank would calm the family. Things always proceeded so smoothly when he was involved. He was very informed in practicalities such as hospice arrangements, social services, funerals, and all the legal necessities that result from someone's passing. He always knew whom to contact under what circumstances.

Hank seemed to live and breathe the Royal Columbian Hospital; he was always there. I noticed that he frequently sat with me in the cafeteria. I would see him come in, look around and then wander over and sit at my table. I would joke with him and tell him that I was beyond salvation. He never seemed to mind and never tried to convert me. Perhaps he thought that by sitting at one of those small cafeteria tables with me, a lapsed Christian, he would strengthen his spiritual immune system fending off my philosophical questions!

One day I jokingly said I should "fee split" with him, as at that time I seemed to be referring so many patients to him.

In reality, fee splitting was unethical and illegal and not a joking matter. Before 1970 it did occur between specialists and family doctors, and sometimes between specialists. Fortunately, it was not common. The practice involved a doctor with a patient who needed specialist care. There may have been several specialists who could provide this care, but perhaps one of them would give the referring doctor a cash kickback if he sent the patient to him. The unethical specialist would thus increase his practice and hence his income, and could then afford to give under-the-table money to the unethical referring doctor. As the number of specialists declined in relationship to the demand, any motivation to provide kickbacks disappeared.

I never knew what church Hank belonged to. I assumed that he was likely a Protestant, but for his work it never seemed to matter. I found his philosophy very interesting because he could so easily interact with the other faiths he encountered at the hospital. He believed that the major faiths of the western world — Jew, Christian, and Muslim — were all children of Abraham, and their god was the same Great Spirit for all of them. He couldn't understand why we had to nitpick over these differences.

Hank had been seen across Canada on television in 1981 when he conducted the very moving funeral services for Terry Fox, the courageous young man from British Columbia whose Marathon of Hope run to raise money for cancer research was tragically cut short when his cancer recurred. I was asked to see Terry for a short time during his final days at the Royal Columbian to see if draining some fluid from his lungs would help his breathing. However, at this point his lungs were filled with tumour cells from his bone cancer and nothing more could be done. He died there and Hank was his chaplain.

I missed Hank after he retired. He was running into health problems while he was still at work and after he retired. When he died, as so often happens, I didn't know about it for several months, but I would certainly have wanted to attend his funeral.

At age eighteen Terry Fox had developed osteogenic sarcoma, a type of bone malignancy, in his right leg and had to have that leg amputated six inches above the knee. After he had extensive chemotherapy, Terry decided to run across Canada from coast to coast on his artificial leg to raise money to help others in their fight against cancer. His cancer recurred and spread into his lungs when he was near the halfway point of his marathon. Terry's legacy lives on, and the annual Terry Fox Run held across Canada and in many countries around the world continues to raise money for cancer research. As of 2008, more than 400 million dollars has been raised in Terry's name. Terry's full story and his legacy can be read at www.terryfoxrun.org

In a hospital atmosphere, it is these medical buddies that make the system function. Many times, as I have been struggling with a problem, one of the scrub nurses has appeared with a different catheter still in its sterile bag. The nurse might stand there until I noticed it. Sometimes it was a gentle hint to try this. Some of these women work all day in the lab, day after day, and they see what some of the other doctors do and find successful. They pass this information on to the other doctors working in the same lab.

Everybody is important. Each person has his job to do. And we couldn't do our work in the heart catheter lab, or anywhere else for that matter, if the housekeeper, the floor cleaner, the wall washer didn't do his or her job correctly. This knowledge has become critically important now, with the appearance of "super bugs," such as MRS (methicillin resistant staphylococcus) and C. difficile (another horrible and drug resistant bug). All our trays full of instruments come from the central supply room (CSR). They are all packaged with exactly the right stuff on each tray, according to a set protocol and, of course, are sterilized and correctly labelled. We couldn't function without all the maintenance personnel, the nursing department, and all the technical staff. In short, it is a huge team effort.

At the Toronto General — at least when I was there from

1961–1968, with a year off when I was working at the "rest home," Vancouver's Shaughnessy Hospital — there seemed to be an unfortunate separation in these various services. In that huge cafeteria, each group sat at separate tables and their various uniforms separated them further. Kitchen staff wore uniforms different from housekeeping, different from maintenance crews, etc., there was little socializing between groups and we didn't get to learn the problems and merits of the people who worked outside our own group.

Even among the doctors on staff at the Toronto General, the juniors and the senior residents sat at different tables. The juniors wore what looked like something that a barber might put over you when he cuts your hair. The seniors wore a shirt and tie, but they still wore their "whites." The staff doctors sat at a long table on a raised platform above the rest of us "untouchables." They wore business suits.

When I came to the Royal Columbian, things were completely different. Anybody could sit anywhere in their cafeteria. And the dress code was, to say the least, casual. There was, of course, a tendency for people to sit with people with similar interests. But there were never any designated areas for the different groups.

I believe that this lack of separation gave the Royal Columbian, and many other smaller hospitals I came to know, a sense of team spirit. Many of us would try to sit with people from different groups, and not necessarily with other doctors, when we came into the cafeteria for lunch. Friendships would develop between these diverse groups. Doctors, as a group, can be boring and stuffy, with a tendency to constantly "talk shop." It was often more stimulating — and relaxing and informative — to sit with these non-doctors.

The Royal Columbian never got to be much more than a 500-bed hospital. But it had all the major services of a trauma and emergency department, and excellent neuro-sciences and cardio-vascular services. Because of its relatively small size, it wasn't a big strain to learn and remember a lot of people's names. And even if I didn't know a person's name, I would certainly be able to recognize and acknowledge almost everyone that I saw in the halls of our hospital. As Harry once declared, "At the risk of sounding like a bloody communist, we are all here to work together to serve the patient."

CHAPTER 10

The Dark Side of Medicine

This was a very difficult chapter for me to write. I have been extremely fortunate to have been associated with, for the most part, sensible people who have been dedicated to the betterment of their patients and to the profession of medicine. But there is, too, a dark side, and it would be wrong for me to ignore or evade it.

SLAVERY AND STUPIDITY (CANADIAN INTERNSHIP AND RESIDENCY IN THE 1960s)

In Ontario, we used to have to go to grade 13 to finish high school. If, however, our marks were good enough, we could get into second year of several universities in other provinces. If we wanted to eventually get into medical school in Ontario, we had two choices. We could go to premeds, a two-year program, and then apply to medical school, or we could take a three-year program in various arts programs, get our BA, and then apply for medical school. In my day, at the University of Toronto, the majority applied through the premed program to save one year.

Medical school itself was a four-year program; the first two years were made up of basic sciences, and the last two years stressed clinical work.

This program was followed by one year of a rotating internship. At the end of this year, we could be turned loose on the public as a GP, or we could apply to enter a residency program in one of the various specialties. After four years of residency, we could sit the specialty exams, and if successful, we could go out and carve up the public, if we were now surgeons, or administer the special poisons, if we were in a medical specialty. Because some of these specialties were themselves becoming so "sub special-ized," it was often necessary to take additional training. I ended up being an "invasive" cardiologist and took an additional eigh-teen months of training in the heart catheter lab under Dr. Doug Wigle. "Invasive" just means that I was one of those guys who push various tubes into people's hearts.

In this prolonged apprenticeship, there were many pitfalls and unfortunate glitches. It wasn't that the people were bad, al-though there were some bad people. Some of the "ivory tower" educators wouldn't know a sick patient if they saw one, and some of the administrators were responsible for some really short-sighted decisions. Moreover, the system itself has promoted a lot of continuing bad decisions. (Of course, it is people who design a system.) Medicine, in some ways, suffers from being in an histori-cal straitjacket, and although things have improved, in my view we still have a very long way to go.

When I was a medical student, and then an intern, and finally a "perpetual resident," we were regaled with stories from our medical superiors about how easy we were having it "now," as compared to "when I was an intern." We, after all, were consid-ered "low life," and the only way we could make it — whatever that meant — was by trying to follow in the footsteps of our great leaders.

Behind their backs, we used to label these stories "Back in the Days of the Giants." That meant working all the time, without any time off. No time was given for even trying to live a normal life. On the surgical side, the residents were encouraged not to get married until they had finished all their training, had passed their specialty exams, and had received an appointment as a junior staff man. In fact, if an intern in a surgical specialty was married or got married during his residency, his future posting might be seriously affected, and his chances reduced of eventu-ally getting his Fellowship exams. (It was not only surgery that discouraged early marriage. The RCMP had a similar policy, and constables weren't supposed to get married until they had been "in" for five years.) Women were not encouraged to even con-sider most of the surgical specialties.

There also was a strong level of anxiety, as we knew that after four additional years of training, there was only a 40 percent pass rate on these specialty exams. A friend of mine, after he had failed twice, went back to his home in Northern Quebec and committed suicide. He was a very competent and kindly guy; he just "froze up" when it came to these horrible exams.

In Toronto, perhaps the worst training job in this regard was that of chief resident in cardiovascular surgery. Unbelievably, he was supposed to stay in residence at the Toronto General Hospital twenty-four hours a day for 365 consecutive days, presumably 366 days if it was a leap year. That was okay, because one assumed that the "Great Chief" of that specialty had had to do it in his days as a resident. Traditionally, the resident would sneak out for two hours on Christmas afternoon, and elaborate precautions were taken to cover him in case some emergency occurred during those two hours. The "Great Chief" was not to know about it, for if the chief resident was discovered to be missing, he could be fired, even on Christmas Day. No one in particular was to blame for this state of affairs. It was the tradition and, no doubt, doctors suffered for generations because of it.

Another major problem was that all the doctors in residency training were very badly off financially. It wasn't that we weren't earning our keep, because before the universal health insurance plan, the resident staff really played a big role in looking after the patients without health insurance, saving the system a ton of money. The medical residents were slightly better off socially, but not any better off financially, than their surgical colleagues. Typically, a junior intern could not afford to live outside hospital, unless he was married to a breadwinner, or his parents lived reasonably close to the hospital. (I was married to a breadwinner, a high school teacher, and my parents had a house in Toronto.) In the second year of residency, if one had taken a clinical program in surgery, the trainee was typically not married, and he only received a very small increase in his "salary." Hence he usually lived in the hospital.

In 1961, as juniors, we received $1,800 a year as our total salary. Even in those days, it was not possible to rent the cheapest apartment, and eat, with such a small salary. The unmarried interns stayed in the intern residence in hospital and, unless lucky enough to have a private room, had to contend with that obnoxious telephone for the roommate who was on call. The Toronto General provided one free meal a day, between 10:00 and 10:30 p.m. This meal was always the same: eggs any style, milk, coffee, and pie with or without ice cream (strictly low cholesterol, of course). Second helpings were allowed, depending on who was the cook that night, and there was never any restriction on the amount of white toast you could eat. I know that many of the interns living in the hospital at the time, took advantage of this free meal and tanked up on the calories in the late evening meal to save money. Some who had had a bad night before in the Emerg, and had gone to bed before ten o'clock, would set their alarm clocks to get up and take advantage of this meal.

A lot of the rotations were "one in two," meaning that the trainee had to stay in the hospital every other night, even if he had outside accommodation. If we were on a "one in three" rotation we considered ourselves lucky.

I went through a medical rather than a surgical program, and I was able to afford to live outside the hospital when I was not on call. Also, I must confess, I tried to pick a varied residency that was compatible with fairly good training, but also had at least some semblance of normality. The trick was, after the junior year, to alternate a clinical year with a year as a fellow to get the mandatory four years, post junior. To be eligible to write the specialty exam, the candidate had to have his training approved by the examining board. They accepted two years as a "fellow" working for an "approved" staff physician, and two years as a "senior intern" only at "approved" hospitals.

In my time, almost everyone graduating from University of Toronto medical school tried to get a rotating junior internship at the Toronto General Hospital. Whether one got the job or not was primarily based on the candidate's marks in medical school, and hence only the upper 20–25 percent, mark wise, from a typical graduating class, got the job. We just did not have the mentality to complain — weren't we getting the best training? And if one wanted to enter a particular specialty, having done a junior year at the TGH was a big help in getting selected. We rotated through approximately nine different specialties in our junior year. Some were awful, in terms of hours, and it was not uncommon to put in 100 hours a week, not counting the number of hours that we were on call, but sleeping in our beds in the interns' residence.

During my junior year, two of our interns had health problems. One person developed hepatitis and was out for six months, and another developed erythema nodosum and lost a number of weeks. The intern with the erythema didn't want to tell the authorities because he knew that if he was sent off sick, he would be making a lot more work for the rest of us. I noticed him one day limping around and when I asked him what was wrong he showed me his legs; they were massively swollen. He just didn't want to quit. I strongly encouraged him to do so, and he eventually confessed to one of the staff men and was given the time off. Poor Murray Jacobs probably still feels guilty, as that simply was our mentality at that time.

All our rotations were "one in two" (on call every other night), except medicine, which was "one in three" (on call every third night) and lasted for three of our four-week rotations. Being on call meant staying at the hospital all night after having completed a twelve-hour shift, and then working another twelve-hour shift the following day. We really appreciated having only to be on call one night in three. (We got one week off on our medical rotation and that was our total vacation time for the year.) But because of the other interns' health problems, we were mostly "one in two" throughout the year. These health problems occurred every year, because the work schedule was so hard and we were constantly exposed to various diseases. My horrible hours on the pediatric rotation are discussed in chapter thirteen. Oh, well, I guess our "giants" had to do this too.

I chose to do my second year of internship at Shaughnessy Hospital in Vancouver. It was more like summer camp, and it gave me time to find out whom I had married just before I had started my junior internship. But my next year I was back into the fire again, working at the Toronto Wellesley Hospital, which was still part of the Toronto General Hospital system, but at least it was "one in three" for the whole year, and now we each got

Erythema Nodosum is a relatively uncommon condition characterized by raised reddened patches on the skin, usually below the knees. It is generally a benign condition that, after a few weeks, gradually disappears. It may be related to various infections, such as strep throat, infectious mono, cat scratch fever, sarcoidosis, and inflammatory bowel disease. Various medications have been implicated, including the sulpha drugs. It probably has some element of autoimmunity, and some cases can be quite debilitating and protracted.

two weeks' holiday, instead of one week. However, we had a very heavy workload, and it was difficult to get home much before seven o'clock at night; our average workday was close to twelve hours.

I chose my next year to be a "fellow," at least in part to try to live a more normal life again, and to have time to study. My boss, Ramsay Gunton, was an excellent instructor and simply a wonderful man. (Ramsay had been the fullback on the football team at Western University, and a Rhodes scholar.) I even had some time to continue some of my hobbies, which I felt I had to do to stay at least partly sane.

During the last year before my exams, I was again in the fire, with a very heavy workload and lots of responsibility. Fortunately, my schedule was again one in three.

The administration at the Toronto General Hospital during this year of training was, in my view, unconscionable. An example was our sleeping accommodation. A health inspector, on a routine visit, had determined that each on-call room had to have an outside window, or at least, some sort of ventilation. There were three rooms in a row, one of which had a window. The other two rooms had no window or any ventilation, and the occupants just slept with the doors open into the hall. The administration, forced to correct this problem, decided to take out the two adjoining walls, making one long narrow room with the one window now serving the entire space.

They then realized that there was space now, with the two walls gone, to jam in an extra bed. There was now no longer a need for the three phones, and four interns on call slept in this long narrow room. Understandably, the single phone was very busy all night, and we would all wake up with each call and have to sort out who should answer each request from the various specialties. This little example illustrates some of the mentality that existed at that time.

The administrator was Dr. Hank Doyle. If he had done his homework, or one of his vice-presidents had actually visited the place, nobody would have made such an inane decision. Although I spent five and a half years at the Toronto General, either as an intern or a fellow, I never laid eyes on the administrator; nor for that matter, did any of us even know who his vice-president equivalents were. They just didn't have a clue what the real prob-

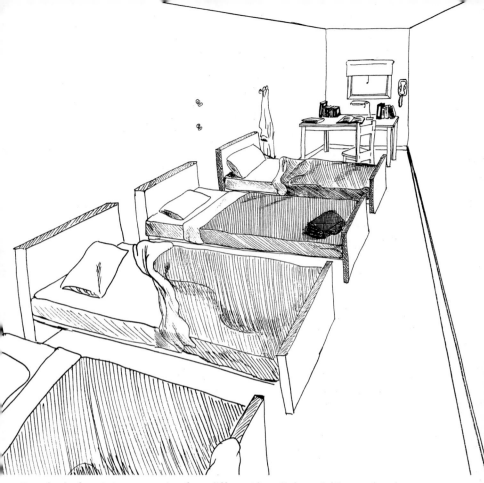

Four beds, four interns covering four different hospital specialties, and a phone that never stopped ringing during the night. Toronto General Hospital administration made sure that their interns couldn't get even a partial night's sleep.

lems were at that interface between the frontline workers and the patients. I think that, if anything, some of these problems have become worse.

I had an easier time than some of my medical colleagues, and certainly an easier time than most of my surgical colleagues. I was able to alternate a very heavy clinical year with a more normal year. I lived outside of the hospital when I was not on call, and I had a very understanding wife. It is no wonder that some of my colleagues from my generation and of course others from previous generations, still bear scars from these training programs. Unfortunately, when we find doctors who don't relate to their patients, throw temper tantrums in the operating room, and are a menace to their friends and families, it may be that some of these personality disorders have been aggravated by five or more years of "slavery" in their training programs.

We have also seen some doctors who have appeared to be money-crazy when they finally got into practice. I have seen examples where I felt that extra procedures were done, not necessarily to the patient's benefit, but more for the doctor's wallet. Perhaps this problem was aggravated by the doctor having lived for a long period in absolute poverty.

I don't want the reader to think that I got through my own medical career completely unscathed. It is always hard to judge oneself, and perhaps it would be better to ask my family and friends about my own mental health than for me to describe it. I know, though, that when I was in a clinical year, I was definitely chronically fatigued. I would fall asleep during hospital rounds, or immediately after the guest speaker said, "Lights out, first slide please."

I remember one very bizarre occasion when my younger brother had invited me to an evening party. I rarely went out; most of us were just too busy or too tired to socialize. My brother had invited a large group of young people, some of whom had been mutual friends. I, of course, had been "out of the loop" and hadn't seen any of his friends for several years. I noticed that they all seemed strangely healthy and vigorous. I then caught myself looking at the veins in the forearms of the young women rather than at their figures. I suspect that most healthy young men of twenty-five years usually do not even notice forearm veins.

While I was at work as a junior, my primary concern had been to try to at least get some sleep at night when on call, and in the late evening we went around looking at all the IVs. If an IV was poor, it inevitably would fail in the middle of the night. We took great pains to retape and find straight veins before trying to get some sleep. Consequently, we always appreciated the patients who had large and straight veins in their forearms.

Just after I had been contemplating this personal revelation of my screwed-up personality, a nice buxom young lady whom I knew vaguely came along and told me, in no uncertain terms, that I was a "professional student" and asked when was I going to go out and get a real job.

During my years of practice as a cardiologist, I saw many of my colleagues as patients. I have noticed that doctors, perhaps more than others, seem particularly worried about their hearts. One just can't help noticing how driven so many of these people are, particularly the doctors in specialties. They don't know how to relax; they take themselves far too seriously, and have an undeveloped sense of humour. Many don't seem to have any hobbies and they inevitably handle retirement very badly.

I think a lot of us don't really know enough about things other than our own specialty and we just don't know how to organize our lives. This is so apparent in some doctors' investment strategies. It's always sad, seeing an elderly doctor shuffling along the hall, still practicing long after he should have stopped, because he can't afford to do so.

I think the same attitude often adversely affects their marriages. The doctor who has been telling people what to do all day, then comes home tired and late, as usual, and his wife, tired and harried herself from herding his "brats" all day, scolds him at the door. And his kids — the noisy little urchins — have the temerity to argue with him! His wife might say that little Johnny has gotten into another fight at school, and what was he going to do about it? He thinks, and maybe says, "Why is this such a big crisis?" After all, hadn't he been saving lives all day? She might even tell him that he had forgotten to take out the garbage that morning, or he wasn't keeping up his end of the household chores. Was she expected to do everything herself? And on and on it might go.

That single, attractive young woman working in his office, or perhaps that little "gem" who seems so nice in the OR, never gives him any hassle. Pretty soon the marriage is in trouble, and three years later he is in his late forties or early fifties, pushing a baby carriage, with his new wife walking behind him. She is perhaps ten or fifteen years younger than his first wife, but now she is also telling him something he doesn't want to know, and is looking a little the worse for wear, and suspiciously like a younger edition of his first wife! This is another place where we screw up and perhaps have to keep working long after we would like to have been able to retire.

Jack Peck, a very capable gynecologist and still very productive, has been through several marriages. He told me that a divorce basically cuts your estate into four equal squares. "The wife gets the bottom left square of the estate and you get the bottom right square. The two opposing lawyers get the top left and right squares." When I asked him when he was going to retire, he said with his usual grin, "I'm going to have to work for five years after I am dead to pay off all my debts!"

It's difficult, sometimes, to step back and see the "big picture." Hopefully, when "god" goes home, he allows his wife to debate some of the issues of the day. If he does, he likely has a happier marriage than a lot of my colleagues.

I think some of this brutal and unthinking training was left over from the wars. In the 1950s and 60s, we were regaled with stories of doctors working impossible hours patching up soldiers at the front in World War II, working in tents with poor equipment and inadequate lighting. Sometimes, they carried on even when they were under mortar attack. Who were we to complain, with only two hours sleep at night and then having to work in the Emerg all the next day?

There's no doubt that being able to work long hours can benefit the patients, if there has been an emergency and you happen to be the only doctor for miles around. However, there was no excuse, in my view, to make it a way of life.

My wife was a high school teacher during my training as a "perpetual resident," and I was able to "work my ass off" at the hospital and to study at home without much interruption, while my wife was teaching and learning her new trade. However, once we decided to start having a family, it was supposed to be a different story. I now had my dreaded fellowship exams behind me, but the training went on. It was at least somewhat easier, of course; I no longer had to study every free minute that I was at home.

When we eventually moved out West and I started out as a cardiologist, my practice soon got out of control and I became a slave to it. For the first eighteen months, I had no one to sign out to, so I literally had no days off and could not even drink any beer because I never knew when there would be another call to the Emerg. Pretty soon, we had four little urchins less than five years of age, and we had bought our farm, which by this time was completely out of control as well. We actually had three kids in a span of twenty-two months, and when a nurse once asked me how come our kids were so close together, I told her that because I was a doctor, my wife got a private room in the hospital and hence we could increase a family more quickly! (In those days, the mothers were kept in hospital for several days after giving birth, something that is unheard of now.) In fact, because we didn't know the fate of our son David, a situation described in the next chapter, we decided to try to establish another pregnancy as a kind of insurance against the possible loss of our second child.

My poor wife had to put up with all this. I guess I was a workaholic, because every minute I had at home I was out in the fields or in one of our barns attending to a problem. When I look back on it, I wonder how she tolerated me, and all these projects that were not really of her making. She was more interested in the arts, while I was a totally hands-on person. I think our boys profited by this difference because they could see there were two broad and different interests to learn about. Perhaps, unfortunately, our kids followed more in my footsteps as hands-on people rather than being interested in fine arts. However, as noted in chapter eight, it is important to have interests other than those related to one's profession. My wife still pursues her hobbies vigorously as I do mine, and we are still getting along well forty-seven years later.

The doctor, after he has reached well into retirement age, may keep practicing because his family has grown up and perhaps his wife has been used to not having him around much and has developed other friends and interests. Without hobbies and friends outside of medicine, he may gravitate back to what makes him feel most comfortable. That they do so may be a good thing, particularly now with such a shortage of doctors, but some of these guys may still try to practice after their "best before date," and ultimately do a disservice to their patients.

I don't think a person has to be particularly bright to get into and survive medical school. The candidate usually has to be good worker, fairly well organized, and has to study hard to get the necessary marks to get into medical school. The occasional very bright person does, in fact, get by doing very little studying, but I believe they are the very rare exception. The majority of medical students are hardworking, focused, and perhaps a little obsessive-compulsive. Medicine is a little self-selecting in this way and the training program, I think, aggravates this type of personality.

Fortunately, the absolutely brutal internship training has been modified considerably. I think, however, the shortage of doctors in modern times has been partly aggravated by the fact that the new breed of doctors just won't accept working sixty or more hours a week, particularly the woman doctors who demand a life outside of medicine. It's certainly a good thing that the internship training has become a little more human, but we have to be careful that the pendulum doesn't eventually swing too far the other way.

In my later years of practice, I often found that the interns on the coronary care and the intensive care units were not available at eight o'clock for morning rounds, because they were having a lecture or, sometimes, they had a bad night on call and hence were sleeping in. At the risk of being in turn labelled with the term "back in the days of the giants," I found, personally, that the most valuable time I spent as an intern was the time I spent with the staff person during morning rounds. The patient's course the night before could be discussed, as well as the future plans for this patient.

Twice in one year, when I asked two different interns what their plans were for the next year, I was told that they were going into "radiation oncology," and hence they were really not that interested in what happened in critical care units. They had to make that choice while they were in third year meds. How anyone could make that choice when they had not even experienced any of the various services at that point in their career, I will never understand. Perhaps the only good thing that I can think of about this particular specialty is that it's strictly 8:00 a.m. to 4:00 p.m., five days a week.

When I was an overworked slave as a junior, I at least had the usual rotation of most of the major services. At the end of my year, I knew that I wouldn't make a psychiatrist and that I didn't have the emotional stamina to be able to work, for the rest of my life, with pediatric cancer patients; but I found general practice, general surgery and internal medicine very interesting. I purposely picked my second year of six months medicine and six months pathology so that I wouldn't close any doors, and could procrastinate even longer. I could go into a medical or a surgical specialty, and I could still go into general practice with some useful extra training under my belt. It wasn't until my fourth year of training, this time with the help of Ramsay Gunton, a cardiologist, that I gravitated into cardiology.

How our present "ivory tower" educators think that the modern medical student can make the choice so early on in their training baffles me. Think how a doctor would feel, and likely treat his patients, if he found that he didn't like what he was doing, or felt he was unsuited to the particular specialty. It used to be that if a GP in private practice decided, after five years or so of general practice, that he really liked, for example, orthopedics, he could at least apply to go into this specialty and his application would be seriously considered. Now the application would not even be given a second look! My colleagues and I were lucky to be able to find a type of medicine that we really enjoyed, and for me, at least, I can't think of a specialty that I would have enjoyed more than cardiology.

SOCIAL AND ECONOMIC PROBLEMS

Our Impoverished Natives

In 1960, during my time as a summer extern at Soldier's Memorial Hospital, I had a lot of contact with the local native band. The area around Lake Couchiching was considered the second most-populated native community in Ontario, and was relatively close to the hospital.

There was a doctor who was responsible for the medical welfare of the Native people. He was a good person and was certainly kind to his patients and to me. He, like the majority of the regular GPs, helped me with the care of the patients, and often would ask the Emerg nurse to ask me to see the patient first and order the tests, such as x-rays and blood tests, that I thought might be appropriate. That not only saved the patient time, but also was good practice for me. He would come in, review my notes, and then see the patient and tell me if he agreed. Sometimes, he would just stand by while I put on a cast or sewed up some lacerations, and other times, he would coach me throughout when the problem was more difficult. This level of care was also popular with the non-native community.

The Natives had a very high birth rate, and often their family life was atrocious. Unbelievably, on two separate occasions while I was there, the admission diagnosis on the hospital's Emerg "green sheet," was abdominal pain NYD (not yet diagnosed).

These two cases were two teenaged girls from different families, but from the same reserve. They were both severely obese and were in labour, and both said they hadn't even known they were pregnant. That was a new cause of abdominal pain NYD that wasn't in any "green book" that I had read.

In 2006 I read in a newspaper that on one Native reserve, up to 40 percent of the infants have fetal alcohol effect. I guess things haven't improved very much since I was a young extern.

The Indian doctor would let me deliver his patients while he stood by and gave me instructions. Sometimes, I would end up giving the anesthetic, which in this hospital was open drop ether. If I wasn't there, it was the nurse who administered this anesthetic. Fortunately, it was a pretty safe and effective agent, the big risk being that if there was an open flame or spark, an explosion was possible. Everything was done to eliminate static sparks and, of course, no cautery was ever used when ether was the anesthetic. I never saw any complications with this agent. It should be noted that I was also often involved in a similar way with the white community, and I never felt that the Natives were ever considered as second class citizens, at least while they were in hospital.

One day, towards the end of my summer at Orillia, a native woman named Florence came in; she was in her early forties. She had what I thought was a really bad case of bronchitis with a very deep cough. I remembered that she was wearing an inexpensive dress with a printed flower design, with a single breast pocket. I ordered the usual chest x-ray and blood work. The radiologist from Barrie was in our x-ray department when she was in our Emerg and he read her chest x-ray as normal; her blood work, too, came back as normal. When I examined her, she didn't look particularly sick; her chest was clear on auscultation and she didn't have any fever. The Indian doctor came in, examined her and wrote her a prescription for the new, at the time, antibiotic called tetracycline. Both the nurse and I saw her fold the paper up and put it in her little breast pocket and she was told now to go to the Indian Agent's house that was just outside of her community and give it to him. He would then get into his car, drive to the local drug store, get the prescription filled, and then deliver the medicine to her house. It was standard procedure at the time.

About five days later, Florence was back, and the same nurse and I were in the Emerg when she came in. This time she was really sick. She was dehydrated, had a high fever, and her chest x-ray showed a bilateral bronchopneumonia. She was still wearing that simple flowered print dress, and when she was being undressed it was noticed that the prescription that she had been given was still neatly folded up in her breast pocket. For some reason she hadn't followed our instructions to give the prescription to the Indian Agent, and hence had never taken the prescription for the antibiotic.

She was now put on pretty heavy IV antibiotic therapy, spent about three weeks in hospital, and after quite a struggle was eventually discharged.

Two years later, during my stint at Shaughnessy Hospital, I was covering Emerg. As Shaughnessy was considered a military hospital, it was supposed to be the main hospital for the Native population in the Vancouver area. On this particular late evening, a big overweight man came in. Apparently he had been in some sort of fight in a local bar, and another patron had broken a beer glass and shoved it in his face. Fortunately, it had missed his eye, but he had the typical curved laceration across the left side of his face and the glass had done a terrible "number" on his left ear.

He turned out to be a very agreeable patient, and although he smelled strongly of alcohol, he was quite co-operative. After washing his wounded area thoroughly, I found that the laceration on his face, fortunately, was not deep. It had gone through the subcutaneous fat, but had not seriously damaged his facial muscles. His ear was a different story, for some of it was literally in tags, and as the earlobe has a lot of cartilage, the blood supply is not very good to this structure. I was forced to trim away a lot of the lobe. After I had got it trimmed as best I could, I then proceeded to try to stitch it up.

There was a relatively new material called "Dexon" for sewing up lacerations, and it came in various sizes or thickness. I requested the six "o," which was the finest suture material at Shaughnessy Hospital. The advantage of this material was that it was supposed to leave less of a scar and it was easy to see because of its blue-green colour, and hence, easier to remove after the laceration had healed sufficiently.

I spent the next two hours sewing and trimming his ear lobe. It was the middle of the night by this time, and nobody else was bothering me. When I had finished, the Emerg nurse and I were pretty proud of our work. I asked the patient to come back in three days so that I could inspect the ear, and I planned to take out some of the sutures, depending on how it was healing.

Guess what? I didn't see him again until about four months later when he was back in the Emerg with another beer glass cut, this time a little further laterally and not quite so extensive. The original laceration had healed up, but nobody had taken out his sutures and they were now overgrown with scar tissue. Because of their blue-green colour, I could see some of them under his scar tissue.

This time, I sewed up his new cut with chromic gut (that is the suture material that dissolves eventually, but leaves more of a scar and is not recommended on skin surface lacerations). I then spent a lot of time trying to extract my suture material from his older cut, but I never did get it all out and my original job was now a bit of a mess.

During this same year, I was visiting my wife's RCMP cousin, Hugh Westheuser, "Uncle Hugh," who worked in Powell River on the BC coast. He was on the night shift and I went with him to a problem on the local reserve. In this single-room house, a woman was sitting on the floor with her back to the wall and was quite dead. Her skin was blue and she had blue foamy spit around her mouth. I examined her to see if she was completely gone and found the characteristic comissurotomy scar across her left chest that was fashionable at the time for somebody that had undergone surgery for a mitral valve disorder. I found out much later that this lady had indeed undergone a mitral valve repair at the Vancouver General Hospital several years earlier, but had never come back for follow up. (The mitral valve is located deep in the heart structure and surgery on it may be very difficult).

All the lights were on in this building. There was a wooden table in the middle of the room and

The blue foamy spit is one of the signs of congestive heart failure. As the heart weakens, it may not pump the blood forward into circulation; the blood then backs up in the lung, causing fluid to escape into the small air sack in the lung, and the patient coughs up the fluid. Sometimes the patient literally drowns in this fluid, which was the result in this lady's case.

on it was a large cooked turkey. There was a "raft" of houseflies sitting on this carcass, and people were just milling about. Some people would go up to the table and break off a piece of turkey and munch on it as they talked. The chief came in, wearing a headlamp. It was difficult to talk to this guy with the spotlight constantly shining in my eyes.

I noticed a wavy line along three walls of the house, and a darker discoloration below this line. I asked one of the ladies who seemed to be attached to this house what that discolouration was on the wall. She told me that in the winter the men were just too lazy to go outside and peed against the wall! The only wall that didn't have this wavy line was where the bed was. It really wasn't a bed; it was a big box, perhaps the size of a triple bed, full of old comforters, newspapers, and burlap. I gather that the whole family slept on it or in it.

The building had no insulation and the uprights were two by fours, some of which were missing, apparently used in their pot-bellied stove for fuel over the last winter. This situation was absolutely intolerable; now, forty years later, a number of reserves are still like this. When I asked who owned this house, one of the women finally explained to me that it was owned by the tribal council and was the house that had been assigned to her family. As far as I could tell, nobody had any employment, and they lived off whatever the tribal council decided to hand out to them. No "fee simple" as all property and houses belonged to the tribal council, and hence no pride of ownership, no democracy, no employment, poor education, families in disarray, and rampant alcoholism plus gasoline or glue sniffing — how can these poor people ever lead productive lives?

I have always had a soft spot for First Nations' people, probably due to my relatively early exposure to this group. My grandfather, in the late 1940s and very early 1950s, hired native Ojibway from the local band near Pointe au Baril, on the north shore of Georgian Bay, to work on the various projects on his properties. Typically, he would hire three or four men that he had gotten to know well. They were excellent general contractors and carpenters, and my older brother and I really appreciated it when, sometimes, they would bring some of their kids who were about our age.

There were no power tools because there was no electricity, and the chain saw didn't appear in our district until the mid 1950s. The men would sometimes start a handful of nails on some planks and my brother and our new friends would try to hammer them down. Sometimes, we would accidentally bend a nail over, and one of the men would come over, and cheerfully help us out.

My brother was given some flint arrowheads that one of these guys had found near his house, and they were a treasured item. On one memorable day, one of the older carpenters, Vic, brought a corn-cob pipe and we promptly crushed up some pine needles, set it alight and passed it around. My strict Presbyterian grandmother was not amused and she bawled out not only us, but also the nice man who had taken the trouble to bring along this pipe.

Occasionally, we would be allowed to go out with some of the Native fishermen and help in their gillnetting of lake trout and whitefish. Our job, as little kids, was to stand as the winch pulled in the net and try to untangle the fish without damaging the net. It was all great fun and a thrill to see so many beautiful fish. When we got back to the dock we continued to clean fish, throwing all the guts to the seagulls. The fish were then packed in ice and sent to New York City by train.

However, trouble was on the horizon. We noticed that many fish, especially the lake trout had lamprey eels stuck on them, or the scars of previous bites. Within the next three years, the fishery just collapsed, the lake trout first, and then the whitefish.

The Natives used to cut lake ice in the winter and store it in "ice houses," basically small wooden buildings full of sawdust that came from the local mill, which also had many Native employees. The fishery used the ice, but summer cottagers from Toronto would also buy ice to keep their food fresh during those hot summer days. Electricity started to arrive in this area in the late 1940s and early 50s, and with the collapse of the fishery, the ice industry collapsed too.

By this time, most of the marketable white and red pine had been decimated and the logging industry folded. To make matters worse, when I was about thirteen, the Indian Agent, a white guy, came along and told the men that if they stayed on their reserve, he would give them money.

We then no longer had Natives coming to work for my grandfather. Their children hence would no longer be exposed to general contracting work and carpentering skills.

I saw where they lived, and if I lived there, I think I would be sniffing gasoline too. It probably wasn't too bad in the summer, the only time that I saw it, but I could just imagine what it was like in the winter, and during the fall and spring "shoulder seasons."

Alcohol was always a problem with this particular group, and because of this, my grandfather would sometimes delay paying them, to avoid the drunkenness that followed, as surely as night follows day. Payment was usually on every second Friday, and the men would often not show up for work until the middle of the following week. On one very sad occasion, long after I had gone, Vic bought a bottle of gin through a middleman (in those days, Natives were not allowed to purchase liquor at the Ontario Liquor Board stores), drank the whole thing, and was found dead on the main street of Midland a few hours later.

In a medical study done in the sixties, a group of Natives and a group of Europeans of similar age, sex, etc. were given identical amounts of alcohol orally, and then the blood alcohol was measured at regular intervals. It was found that the Natives obtained a much higher level of blood alcohol, and it persisted longer in their circulation than with the white group.

Also, when the enzyme alcohol dehydrogenase, which is responsible for breaking down alcohol, was obtained through liver biopsy measured in both groups, the Natives were found to have a much lower level of this enzyme. Compared to his white counterpart, when the Native drinks alcohol, it is almost as if he is taking it by IV. Presumably, the European has been exposed to alcohol for perhaps thousands of years, while for some of the Native groups, it is a relatively new thing and they haven't had time to adapt to this "poison."

Because of my interest in the welfare of First Nations people, I tried to visit reserves whenever I got the chance. In my retirement years, wandering in the north with my little home built aircraft, I have had the opportunity to visit many remote spots in northern BC, the Yukon, the Northwest Territories, and northern Alberta and Saskatchewan. (Because of problems obtaining aviation gas, I didn't get to Aklavik, or points east of Tuktoyaktuk along the north Arctic coast.) I just don't know how anybody would want to live in some of these places, particularly when the conditions may be appalling. I think a lot of these people don't even know there are alternatives.

In some of these communities in the far north, there is no chance of having a productive existence. Their whole way of life has collapsed. Nobody wants to wear furs, the caribou have disappeared in many areas, and we are now in a whole different time period.

Moving communities from one remote area to another remote area is completely wrong-headed. These communities should be encouraged to go where there is a chance of education, diversity and employment. Tribal councils should be completely abandoned and some sort of democratic municipal government should be put in their place.

If a Native person wants to leave and go to the south, he will lose his house, and it may be some time before he gets the government funding he has been accustomed to receiving. He has a real disincentive to moving out, leaving everything that he knows, and with uncertain funding in the future. He is basically trapped.

If there was "fee simple," the Native might at least have pride of ownership and be more interested in keeping his home in good repair. He could sell his share of the band's assets, including his share of land claims. Besides giving him a bit of a "grubstake" for his future, if a non-Native were allowed to buy his share, over time, these disastrous ghettos would be broken up. Remaining in these "ghetto" systems doesn't allow those who live in these communities to be exposed to different ways of living.

The system of hereditary chiefs with real power is feudal, and western countries long ago abandoned that type of government. Tribal councils, in my view, are Soviet-style communism. Surely our Natives deserve better than this. Of course, the chiefs at the top of this pile don't want any change, and fight it tooth and nail. The white government bureaucrats, likewise, don't want change; they want to protect their pay cheques and their fat pensions.

Some of my grandchildren are now at least sixth-generation Canadians. When will these grandchildren ever be considered to be equal to everyone else in Canada? We claim to be against racism. But the Department of Indian and Northern Affairs has "institutionalized" this racism, even to the point where a Native has only to show his racial heritage to be able to get advantages, such as free university education, and exemption from paying income tax and, of course, handouts.

Questions of race are always complicated. If your grandmother, a Native, was unmarried when your mother was conceived, even though her boyfriend, and therefore your grandfather, was white, does that make you a full-status Native even if your father was also white? Apparently it does.

These race-based distinctions should be phased out over the next generation. The mindset is frozen in the past. Whatever the government has done, sometimes with good intentions, just hasn't worked in the past 100 years, isn't working now, and will continue to fail in the future.

Radical "surgery" on the government bureaucracy is urgent and necessary. The Department of Indian and Northern Affairs should also be phased out over time — within one generation. Throwing government money at the problem may actually be making the long-term outlook worse. (Approximately 400,000 Natives live on reserves representing 1.3 percent of our Canadian population. We, the taxpayer, spend eight billion dollars on this population, amounting to 20,000 dollars per year for every man, woman, and child living on these reserves. In a household of five people that would be 100,000 dollars.) Do these people ever see this money? Not directly. It first has to filter through a huge bureaucracy and then go to infrastructure problems, then to the tribal councils and finally, only a fraction filters down to each household. Also, it is much more expensive to live in remote areas of Canada, so the Natives' costs for household goods may be two or three times as high as the costs for us living in the southern regions.

In so many remote Native communities there is no local industry to add anything to the tax base, and of course the Native households are immune to federal taxes. Despite all the money being spent by various levels of government, our First Nations people are often living in abject poverty. It's an embarrassment to all Canadians. The recent introduction of hard drugs and HIV into these communities has compounded the problems.

This money would be far better spent bringing these people to centres where there is useful employment, education possibilities and good diet and medical help, and perhaps most importantly, a chance to join the twenty-first century and leave their third-world conditions behind.

One day, after I had just seen another tragedy, I saw my buddy Harry and started to rant about all these Native problems. Harry had once told me that he never felt comfortable in a conversation unless he did at least 85 percent of the talking. Nobody usually minded, because Harry was so bright and entertaining that most of us learned more than we ever contributed during these conversations. However, on this occasion, I told Harry to just "shut up and listen!"

"Harry, your father was a big-shot surgeon at the Toronto General during the 1930s to at least the mid-50s and he must have seen lots of these same problems. He just handled these problems one patient at a time. He likely never did anything to change the system itself. We have covered the scene from 1960 to the present and have watched these things go on and on.

"What have you done? What have I done about this systemic problem? Not a thing. We just go about our business and try to help the individual patient, ignoring the big problem.

"Aren't we supposed to advocate for our patients? We just keep our mouths shut and carry on as if the problem didn't exist! We send our young troops off to Afghanistan to force 'democracy' on the Afghan people, but we do nothing about the lack of democracy on our own country's reserves. We even allowed Trudeau to enshrine this legislation in our new constitution with this self-government nonsense!"

I walked off before even Harry had a chance to collect his thoughts. It was probably the only time that I contributed 100 percent of the conversation and Harry none.

DRUGS, DRUGS, AND MORE DRUGS

In the 1960s, working in the various emergency departments, we saw the usual Saturday night drunks, the tragedies related to drunk driving, and family disintegration due to alcoholism, but we saw far less of the drug problems that are so common now. In downtown Toronto there were some heroin addicts, but drugs were not the huge problem that they have become today.

In my later years of practice, I continued to frequent the Emerg, because, due to the nature of their illness, so many of our cardiac patients ended up there. Our cardiac patients would usually be "hived" off in a quieter section. However, it was the drug people who caused the most disruption in the department.

Most large emergency departments have a locked room where the really disruptive and sometimes dangerous patients can be put. There is no furniture in these rooms, only a mattress on the floor and some bedding. A peephole in the door and usually a video camera allow the staff to monitor these patients.

Coming into the Emerg during the night and hearing that characteristic banging on the door to the "locked room" would bring a smile to my face, because I didn't usually have to see these patients unless they had a rare arrhythmia related to such drugs as the amphetamines. However, this group of patients was very disruptive to the Emerg and tragically, to society as a whole.

One day, while I was off in my little alcove looking after the cardiac patients still awaiting assessment in the Emerg, a very disruptive man was in the bed next to this alcove. He was literally yelling and screaming, swearing at the nurses and my patients, and when he caught my eye, he "put me in my place" with pretty colourful language. He had been found lying on the sidewalk several blocks away, unconscious, barely breathing, and likely suffering from some degree of hypothermia. He had overdosed on heroin and on arrival in Emerg had been given an IV dose of Naloxone, an antidote to heroin and other opioids. Apparently he didn't like being "saved," because the Emerg staff had, in his view, spoiled his high.

He was eventually discharged after he had been rehydrated, fed, and warmed up, a process that kept him in our Emerg for the better part of a day. Exactly six days later, when I was again on call, looking after a different group of cardiac patients in the alcove, the same man was brought back in. Basically the same scenario ensued, and his vocabulary had not improved.

Some people might think he should just be left lying on the sidewalk. It seems to me it would be more humane to admit him to an institution, where at least he could be warm and dry and would not run the risk of killing himself or someone else. Perhaps, he might even, over time, be rehabilitated. I suspect the treatment would be cheaper than allowing him to continue to engage in whatever criminal activity that he had to undertake to feed his addiction, arresting him, convicting him, and continuing to release him back into society.

The "revolving-door" criminal justice system with its continual conviction and release scenarios for individuals like this simply supports ongoing crime and does nothing to address the root of the problem. It simply puts the problems back on the doorsteps of communities that are unable to help in any meaningful way.

Closing the big mental institutions (in our local area, the Riverview Hospital in Coquitlam) was a tragic mistake. Seriously ill mental patients released from hospital often end up in economically depressed, drug-infested, run-down areas and, perhaps in an attempt to lessen their distress, become drug addicted. They may then have a dual diagnosis: their original mental illness with the addition of a substance addiction. Why can we not keep these poor souls in appropriate institutions when it has been reasonably determined that they are only going to continue hurting themselves and society in general? They need to be admitted, assessed and treated, with eventual release dependent on this continued assessment.

Building social housing at great cost is not the answer in a large number of cases because these hopelessly addicted individuals and/or, mentally ill persons just simply trash their accommodation in short order. We then feel sorry for them and want to build them new structures.

Putting them in safe institutions is, in my view, the less expensive and more compassionate answer to at least some of these desperate problems. It's not really rocket science. Our former prime minister, Mr. Trudeau, with his charter of rights and freedoms, although perhaps well intentioned, has in these circumstances simply aggravated problems instead of solving them.

CHAPTER 11

Obstetrics —
A Tough Job

A lot of the old-time family doctors back in the 1960s really liked obstetrics, despite the awful hours, and I could see why. The mother and the GP had arrived at the end of a successful pregnancy, and now the fruits of this combined effort had arrived.

By this time, the delivery room was usually quiet. The nurse, or often the doctor, had taken this "bundle of joy" out to the father who had been anxiously waiting in the hall. In those days, the father was not allowed into the delivery room. The wrapped-up infant was then quietly sleeping on the mother's chest or in a small plastic open box on a small table beside her, and the mother was happy and was now recovering from her long ordeal. Some mothers at this point were quite chatty; others would be quietly sleeping with their infants.

The doctor would be filling out those interminable forms or sewing up the episiotomy.

The doctor was usually relaxed at this point and would be exhausted or even a little "punchy" after being up most of the night. Obstetrics was very pleasant, at least 95 percent of the time.

It was that *five percent or less* of the time that caused all the trouble!

An episiotomy is an incision that the obstetrician makes, usually on a diagonal line at the entrance to the vagina, to allow a wider birth opening. The tissues in this area will stretch to a certain point, but if the obstetrician feels that the area will be torn by the passage of the infant he usually makes this incision to have a "controlled" tear, and avoid the possibility of the tear extending into the rectum.

It was 1961–62, my year as a junior intern. I had just arrived for my four-week rotation on the obstetrical service at the Toronto General Hospital. In fact, two of us were assigned for each four-week period; on this occasion, it was my old classmate and friend, Henry Singer and I. We rotated one day on the delivery service, and one day on the ward and OR. From what we had learned from our predecessors, it seemed we could count on doing at least two deliveries every other day. With any luck, the two of us would each get at least twenty deliveries during our obstetrical stint.

Our resident in obstetrics, Dr. Bill Thomas, asked if I had any previous experience. As it turned out, I was one of the few juniors that year who had done an "externship" the previous summer in Orillia in 1960, as described in chapter two. During that summer I had scrubbed in on about forty cases. On at least ten of these, I was the only "doctor" in the hospital when the delivery occurred, so I had actually been a temporary obstetrician for those cases.

The first normal delivery that I was supposed to be involved with at the Toronto General was going to be demonstrated by Dr. Thomas, and I was just putting my gloves on when all hell broke loose.

When the delivery nurse pulled down the bed sheets, the umbilical cord was out of the vagina and a small portion was actually lying on the bottom sheet of the bed. To me it looked like a cross between a huge varicose vein and a large hemorrhoid!

In the scheme of things, this isn't supposed to happen. It is a rare event. The cord is getting all its oxygen and nutrition from the placenta, and is supposed to transfer these to the about-to-be-born infant. If, for some reason, it drops down through the mouth of the womb (the cervix) in front of the head of the fetus, it will be squashed and the fetus will be starved of the precious oxygen it needs to survive.

This rare occurrence is a huge disaster and may result in death to the fetus, or perhaps even worse, irreparable brain damage. It's basically "game over" for the fetus if it should happen where those in charge are inexperienced, or in a small centre without all the emergency equipment, or during a home delivery. I dread to think what would have been the result had this occurred during the night at Soldier's Memorial Hospital in Orillia when I was the only doctor in the building.

While I was standing there with, undoubtedly, a stupid expression on my face, Dr. Thomas was rapidly giving orders. Having called for the anesthetist, and quickly raising the foot of the bed very high, he had his hand on the head of the fetus pushing hard to take the weight off the cord. The anesthetist was soon with us, and once he had put the patient to sleep, the uterus relaxed, thus taking the pressure off this precious cord. Dr. Thomas wasted no time. Within two minutes he had delivered the fetus by cesarean section.

By this time, the delivery room was full of people, and I either was pushed or had backed up voluntarily against the wall. This had been an emergency requiring quick, skilled action, and I was surplus to requirements. I was very thankful that Dr. Thomas was on hand; it had given me the chance to see "how it was done." The little girl didn't look too good at first, but very rapidly she pinked up and it was felt that she wouldn't be any the worse for wear.

Just over two weeks later when I was doing my on-call day for the delivery service, I went to check on my patient (the public patients in those days were looked after by the resident staff, as there was no general insurance scheme). I pulled back the covers; and, unbelievably, there on the bottom sheet of the bed was another cord!

This is supposed to be a rare occurrence, yet here I was seeing my second case within two weeks, and I was only a junior! I found myself hollering for somebody to get the anesthetist and the surgeon. At the same time someone raised the foot of the bed, and I pushed like mad on the fetus's head.

Again everything went like clockwork, and the outcome was very satisfactory. Dr. Cannell, the big chief, subsequently heard about the incident and asked how I had known what to do. When I told him it was my second case, I think he initially thought I had somehow caused these two cords to prolapse. But eventually he was reassured, and I was off the hook.

I wasn't very fond of Dr. Cannell. I found him cold and distant. He never introduced himself, never even asked me my name. And we were told, in no uncertain terms, that we were *not* allowed to give any public patients birth control advice of any kind.

In 2008 this seems draconian. Even at that time, we thought this directive unduly harsh. Many families, for various reasons, were not even able to cope with their existing brood, let alone handle yet another child. The public patients had a pre-natal and post-natal clinic, and we saw a lot of their problems firsthand. We also worked in the public gynecology clinic, and again saw a series of problems where proper birth control advice would have been of great help. I believe most of the intern staff took a similar view, but we were under Dr. Cannell's orders. We simply had to do what we were told.

AN AVOIDABLE TRAGEDY

My classmates and I had known a beautiful woman, L P, who was in our class from 1955 to 1958. She was a little older than the rest of us, perhaps twenty-five years old. She had been born in Egypt and spoke Arabic, elegant French, and English, probably better than most of us. She was out-going, friendly, and kind, and fitted very well into our class. Perhaps because she was so beautiful, we naturally elected her class president. (There had always been a friendly rivalry between the engineering school and the medical school, and I think that because at that time there were very few, if any, women in the engineering school, we felt that having such a beautiful lady as our president would make the engineers jealous!)

Sometime in 1958, L P became pregnant, and in those days abortions were illegal. She couldn't afford to have a baby at that time in her life and career and sought a "back street" abortionist. Most tragically, she became septic and eventually died from complications.

I think this tragedy affected all of us. It was a terrible loss, as well as a waste of a wonderful life and a first-class talent. Most of us felt that if someone is determined to get an abortion, then surely a proper doctor with modern equipment should be able to do the job. Why have to take the risk of having some amateur abortionist stick a dirty knitting needle through the cervix, or worse, the wall of the vagina into the peritoneal cavity? We grieved for L P and missed her greatly. Indeed, I can see her today as I write: that beautiful face and figure, that laughing animated presence. I think we were all secretly in love with her.

Several years later an "infamous" GP, Dr. Henry Morgenthaler, was hauled before the courts over his conducting of — still, at that time! — illegal abortions. I closely followed his story in the

278

newspapers. He was an active general practitioner who became interested in this problem and he felt he could offer a much safer alternative. I am certain he didn't do it for the money, and in fact, in those days a general practitioner could make a decent living doing a legitimate practice; and it was, of course, much safer than doing illegal abortions.

Dr. Morgenthaler eventually went to jail, and in jail he suffered a heart attack. He needed help with his legal bills and I actually sent him a thousand dollars, which was a lot of money in those days, and probably more than I could afford. I included a letter, and described the story of our late friend, L P.

Then, by a total fluke, years later as I was having lunch with my wife and her brother and sister-in-law in a downtown Toronto restaurant, sitting at a table beside us was Dr. Henry Morgenthaler.

I went over and introduced myself, and he immediately recalled the letter that I had sent him. He told me that "back street" damage suffered by desperate young women was the type of thing he had seen too often in his practice. It was what had induced him to become an illegal abortionist.

I think he was a good man, but unfortunately for him, Mother Nature had given him that shit-disturber chip of Harry's.

I am just sad that Dr. Morgenthaler's skilled services weren't available for our classmate.

In 2008 Dr. Henry Morgenthaler was appointed a Member of the Order of Canada for his commitment to increased health care options for women, his determined efforts to influence Canadian public policy and his leadership in humanist and civil liberties organizations. The Order of Canada is Canada's highest civilian honour for lifetime achievement.

PLACENTA

Because the resident staff looked after the public patients, we often saw a different clientele from the ones we would see in such numbers after public insurance came in. In the early 1960s, there were about 200,000 first-generation Italians living in the greater Toronto area. The majority didn't speak English well, and of course many were at the bottom of the socio-economic scale and didn't have medical insurance. The Toronto Western Hospital got a large percentage of these patients, but certainly the Toronto General also got its share.

These people made good patients and always treated the interns very well. They were always most appreciative of any service that we could give them, and we especially enjoyed the homemade wine they freely brought for us. Some of the interns with more sophisticated palates said the wine was "no good." But I don't remember a single bottle of wine that I didn't like!

We also dealt with some of Toronto's most "down and out" people, and members of the hippie movement, which was just in its infancy. The drug culture was just getting started then and it was tragic to see. In the United States some of these folks would be called white trash, but calling them that in Canada would not have been considered "politically correct."

One day, just after completing a totally uneventful delivery, I was talking to the mother's boyfriend. Out of the blue, he asked if he could have the placenta. I had never heard anyone ask for that before. Apparently the hospital would give it out, but only with the mother's permission.

I was very curious and, of course asked him why on earth he would want to take "that thing" home? After some pushing, he finally told me a bizarre story.

He said he belonged to a "group" (translation, "commune") and to make everybody feel that they were sharing, they would take the placenta and put it through a blender and would add various spices and other things along with a generous amount of "Crabeen rum." I said, "You mean, Caribbean rum?"

He nodded, "Yeah, Crabeen rum."

I was horrified and asked, "Then, you drink it?"

"Yeah, it binds us all together."

It turned out that he belonged to a group that consisted of about twenty people who all lived together in what I gathered were appalling conditions. Most were on some sort of welfare, and several members had bad drug problems. I asked him if he was sure that he was the father, and he said that he was "pirty sure."

Years later, when I told Harry this story he said that they were just "ahead of their time." He could envision a time when every newborn infant would have cord blood drawn and preserved indefinitely, as these valuable cells could come in handy for a whole list of diseases in the future. He then added that putting these valuable cells through a blender was no way to preserve them; and of course if the cells were taken orally, the stomach acids wouldn't be good for them either.

These hippies, declared Harry, were certainly on to something. They just hadn't gotten the drill right! However, he suggested that all the fibrous material in the placenta might be good roughage, and might help to relieve some of the constipation in the group's heroin addicts. Harry had answers for everything.

Animals often eat their placentas. Cats usually clean up well after giving birth, and herbivores also may eat their placentas. As a kid, I watched in awe as a cow ate her own placenta. I am told it is a sort of camouflage to prevent would-be predators from knowing that there has been a recent delivery. Rabbits do it regularly.

MAKING BABIES — PART I

On another occasion, when I was not on call for any deliveries and was covering the ward — my friend Henry was doing the deliveries — a student nurse grabbed me by the wrist and started leading me down the hall at almost a jog. She was really excited, but wouldn't say anything. I expected her to say that the patient in room so and so was bleeding badly, or some patient had no blood pressure, or perhaps that someone was very septic. If she had said something I could have prepared myself mentally for what I was about to see.

When I stood in the doorframe of the patient's room there was a "semi-naked hairy beast" lying on top of the patient, "doing his thing." He was indeed semi-naked as he had pulled his pants and underwear down to just below his knees, but he still had his shirt on and his shoes and socks. I was dumbfounded. Remember, I had been brought up in nice, god-fearing, Presbyterian family. We weren't supposed to do that sort of thing. The stork brought us into this world, right?

I mustered up my loudest "parade square" naval language and barked at this fellow, who was seriously "on the job," to "Get up! Pull up your pants! And get out!" I pointed with a stern and dramatic gesture towards the door. The poor guy stumbled to his feet, and while re-arranging himself and "hoicking" up his trousers, hobbled out the door and off down the hall, with me berating him like a parade square Sergeant Major. I followed this "gentle-man" all the way down the hall to the elevators, berating him continuously, and didn't let up until he was safely on the elevator.

When I went back to the patient's room the student was there, along with the assistant head nurse. The patient thanked me profusely. I had delivered her the previous afternoon, and it was now mid-morning the following day. Sexual intercourse so soon after childbirth can cause infection. And certainly the wife/partner was by no means a "willing party." In fact, it was difficult to tell whether she was more embarrassed than angry and frightened. In those days spousal abuse was not considered a hospital problem, and the family doctor may or may not have been informed, if indeed the patient even had a family doctor. Fortunately, in more modern times, in cases like this, social services would probably be involved. Hopefully in the course of time, this would result in at least some of the family problems being straightened out. Today, of course, she'd be home the very next day. Maybe her harridan mother would be there to handle the beast.

Later that afternoon, the head nurse, a great salt-of-earth character, and a battleaxe typical of her kind, said she had heard all about the morning's "comings and goings." She paused, looked up at me, and with a perfectly straight face, asked, "Do you take off your shoes when you have sex with your wife?" What had apparently really riled up the nurses was that, not only had our "visitor" not taken off his shoes, but also these shoes were very dirty. The staff, therefore, had to change not only the sheets, but the blanket and the bedspread as well.

I thought for a few seconds and replied, "No. Actually I have a fetish about leaving my shoes on. But at least I have, some class."

"Really," she said, "and how is that?"

"Because I *always* wipe my shoes on the bathmat before I get into bed."

MAKING BABIES — PART 2

While I was a senior resident at the Toronto General Hospital my wife and I thought it was time to start a family. We had been married for just over four years and I was approaching 30 years old, and our first pregnancy had ended in a spontaneous miscarriage. The problem was that getting pregnant might not be as easy as "falling off a log." Up until a year before we had been faithfully using birth control and now we were getting anxious.

So, we had to consider things like the "right time of the month," "temperature," "being relaxed," etc. My wife had purposely stopped teaching, but my job as a "slave to the medical system," was perhaps not conducive. On one particular day, while I was on call and staying in the very Spartan interns' residence, my wife decided that it "was the time" again. She dutifully came down to the residence early one evening.

I informed the hospital telephone operator that I would be "sleeping" for a short time in the residence if they wanted to get me. We dutifully did our business, almost in a clinical fashion. Unfortunately, one of the female staff doctors, Dr. B H, had been looking for me, and thought she could easily find me either on the ward or in the Emerg. When she didn't find me she was a little annoyed, and for some reason didn't think of phoning the hospital telephone operator.

When I showed up on the ward, and I was already behind in my hospital chores, I could tell that she was a little miffed. She asked me where I had been and when I told her, she asked what I was doing in my room at this early hour in the evening when there was more work to be done. I was tired — we were always tired in those days, sleep being in short supply — and I felt that, in any case, it was none of her business. For some reason, I just blurted out that I was making love to my wife. (I actually had another word for the same type of activity on the tip of my tongue but we didn't use that word to a staff person, at least not in those days.)

I then went on to explain what the problem was, and that my wife had had a previous miscarriage and we were having trouble getting pregnant again. Her face turned red and I could see that she was obviously embarrassed. (Actually she was a very nice lady and I always got on well with her.)

About three months later, I was walking down the hall and saw Dr. B H and she came right over and said, "Well, were you?" At first, I didn't know what she was talking about, but after a few seconds I answered, "Yes, as a matter of fact we were successful, and we are now three months pregnant!"

She broke into a big smile, walked over gave me a big hug, kissed me on the cheek, made a few flattering comments, and walked off.

JUST PLAIN BABIES

St. Mary's Hospital in New Westminster was really too close to the Royal Columbian to function effectively. When I first arrived in this area in 1968, however, it still had an active obstetrics department. The local GPs often admitted their patients to St. Mary's, but there were often no doctors in the building after eight or nine at night, and it was "hit and miss" over the weekends. Because of our heavy work schedule at the Royal Columbian, and my desire to avoid regular hours at St. Mary's in order not to run into GP's over there (as discussed previously), I was often at St. Mary's late in the evenings or very early in the mornings.

On three separate occasions while I was at St. Mary's during these off hours there was that dreaded call: "Any doctor, case room, stat!" ("Stat" means right away) How I hated that!

The first time this happened it was about eleven o'clock at night. I arrived in the delivery room breathless and definitely terrified. Several nurses were already there. I just said, "You guys know what to do. I'll just stand here and I guess take the blame." Where were those midwives when you needed them?

My suggestion was ignored and I was immediately told, "You have to hurry and get your gloves on! There's no time to scrub up!"

It had been almost ten years since I had been involved in this delivery business. *Homo sapiens*, the naked ape, had been popping out little naked apes for thousands of years without medical help, so why was I panicking now? And besides, I had about sixty deliveries under my belt and wasn't this delivery business something you don't forget, like riding a bicycle? I earnestly hoped it would all come back to me, and quickly!

There bulging in front of me was a very wrinkled and hairy scalp at the vulva, and the mother at this point was pushing like mad. No wonder the nurses had told me there was no time even to wash my hands. I thought this mother's whole bottom was going to rip open.

Then, very fortunately, I noticed a thin scar running at a forty-five degree angle away from this threatening hole with the wrinkled scalp. At this point the mother stopped pushing; and then I remembered what that thin scar was all about. It was the sign of a previous episiotomy.

It started coming back, and I felt that I was a little more in the "driver's seat" again. I did the episiotomy with the scissors that one of the nurses handed to me, a bit like following the dotted line, carefully "snipping" along that thin scar. Then to the great relief of us all, with the next push, the head was born, followed swiftly by the rest of the body.

Although this was considered a "precipitous delivery," because the infant was born so quickly, the little girl seemed just fine. The placenta followed without a problem, and at the nurses' suggestions, I ordered the injections that were fashionable at the time to make the uterus contract down and reduce the risk of postpartum bleeding.

I expected that, as was the custom, the GP would soon arrive and do a better job of sewing up this episiotomy than I could. But I was in for a surprise. The nurses told me that this GP had just left the hospital, and he lived in Cloverdale, about twenty miles away. As there had been no sign of labour, he apparently had left, confident in the belief that she would not deliver until sometime the next day. There were no cell phones or pagers in those days; and anyway, it would be more than an hour before he could be back at the hospital. So I now had to sew up my own episiotomy.

I asked the nurses what suture material was now in fashion, and gradually the cobwebs were clearing from my brain, and the rust from my fingers. While sewing up this wound, I remembered being told years earlier to sew it up snugly, as the patient's husband would appreciate it!

By the time the family doctor was finally contacted at his home, all was well and he decided not to come back until the next morning. Nice guy! He was actually one of the older family doctors, and I must say I didn't blame him.

I was "caught" twice more at St. Mary's Hospital in a similar fashion. The next time was worrisome for me, because the baby was a pretty large boy, and the pregnancy was this lady's first. When the head came out though, I thought the problems were over. Not so. This time there was a struggle with delivering the shoulders. But by pulling up and down vertically I soon had the shoulders out, and the rest quickly followed. I guess this kid was going to be a football player. Fortunately, the family doctor arrived soon afterwards and he had the task of sewing up my new episiotomy.

Obstetrics the easy way.

By the time of my third and last delivery it was beginning to be "old hat." I now even knew some of the names of the nurses on the night shift. I don't know to this day why we were treating patients this way, with a clown like me, the only MD in the building and that only by chance, when a full-service hospital was only a half-mile down the road, with a very active preemie (pre-mature baby) nursery, and an obstetrical anesthetist and a fellowship obstetrician in the hospital, plus resident staff.

Several years later the obstetrical department was closed. Then approximately three years after obstetrics had been shut down, Sister Mary Michael, the CEO equivalent of St. Mary's, asked me why the doctors in our cardiac department at the Royal Columbian only put very old cardiac patients in St. Mary's so-called "coronary care" unit. Apparently the mean age of the cardiac patients we sent to St. Mary's was eighty-four. I explained that we could only put those patients who had a negative "code status" (meaning if they should arrest the staff would not try to resuscitate them) in her unit, as there was little prospect of successfully resuscitating our patients at St Mary's during the night if they should sustain a cardiac arrest.

To correct for this, she hired a specially trained doctor to stay in St. Mary's hospital overnight, but funding soon fell short and this attempt was abandoned. The coronary care unit was eventually closed as well.

When the government of the day finally got up the nerve and decided to close the whole hospital, there was a great hue and cry from various groups, and many articles in the paper opposing this closure. I know, however, that many of my colleagues were relieved, particularly me. I believe this was a good decision. The patients generally would be a lot safer at the Royal Columbian, and the poor taxpayer would be spared at least some expense from duplication of service.

Not surprisingly, those with a vested interest wanted the hospital to stay open. This included the medical and non-medical/ancillary staff, the unions, the local politicians, and community activists. And of course, the Roman Catholic Order, to which the hospital belonged, fought the government tooth and nail. But all these interested parties forgot the most important thing, indeed the reason for the hospital's and their existence — the patient.

The fact is that sick people in the system were far better off being treated in a full-service hospital.

St. Mary's had a long and proud tradition, however, and it was a sad day when it was closed. Perhaps it could have been turned into a higher intensity nursing home, or retained for specialty endeavours such as ear, nose and throat (ENT), ophthalmology or plastic surgery. But this didn't happen. Certainly, the problems confronting St. Mary's were not unique. The same thing occurred at St. Vincent's Hospital in downtown Vancouver, and indeed at many other small hospitals in urban settings across the country.

In rural communities, where there is no alternative, these smaller hospitals serve a very valuable function. Obviously, in a community of a few thousand souls, it is not realistic to expect to have MRIs and full-service heart catheter labs with angioplasty and other special procedures. Much, therefore, may depend on an efficient emergency transport system. If, however, there is a thick fog over a place like Alert Bay, and a medical problem requires emergency high-tech equipment, there may not be a happy resolution. This is a fact of life, a reality for those living in distant, often isolated communities.

Twenty-five years after the obstetrics department at St. Mary's had been closed, I was at a large house party and noticed a particularly attractive young woman. She rapidly came towards me and said she had always wanted to meet me again. I was, of course, flattered and delighted. She then proceeded to give me a huge hug, right in front of my wife.

I didn't have the foggiest idea who she was and thought I must be getting senile. After all, who wouldn't remember such a beautiful young woman? She then told me I had delivered her at St. Mary's Hospital and while I was sewing up her mother's episiotomy, I apparently had told her mother that I was getting a "little rusty" at delivering a young *Homo sapiens* but had had a lot of recent experience delivering calves. I had apparently told her, in fact, that delivering human babies was a whole lot easier than delivering calves.

I had probably been overly tired, "punchy" and a little chatty. Her mother got a lot of "mileage" out of this conversation.

CALVES

When I reflect back, on my earliest "calving days," I remember asking one of my farmer neighbours, "How hard are you allowed to pull on these pulling-chains?"

A pulling-chain is a strong but fairly light chain, heavily chromed so that it can be cleaned, and has a small metal loop at each end that can be fastened into a choke collar. Each end is then slipped over the calf's two ankles and the loop, or "bite," can be pulled on by hand or attached to something that will provide a stronger extraction force.

I had a young heifer (a heifer is a first-time mother that has not yet calved) that was lying on her side in the rain in our barn-yard. The calf's two front legs were sticking out of her vagina, but it was apparent that the mother was completely exhausted. I had attached the two ends of the pulling-chain one to each ankle of the calf. I first tried pulling by hand, but to no effect. So I jumped on my tractor and attached the loop of the chain to the back of the tractor. When the heifer started pushing again I gently let out the clutch. Pretty soon the delivery was over. The calf, although she walked with rather straight front legs for a couple of days, was soon completely well, and the young heifer turned out to be a good mother.

To answer the question, "How hard are you allowed to pull on these things?" my neighbour answered, "When the cow starts to slide on dry pavement you are probably pulling hard enough!" It had been raining, and the heifer didn't even slide on the wet pavement, so I guess I hadn't pulled too hard.

Some of my worst experiences in calving involved trying to "fish out" the second front leg, when only one leg and the calf's nose have appeared at the vulva. For those folks who never saw that TV vet program, *All Creatures Great and Small*, a normal delivery of a calf happens when both front feet of the calf are sticking out with the flat side of the feet facing towards the ground if the mother was standing up. In the case of only one foot sticking out alongside the nose of the calf, the cow may be lying on her side, is often exhausted and refuses to get up. So it's back to lying flat on my chest, then reaching up and trying to wrestle that stupid second leg down and out. By the time it's over I am never sure who is more exhausted — the cow or me!

Haven't cows been popping out calves for at least thousands

Obstetrics the hard way — at the outer limits of my endurance.

of years, too? The problem is probably that we have been breeding cattle to be bigger and faster growing. Which may be all well and good, but it would seem that sometimes we forget about "easy calving" in our breeding program.

On our farm, we started breeding Simmental cattle. They are like really big Herefords (cowboy beef-type cattle), are usually quite docile, put on a lot of meat quickly, are fairly lean, and have lots of milk for their calves. The problem is that some of our calves weighed 120 pounds at birth. When I was a kid, I never knew that calves could be that big. Sometimes it was necessary to carry a newborn calf to the barn — not easy when it is wet and slippery, and often quite limp right after a difficult birth. Sometimes fighting off the mother and carrying a 120-pound "slime ball" to that barn took me to the very limits of my endurance.

So, you see, delivering little "naked apes" can be a whole lot easier than delivering some of these problem calves.

DELIVER YOUR OWN INFANT?

One day one of our cardiac nurses was musing, and said it would be "wonderful" to be a doctor and be able to deliver your own infant.

So, I launched into the story of my delivery of our son David, one of the most horrible experiences of my life.

Even now, when I tell people the story it invariably brings tears to my eyes, and sometimes I even break down. Our unnamed obstetrician was indeed a scoundrel, in my view. But in hindsight forty years later, I think we were all collectively somewhat guilty, because nobody expected this little boy not only to survive, but also to grow up normally.

As it eventually turned out, two parents could not have asked for a better son. My wife Elaine's first delivery was under difficult circumstances, but everything was done very professionally, and after a few hours our little boy Michael progressed well. My wife's second delivery — David — was a total disaster.

At twenty-eight weeks Elaine went into labour, there having been no warning that something was wrong. In downtown Toronto, everybody had an obstetrician to deliver their babies, and not a family doctor. I don't know why this was so, but it was the system. It meant that these obstetricians did a huge number of normal deliveries. And of course there were a lot of obstetricians in this local area. Some of them, therefore, lacked experience in the difficult deliveries that an obstetrician would see in an area where the family doctors did the routine stuff, and the more complicated problems would be referred to the relatively small number of obstetricians.

I phoned our obstetrician at about ten o'clock at night and told him that my wife seemed to be having pretty straightforward labour pains. He, however, said that this was pretty unlikely at twenty-eight weeks, and asked me to inject her with 100 mgs of Demerol. He phoned the drug store, and I dutifully went to the pharmacy and obtained the syringe, needle, and medication, and came home and injected the drug as the obstetrician had suggested.

The labour pains, however, did not settle down. So I drove her to the Toronto General, where she was admitted to the obstetrical department.

While she was in the labour room, a nurse came in with a

syringe of Demerol. I told her that my wife had already received 100 mgs of Demerol before she was admitted. The nurse told me that our obstetrician knew that, but felt a second dose would likely settle her down. The injection was dutifully given, and the pains slowed briefly, but started up again and were frequent and severe.

Soon my wife started pushing. The nurses were about to take her to the delivery room when my wife said the baby was coming. I immediately pulled down the bed covers and saw that our little boy was now half out. With the next push he was fully delivered.

It was a big shock for me. He was very small, almost tiny, weighing two pounds, eight ounces. He was dark red, wrinkled, and did not really look human. We were all quite surprised when he gave out a feeble cry. With the amount of Demerol he had on board it was surprising that he could even cry at all. I clamped and cut the cord and he was whisked away to the preemie nursery.

My wife was quite drowsy with the two shots of Demerol, but seemed otherwise quite well. The placenta was soon delivered and there was no particular post-partum bleeding. At this point, I didn't think our little boy had a hope in Hell of surviving. Back in 1967 very few infants in this weight class made it.

After my wife had settled down, I phoned the preemie nursery and was told that he still had an apex beat. (This is the pulsation that can be felt on the left side of the chest. It is the heart pumping against the side of the chest wall, and is particularly easy to feel in newborns, and especially so in premature infants, and is often easily visible). Because he was now deeply cyanosed (blue in colour suggesting his oxygenation was very poor), they put him on a mask-type positive pressure breather.

Our obstetrician never did show up, although the nurses had phoned him several times, and no MD had yet seen the baby in the preemie nursery. Everybody expected him to die shortly. But with the breather, he had apparently pinked up a bit. Because he was still alive the next morning, about six hours later, he was then transferred across the street to the Sick Children's Hospital. Amazingly, an intensive care unit for preemies (ICU) had just been set up, one of the first in the world, especially designed to care for premature infants.

Suddenly our baby was getting all the high-tech equipment and investigations that were available at the time. He was intubated, his arterial blood was drawn for blood gases and acid base, and he was put on a cardiac monitor, which was very revolutionary at the time. (I think they dragged their feet a bit at the Toronto General because they weren't yet fully aware of this fantastic help that was so close by.)

The head of this unit, a very dedicated man, Dr. Paul Swyer, met with me several times. He told me that if our little guy should survive, statistically he had only about a 5 percent chance of being neurologically normal. It was a pretty depressing situation all around; and just to top it off, our son Michael, who had been at home, and was now about ten months old, had to be admitted with an acute asthma attack. My poor wife was still at the General, and our two little boys were both in the "Sick Kids" (the Toronto Hospital for Sick Children).

Elaine was soon home from the hospital, and Michael recovered rapidly. However, David was in the intensive care unit for the next two months, and spent his third month in the preemie nursery back at the Toronto General. He had one crisis after another. A portion of his lungs collapsed because they were so immature; and when he got over this, he developed some form of bacterial infection causing severe diarrhea. They put him on a new antibiotic called Kanamycin, which could cause deafness, but they felt they had no choice. He also developed periods of apnea (the patient for some reason just stops breathing and has to be stimulated to get him to start breathing again).

I was working at the General right across the street from the Sick Kids and would visit this intensive care unit twice a day. I had the feeling if the nursing staff saw me every day they would somehow give our little boy extra care.

I also went because of curiosity, but probably of more importance, because of a feeling of guilt that I could not explain. It was very profound, even though rationally I did not know why I should blame myself. To make matters worse, I was even half hoping he would die if he were going to have a significant neurology problem. Because I saw him every day, he didn't seem to change much, and he still didn't look completely human, more perhaps like a wrinkled red monkey. He certainly got excellent care, however, and the staff was very careful not to give him too much oxygen, for that could result in blindness. (A very high oxygen level in premature infants could lead to fibrosis of the retina, retrolental fibroplasia.)

He weighed 2,300 grams (about five pounds) when we finally got him home, and had been less than 900 grams (about two pounds) at his low point. Our problems were, however, not over. He had a terrible feeding problem, and would often vomit everything my wife tried to feed him. When he cried, he sounded as though he were crying from the bottom of a deep tin can, producing that characteristic raucous cry that I had associated with children with cerebral palsy.

Finally, he seemed to enjoy his bottle, but later on whenever we presented him with a spoon of Pablum he would immediately start crying, and would refuse to eat this cereal. I noticed that when we got the spoon close to his face he would start crying. At least he was consistent, and his behaviour established that he could see and apparently could remember. We got the bright idea of feeding him his Pablum out of a bottle with the nipple cut off part way down to make a large opening. He seemed quite happy to eat his Pablum this way. Why he didn't like the metal spoon we will likely never know.

Fortunately his feeding problems settled down completely. After another month, he would accept a spoon without any fuss. He was very active in movement, able to pull himself up, and indeed started to walk at a corrected age of ten months (subtracting three months from his real age). He was, in fact, now passing his milestones normally.

As time and the years progressed, we noticed he had a pretty good vocabulary, although he had a speech impediment. Elaine got a speech therapist for him and this problem was soon corrected. In the first two years of his life he seemed a little clumsy, perhaps just taking after his father, but that too gradually disappeared. We then slowly became aware that he had a huge learning ability. Indeed, just by sitting, listening, and watching my wife reading bedtime stories to his older brother, he learned how to read.

At the beginning of grade three, when the whole class had some sort of a reading test, it was discovered that David had a grade-six point-six score, meaning that he was reading at a grade six level. David's coordination became absolutely normal and he eventually became a very proficient snow boarder and mountain biker. He went through law school on a scholarship. Talk about having horseshoes up your ass!

My wife has kept in touch with the head nurse of the preemie nursery at the Toronto General, Mrs. Abel, who was there during the traumatic beginning of David's life, and in 2007 we visited her at her home. She is healthy, in her eighties, and was gardening when we arrived. It was only through the fabulous care of people like Mrs. Abel, and cutting-edge technology at the Sick Kids, that our son survived unscathed from his early ordeal.

"Delivering your own son would be wonderful," the cardiac nurse had said. Maybe, on the other hand, the experience is not all it is cracked up to be.

And obstetrics is not, in fact, all that easy either.

CHAPTER 12

Crabs —
Little, Big & Crabby

LITTLE CRABS

I knew nothing about lice until my father got me a three-month summer job in Northern Quebec. I really needed this job to buck up my language marks, at least in French, if I hoped to go to the university of my choice.

I arrived at the lumber camp in Northern Quebec in the summer of 1954. I was unilingual, and so were all the men with whom I was supposed to work. Too bad we spoke different languages! However, you couldn't find a nicer bunch of guys. Even though initially I had a lot trouble communicating even the simplest of things, we got on famously.

In those days a large proportion of the older lumberjacks *(bucherons)* in this area were functionally illiterate. Also, it appeared that most of the men over thirty literally lived in their same underwear all summer, and didn't put on clean ones until they went home at the end of the summer during changeover before the winter cutting season.

One Sunday (no one was allowed to work on a Sunday back then) one of my new friends was sitting on his bunk, scraping along the seams of his summer long woollen underwear with a penknife. When I asked him what he was doing, he said, "Toma, j'ote les nids." Sounds like, "Tom, I out the nits," doesn't it?

When I watched, now completely fascinated, he showed me how he did it, as he still had a lot of seams to go. Piled up on the edge of the blade of his knife was a slimy grey-white mass of nits. (Nits are the eggs of the new population of his body lice ready to hatch out.) Periodically, he would wipe the knife blade off on the knee of his trousers.

After that, needless to say, every Sunday, rain or shine —

"Toma, j'ote les nids!" (Tom, I'm outing the nits!)

mostly rain, in fact — I would jump into the lake nearby, soap myself completely and wash my clothes as best I could. These body lice were quite endemic in that part of the country, and a close cousin to pubic lice or "crabs." Body lice prefer to lay their eggs, or nits, on clothing, I guess due to the relative lack of suitable body hair on *Homo sapiens*.

Pubic lice, on the other hand, prefer to lay their eggs at the base of pubic hair. I had my first exposure to pubic lice when I joined the University Navy in 1955. Pubic lice are usually contracted by sexual contact, and were a "favourite" malady of Canadian sailors shipping into foreign ports.

During my first summer in the Canadian Navy in 1956 we "sailed" to London on a frigate called the Fort Erie. This ship was a World War II relic and was crammed with 150 men.

I guess it was probably inevitable that a few sailors developed crabs that would be diagnosed during "sick parade." (Any of the crew wishing to have non-urgent medical attention would muster outside the sick bay at an appointed time. On a small ship it would be a paramedic rather than a nurse or doctor that dealt with sick parade.) The afflicted personnel would have all their pubic hair carefully shaved off and would be dusted with some sort of white powder. I was disappointed that they had shaved these sailors and powdered them before I got a chance to see what these crabs looked like.

I have no idea why pubic lice are called "crabs." Most of my friends assumed that the "crabs" were just a smaller edition of the little crabs seen on the seashore scrambling over the rocks. These sea crabs are very fast and, until one gets the hang of it, a bit difficult to catch. When these little beasts are caught, watch out, because they can give a sharp pinch. Most of the sailors and cadets

Dog fleas were a different species altogether. My brother and I used to search for them on our dog, and were always amazed at how far these fleas could jump. Any flea worth its salt could do a jump of six inches. They were also hard to kill because they had a hard outer shell; the only way to kill them was to squash them with a fingernail on top of a hard surface. Fleas, originally from rats, were responsible for the infamous "black death" of the middle ages.

who didn't actually catch a dose of the crabs actually did think these creatures were similar to sea crabs, only much smaller. I suspect that I was one of the few who knew that these pests were like minute soft-shelled snails or slugs. They weren't crabs at all and they certainly couldn't jump; they were just cousins of body lice.

Soon after sick parade, one of the medical officers sectioned off one of the toilets to be used exclusively by those members of the ship's company who had these crabs. The particular toilet was suitably labelled "crab toilet," and the rest of us avoided it completely, not even wanting to sit in the john next to the designated toilet. An enterprising member of our group of cadets stencilled, in very official script, under the crab toilet sign, "Don't sit on the toilet seat because crabs can jump 6 feet high." This joker then claimed that early the next morning when he went into the bathroom, he actually saw a sailor standing on the toilet seat trying to do his business while holding onto a pipe overhead.

A few years after I went into practice at the Royal Columbian, the GP covering the Emerg asked me to see a young pharmaceutical rep, Mr. C, age 42. I had seen him occasionally around the hospital, flogging his particular brand of drugs.

Drug reps had a difficult job; they had to be salespeople in the truest sense of the word, because their clientele was somewhat skeptical by nature, their market was very competitive, and often there was very little difference between the various choices of similar drugs. The price, of course, varied tremendously, but the doctors, unfortunately for the taxpayer, often didn't concern themselves about this because the government paid for medications for hospitalized patients. A "new" drug, with a slightly different formula from a previous one, was always more expensive, and usually the increased benefit was, at best, questionable.

The job had a lot of drawbacks. Sometimes they would have to wait for hours in the waiting room of a busy doctor's office for perhaps only two minutes of conversation. Often, the doctor would be called away at the last minute and all that waiting had been for nothing. They would then have to come back another day, perhaps to be frustrated all over again. Another thing that was hard on these salespeople was that they had to travel a lot, often to travel to small northern communities, staying in very small hotels, and being alone much of the time after the doctors' offices were closed.

In general, the drug reps would do almost anything to get an audience with those doctors who would be likely to prescribe their company's particular antibiotic, or for that matter, any specific drug that their company made. Sometimes, there would be what I would frankly call bribery going on. The drug rep would take the doctor out for lunch or provide tickets to a professional sports game, or even in some cases other "perks" such as fully paid trips, in order to discuss his particular drug, "the flavour of the month." However, as new drugs come along, they are always written up in peer-reviewed medical journals and this information tends to remove a lot of bias. But the drug manufacturers know that the busy doctor often just doesn't have time to keep up with the latest information in the monthly newsletter, "Medical Letter," or the equivalent journal, and hence send out their battalions of reps. This lobbying must pay off, because during my time there was one detail rep for every two doctors in active practice. As we know, these big companies don't do anything without thinking of the bottom line.

Our patient, Mr. C, was a nice guy and I don't think his amiability was artificial. He had that necessary open and pleasant personality, basically a prerequisite for his job, but in his case I think it was completely natural. One day when I met him in the hospital cafeteria, he joked that the specialists in the Fairmont Medical Building in Vancouver were bad for his business because they only ordered ASA and cold cream. Apparently, he had found the same thing in the Royal Columbian Hospital community. If it weren't for the general practitioners, the ones ordering the newer, more expensive drugs, he would be out of business.

It was a very short time later that he came into our Emerg as a patient. Unfortunately, he had developed fairly severe chest pain when staying in some hotel in one of the smaller northern communities. He didn't want to be admitted to the local infirmary and had decided to tough it out overnight; in the morning, fortunately, he felt somewhat better. He then chose to drive himself down to the Royal Columbian Hospital. His estranged wife and children lived in our local area.

I was the cardiologist on call, and when he had an ECG done it was apparent that he had likely suffered a small heart attack the night before. He was already over the worst of it and in all probability would do well. His physical examination suggested that he was, otherwise, in pretty good shape. He was fairly slim, had normal blood pressure, and had given up smoking about two years previously. The only thing that was remarkable was the fact that he had a big rash over his pubic area, obviously aggravated by heavy scratching. It looked fairly raw, and when I inspected it closely, I could see that he had nits attached to the base of his pubic hairs. Although I looked carefully, I didn't see any of the creepy crawlies. He had probably scratched them flat, or they had temporarily crawled away.

I wrote the usual orders on the order sheet, including the sedation, etc. that was customary back then, and he was dutifully monitored with an ECG monitor and transferred to our coronary unit. He, unfortunately, didn't have a GP and so I took it upon myself to treat his crabs. We didn't have the convenience to call the pharmacist in those days, so I wrote up what I had remembered from my ancient reading in our various insufficient courses in parasitology. I wrote him up for 5 percent DDT powder twice daily. It was the usual busy day on call for Emerg, and I was the only available cardiologist. I was soon busy with other patients, and Mr. C was, temporarily at least, out of mind.

A few hours later at lunch, I sat down with the usual bunch of nurses and the typical conversations ensued. One older nurse, whom I always enjoyed because she had a great sense of humour, was already sitting at this table. She was the head nurse on the cardiac ward and, unfortunately, near to retirement, and had literally seen it all. She also knew how to keep the new young specialists like me in line, and in many cases, keep us out of trouble.

In her usual loud, authoritarian voice, but always with a bit of a twinkle in her eye, she said, "So we are big game hunting today are we, Dr. Godwin?" I was confused and didn't know initially what she was referring to. Then she announced that, "You only have to use that DDT stuff once, unless there are any nits left," not twice daily as I had written on the order sheet. I dutifully went back to the ward and rewrote my order.

Mr. C made a completely uneventful recovery, and I saw him once a year for many years afterwards for his routine treadmill test. But I'll always remember him, not so much for his heart attack, but for the thought of his crabs, which always makes me smile inside.

BIG CRABS

One day at lunch, I was sitting with Harry and my beloved (and now late) family doctor, Dr. Fred Harder. Although this story is secondhand, as mentioned in the Foreword, Fred assured me it is absolutely true. He had been our family doctor for several years by this time, and had looked after my wife during her last two pregnancies, so of course I trusted him completely. The reader might think it strange that doctors would even contemplate discussing some of the things that we talk about while eating our lunch. However, if we can eat our lunch in the anatomy lab as medical students, then anything is possible for discussion later in life, even while eating lunch.

When Fred first went into practice as a GP in 1955, he initially worked part time for the coroner's service, until his practice got established. Occasionally, he would get called from New Westminster to downtown Vancouver to pronounce someone dead who had suffered some mishap. He would dutifully get in his car, drive downtown, examine the body, fill out the appropriate papers, and drive home again.

On one particular occasion, he was called to pronounce a "floater" whose body had been picked up floating in English Bay. As was the custom, the body was in the back of the coroner's van. When Fred crawled in and had a look at the body, he noticed that something was moving under the dead man's windbreaker, and with difficulty, he managed to get the now corroded zipper undone. To his horror, he found two good-sized Dungeness crabs living under this guy's jacket and saw that they had eaten a large hole into the man's chest cavity. In absolute disgust, Fred threw the two crabs over to the side of the van and, again with difficulty, zipped up the man's jacket again. He imprisoned the two crabs by laying a spare stretcher on top of them.

He then went into the coroner's office, filled out the appropriate forms, and informed the somewhat unfriendly man sitting at the desk that crabs had been eating the man's body. The unfriendly man barely looked up and said he would tell the morgue attendant when he next came out from the cooler.

A few days later, when Fred was back in the coroner's office on another errand, he asked the same unfriendly guy at the desk what had happened to the crabs. The man looked up. For the first time that Fred could remember he had a big smile on his face and said, "Oh, the morgue attendant took them home and ate them!"

I was at loss for words at this horrible story, but Harry, it seems, was never at loss for words and quickly said that it was proper "recycling." When I started to protest, Harry said, "If you found asparagus growing in a cemetery, you would eat it wouldn't you? So, what the hell is the difference?"

I know what garbage hounds those crabs are, and every time I eat Dungeness crabs now I wonder where they've been in the recent past.

CRABBY DOCTORS

When my friends in Toronto heard that I was planning to practice cardiology in British Columbia, they always made some comment about the "wild west." It was all in fun, of course, but when I arrived in 1968, I heard that the year before two doctors had got into a fistfight on the front steps of the old part of the hospital. They had to be separated by the other doctors, who were standing around before a meeting, to make sure that nobody got hurt. I got to know one of the combatants, and he was certainly a very amiable fellow and very concerned about his patients, but I could see that he might, under the right circumstances, have a short fuse.

"Black Balls"

The year after I arrived, I had met a friendly, middle-aged radiologist who wanted to take a scuba-diving course. He knew of my interest in this activity, and wanted to have a physical examination to be sure it would be safe for him to proceed. In those days, doctors never charged a colleague if the consultation wasn't covered by the medical plans. Because this was a non-insured item, and this man was a particularly nice guy, I was very happy to help. I didn't find any problems and he passed his test. I also did a treadmill test on him because it is a good screening test to rule out hidden heart disease. In fact, his exercise capacity was above average for a North American man in his age group.

He started his course and, as far as I knew, there were no problems. Then he arrived in my office late one afternoon really upset and wanted me to examine him as soon as possible. I initially was afraid that he had run into a scuba-diving problem. He stripped down immediately when I had him in the examining room and, to my horror, I saw that he had a huge swelling on the left side of his scrotum, and some of this swelling had tracked down the inner side of his thigh.

Apparently, he'd had some sort of argument with the chief of his department. He then claimed that his chief had brought his knee up abruptly into his groin area without any warning. The damage was acute and obvious, and was about six hours old by this time. I was smart enough to know that I would have to take a lot of detailed notes and only wished that I had a camera to document this damage further. Fortunately, there was no increase in pressure against his testicle that would require evacuation of the hematoma (big bruise). Sometimes, these injuries cause so much pressure on the poor testicle that the testicle dies and shrivels up over a period of a month or so.

He then told me that his boss had been admitted to St Mary's hospital, because he had struck his boss back with his fist, knocking him to the floor and apparently causing a depressed fracture on his opponent's face. It had broken the zygoma bone, which is just under the eye and forms part of the orbit, and unless it is elevated again, the patient's eyeball will look downwards. Without corrective surgery it is quite a disfiguring injury, and the patient will suffer double vision. It's a pretty common fracture, and usually a plastic surgeon makes these repairs. It's quite an ingenious repair. The surgeon lifts the upper lip, makes an incision under the lip, and then slips his instruments up under the flesh over the side of the cheekbone and pries up the depressed bone under the eyeball. In this way, there is no surgical scar on the face. Fortunately, in this case the chief had a good cosmetic result and no visual problems.

I asked my patient to come back each day for several consecutive days so that I could document the damage further, and I understood that his wife took photographs in case all this came to court. It's usually about three to four days later that the injury looks the worst, when it comes out in all the Technicolor of the bruising process.

My patient asked me what I would have done if his boss had kneed me in the crotch. I said that, if I could have got up after this injury, I would have literally killed him, not just give him a little fracture of his zygoma.

Of course, the word was out in the hospital and we all took sides. My patient was the favourite by far. Unfortunately, because the chief had contacted the hospital administrator, and didn't mention the fact that he had initiated the physical side of the argument, the administrator in turn contacted the police department. My patient was served with an injunction prohibiting him from coming into the hospital.

I had a nice chat with our administrator, Dr. Richard Foulkes ("Dickie," described in chapter two). I outlined the extent of my patient's injuries. I had always liked Dickie and I knew that he would not take sides once he knew the other side of this story. The word got back to the chief residing in St. Mary's hospital, and the original charges against my patient were dropped.

I was a little disappointed that my patient wasn't prepared to fight this problem in court. He ultimately left our community and moved to the interior of BC and practiced his specialty in a smaller hospital. He was a very good person and a very competent radiologist, and I guess our loss was some other community's gain. Later, the chief got himself into some administration difficulties and was, in turn, forced to resign.

Doctors, of course, are just like everybody else. We have our passions and our bad tempers, but particularly in the old days, we were perhaps held to a slightly higher standard. We were supposed to wear a shirt and tie, and usually a suit. The car we drove to work, or drove when we used to actually make house calls, was a conservative model and usually dark in colour. When I first arrived at the Royal Columbian in 1968, I was quite surprised to see a family doctor wearing a turtleneck sweater with a fake gold chain hanging around his neck, with some big medallion suspended below. Working in the downtown Toronto hospitals, I was not used to seeing such things. I must say I felt more comfortable when I saw that we could be more casual. I think, in some ways, less formality may even put the patient more at ease.

We had been lectured at medical school never to sit on a patient's bed. We were supposed to stand, or find a chair before we sat down. Often, in the real world, however, there is no chair, or even space for a chair. Usually, by the end of the day, my feet were just killing me. I didn't have the luxury of the eight-hour day that those ivory tower professors had.

I often found that the patient would just move over to make

a space for me to sit down. I think it was also a little friendlier. I liked drawing pictures for the patient, particularly when I would be trying to explain the nature of his heart disease. A picture is literally "worth a thousand words," and sitting on the side of a patient's bed and drawing a picture of where his vein bypasses have been implanted is, I think, reassuring to the patient.

I have often seen a patient who brings his picture drawn by the surgeon to my office to ask some further questions. In our old heart catheterization lab, the machine could make still frames at the same time as it took a 35mm movie, and we would often give these pictures to the patient for souvenirs. If we could set up the video so the patient would be able to watch his own heart, we would do so, unless the patient specifically asked us not to. The more knowledge a patient has about his heart, the better, and the more compliant he is likely to be. One patient told me his pictures provided "ammunition" for him when his aunt was describing her long-past gall bladder surgery for the tenth time. He popped out his pictures and showed her the blocks in his coronary arteries and then his subsequent bypasses. He felt that he had "trumped" her on that occasion!

A lot of the tubes that we use to inject dye into the patient's heart or measure the pressures were "for one use only" and we often gave them to the patient for a souvenir after the test was finished.

These cold-hearted professors always told us never to show emotion, never show any affection and, never, never, put an arm around a patient. What are you supposed to do when that's really what the patient needs at the time? It's a bit of a delicate area, and there have been some high-profile cases that would suggest that one should always be "formal." That, however, was never my style, and I would not have been able to practice humanely if I hadn't been able to show complete empathy.

CHAPTER 13

Do doctors cry?

O f course doctors cry — and sometimes, perhaps — too often and too long. Some specialties are extremely brutal in this regard, and perhaps one of the worst is pediatric oncology (basically the care and study of children with cancer).

When I took my training, because of the scheduling system I ended up doing twelve months on oncology, and some of it involved little children. I still have no idea how the doctors in this specialty can cope with the agony of seeing so many young people dying year after year and, in many cases, dying horrible deaths.

The resident staff used to call the leukemias and Non-Hodgkin's lymphomas the "liquid tumours" because they were widespread and had no known solid mass from which the tumour had originally spread. In adults, myeloma and often melanoma, which may have started from a seemingly insignificant mole, we also sometimes classified as liquid tumours.

In the early 1960s there was no talk of radical chemotherapies, which virtually wipe out many of the blood-forming cells and hence, hopefully, all of the "bad cells," followed by marrow transplant or, more recently, cord blood transplant. Cord blood is obtained from the umbilical cord immediately after birth, analyzed, and usually discarded. However, nowadays the cord blood may be frozen and kept indefinitely, for use at some future date if it becomes necessary. These modern patients at least have a fair chance of a complete cure.

However, when I worked on oncology during my training, none of these options had yet been discovered. Our patients with these liquid tumours all died, and most were young and completely innocent. I suspected, at this point, that if there was

Cord blood contains very immature or stem cells that can be used to replace malignant cells that, it is hoped, have been completely wiped out with massive chemotherapy plus or minus radiation. The immature stem cells have the capacity to develop into various types of cells found in the marrow. The cord blood could be used on the original infant in the future, should that person develop one of these diseases later on, particularly the leukemias. A big controversy exists now where a "saviour" fetus is selected after in vitro fertilization. The multiple embryos produced by in vitro fertilization are assessed to see which one is the best match for an older sibling who has leukemia and that embryo is implanted in the mother's uterus and the other embryos are discarded.

a "force" in the sky, he had lost interest, didn't care, or was a psychopath. So much for "He sees the little sparrow fall" that we had all sung so lustily as little kids.

There is no end to horrible diseases that claim young innocent lives but, fortunately, they are relatively infrequent and the majority of families don't have to go through this anguish. However, when one works in a hospital and just about every other patient on some of these specialized services is seriously ill, sometimes it becomes difficult to keep perspective and realize that not every kid has an aggressive lymphoma, blast cell leukemia, or a brain tumour.

And it's not just the cancers that are so sad, but also major organ failures, particularly before the hope of transplant. And accidents, so many accidents, particularly with young people, often make the lives of emergency personnel sad day after day.

In my own specialty of cardiology, there was so much that we could do (particularly as the years progressed) to help the patient that the very sad cases were "diluted" by the cases that had a very gratifying outcome. As well, the vast majority of our patients were older, in most cases having lived a full life. Moreover, although it might seem a shocking thing to say, a lot of our cases were perhaps partly "self-inflicted," the result of a combination of smoking, poor diet, and no exercise. Those of us in this field had to rationalize in this way to lessen the emotional drain when we could no longer help the patient.

My colleagues in some of these other specialties just didn't have these benefits and would see, day after day, a catalogue of disasters. I think it's pretty hard to maintain a normal outlook on life in these really difficult specialties, and these doctors have to have the "right stuff" to survive emotionally. I quickly found out that I certainly didn't have the right stuff to work on an oncology service.

LESSONS IN ONCOLOGY

In 1963–64, I had the honour to work for Dr. Arthur Squires. He was a very kindly and very knowledgeable guy, and always went out of his way to help his resident staff. He spent a great deal of time with us looking down the microscope at blood smears and bone marrows. We soon got to recognize the difference between a marrow from someone with a B12 vitamin deficiency and someone with acute myelogenous leukemia.

In the case of the leukemic patient, once the diagnosis had been made, the real problems began. The treatment in those days was fairly standard — horrible! However, how do you break the news to the patient and the family?

Dr. Squires saw patients from all over the province of Ontario, and it usually fell on him to confirm the diagnosis and to manage the patient. The patient frequently came with a bunch of slides sent from an outlying hospital and, understandably, the referring doctor had not told the patient the bad news, as the diagnosis had not yet been adequately confirmed. We sometimes saw the slides, if available, and most of the time the notes of the referring doctors, before we saw the patient. Often, however, we had to take our own blood smears and bone marrow specimens, as they hadn't been done or were considered inadequate or out of date.

When all the information had been gathered, Dr. Squires would arrange an interview with the patient and the family, basically to discuss the diagnosis and the proposed course of treatment. This usually occurred in the afternoon in Dr Squires' office if the patient had not yet been hospitalized, or on the ward if the patient had already been admitted. The resident staff was usually intimately involved with these patients as we had to take a complete history, gather all the pertinent lab material and X-rays, and often take multiple blood specimens and assist in getting the bone marrow specimens. Sometimes we also assisted in lymph node and lump biopsies.

By this time, we usually knew the patients quite well and, in the majority of cases that had to be hospitalized, we also got to know the family. The history alone was usually very suspicious in the serious cases, and frequently before we even looked down the microscope, we pretty well knew what we were going to find. However, it was those afternoon interviews that "separated the men from the boys" and I was definitely a "boy." Sometimes as I would hear the words that Dr. Squires said, I just sat there feeling as if I were in some sort of a fog. I think that often the patient and family heard very little after the dreaded word leukemia was mentioned. Occasionally the patients would be surprisingly matter of fact, but that was unusual. I think that with the majority of these patients the cruel words just had not had time to sink in, or some of them had already figured out their diagnosis. While these interviews were going on, as a defence mechanism I would try to think of something absolutely ludicrous to try to distance my self emotionally from what was going on in that consulting room. (Remember that in the early 1960s there was no hope for these patients, and most were dead within a year).

I think if you can tell a nice young couple that their four-year-old son or daughter has blast cell leukemia and then just go home and have a full supper, you've obviously developed a good defence mechanism. Surprisingly, many doctors have developed such a mechanism. However, I think that for some doctors these cases take a terrible toll in the long term.

After the big interview, the patient, if not already admitted, was soon in hospital and treatment was started immediately. During the first few days the patient and the family always had numerous questions, so many of which had no answers or only incomplete ones. Dr. Squires tried to answer these questions, but he wasn't always available. Fortunately, he had tremendous confidence in the resident staff, and always allowed us to proceed as best we could. We usually reiterated what Dr. Squires had said, and discussed the side effects of the various drugs that we were administering. We weren't very good at being completely honest, however, and were evasive when asked such questions as "What happens if this drug stops working?" or "Will I be home for my birthday party?"

I don't think that even with the adult patients we really were as honest as we might have been when asked a direct question about the ultimate prognosis. You always have to leave the patient hope, but it's also hard to justify deception.

Despite what the medical students are taught by their professors, some of whom haven't taken care of the whole patient for years, it is probably impossible not to become friends with and emotionally attached to these patients. We see them every day, sometimes for weeks on end, and they discuss their intimate problems with us. We may end up sitting on their beds, holding their hands. We may draw them sketches of their anatomy, talk to them just before they go under some really tough procedure, and talk to them again when they first wake up. If these patients don't become our friends, it would be contrary to human nature. Consequently, it is really tough when your friend runs into serious trouble, even when you know it's inevitable.

In those days, the Toronto Wellesley Hospital was intimately involved with the Princess Margaret Hospital, which was the cancer hospital for Ontario, and we shared the same building. Consequently we saw far more cancer patients than we would have seen in a similar sized general teaching hospital.

A YOUNG WOMAN FROM RICHMOND HILL

One day while I was working for Dr. Squires, I was sitting with him in his little office and he showed me some slides of a bone marrow with the characteristic findings of acute myelogenous leukemia. The slides, which had been sent down from a hospital in Richmond Hill, were of good quality, and there was no doubt about the diagnosis. Shortly afterwards, Dr. Squires ushered a mother and her twenty-two-year-old daughter into the room. The daughter, of course, was the owner of these bone marrow slides. This young patient had just finished teachers college and had begun teaching at the local public school before being taken ill. She didn't look really ill at this point, however, although she was a little pale and she had a few blisters on her lips.

Both the patient and her mother were very bright, and there was a strong family resemblance. They obviously had a good relationship. Both were also very attractive, even beautiful. The daughter had very white skin, probably exaggerated by her anemia and very black hair. Maybe she was of "black Irish" descent. In any case, she was very striking and had a very appealing personality. I could identify with her immediately; my wife was also a recent graduate of the same teachers college and was only one year older than our patient.

Dr. Squires used all the tact and kindness that any man could muster, but he had to mention that dreaded leukemia word. I put myself into my daze, but I could still hear his words, as if they were in a dream. For some reason, I almost found it easier to give very bad news myself than to hear it second hand. Perhaps our brain is mercifully distracted when we have to think of what we are going to say, but not when we hear it spoken by someone else. As a third party, I think we sense how other people's words hit home more sharply than when we are speaking ourselves.

I was asked to find a bed for the patient; I was very glad to be asked to do something even slightly useful. It was good to be distracted even with the simple job of having to remember the phone number for the admitting department.

This beautiful creature was admitted, and the poisons were dutifully ordered up from the pharmacy in the Princess Margaret Hospital. In the early 60s no one survived acute myelogenous leukemia. I used to think that perhaps the patients would have been better off just going home rather than undergoing the regimen we had planned for them. True, we made them live longer, but it sometimes seemed to me that we just prolonged the agony. The theory was that they were living longer and someday they might live on indefinitely with the right combination of drugs. That could only be found by trying these various methods, but so often I "could not see the forest for the trees," and used to be really upset at how we really were stretching out the suffering on all sides. Besides torturing the patients, we were also torturing the family, in this case the mother and the patient's entire family and many friends.

She was given 6 MP and a big course of prednisone, standard therapy for this disease. The 6 MP was an anti-metabolite that interfered with the growth machinery of the tumour cells, but also wreaked havoc on normal cells. Over several weeks, the patient started to improve and she was discharged. There were no more leukemia cells in her peripheral blood, and she said her sore throat had gone. She felt well, and was ready to go back to work. Indeed she insisted on going back to teaching her class at school. Dr. Squires and I saw her weekly in his office. She continued to improve, and although I knew intellectually that she was on borrowed time, it was hard to convince myself that she had no chance and would likely be dead within a year. I think her enthusiasm even led to false hope for her family. I think, too, that even we began to believe that this time the outcome was going to be different. I have no doubt, in retrospect, that we all harboured the hope of some miraculous exception to the rule.

Reality came back with a vengeance, and within two months of her discharge she was back in hospital, this time worse than before. We again put her on more 6 MP and a bigger dose of prednisone. Her response this time was muted, and after she had been home for only about ten days, she was back again. She was very anemic, her platelet count had dropped, and she now had a few bruises.

She was then started on "second line" chemo, but the response was short-lived. She had one more, brief, period out of hospital and then she was back again. This time she was covered in large bruises and was severely anemic, and we started giving her blood and fresh platelet transfusions. She was now scarcely recognizable except for her smile and beautiful personality.

She subsequently got various infections and was put on multiple antibiotics. Then she developed some sort of fungus infection and was put on intravenous amphotericin, which the interns used to call "amphoterrible" because of the numerous and very awful side effects. Eventually, she was covered with strange red blotches, her mouth was covered with sores, and she was bleeding from her rectum. A week before her death she asked that her friends not come to see her anymore, because she felt her appearance would be too hard on them. On the weekend of her death, she told me I was spending too many hours at work and looked overly tired. She also told me that she was really worried about the effect her illness was having on her mother, and that she hoped her mother would be able to cope after she was gone. When she died, I was too much of a basket case to go to her funeral.

The amazing thing was that I saw many cases that were somewhat like this. This case has remained in my mind more than others because it was one of my earlier introductions to these leukemias, and because she so reminded me of my own young and beautiful wife. Her death seemed so unnecessary and inexplicable. As a relative of one of my patients once said, "If there is a God, he must be a bloody psychopath."

At the end of my year at the Wellesley Hospital, Dr. Squires said I should consider specializing in hematology or oncology, as he said I seemed to understand the science and had a good way with the patients. It was obviously a very interesting science — if the slides weren't attached to some poor patient and if it could be studied as a purely academic pursuit. However, I clearly wasn't "the right stuff," and I honestly believe that if I'd had to work as an oncologist for the rest of my career, I would have either killed myself or got out of medicine completely.

OTHER REASONS TO CRY

However, I don't want to give the reader the impression that only the oncologists get the emotional problems. When I first started working at the Royal Columbian Hospital in New Westminster in 1968, I was called to all the cardiac arrests. Every summer a number of drownings were inevitably brought in. At that time, my wife and I had four small, very energetic, blond boys, a year apart in age.

When I would arrive in Emerg and see a little blond kid lying on a stretcher surrounded by heavy equipment, as soon as I had done the very immediate things I was supposed to do, I would lift the endotracheal tube or oxygen mask slightly away from the face to be certain that it wasn't one of ours.

How would the parents feel? Each time I looked under the mask and was thankful the child wasn't mine, somebody else had to take the grief. What about the Emerg docs and nurses who had to sit down with parents, time and time again?

I will describe a few cases of grief that have not faded from my memory. Some things stick in our minds because of the peculiar story, but other things stick because of a feeling of some sort of guilt that perhaps we didn't do the right thing at the time or, more likely, that we just felt absolutely inadequate.

My first year as an intern, in 1961, I had to do my four weeks as a junior at the Sick Kids Hospital in Toronto, to fulfill the eligibility requirements for going into general practice or one of the specialties the following year. I think most of us at the time felt inadequate generally, even after a year of internship; although we had developed a little increase in confidence, we still felt inadequate to face the public.

However, nowhere was that truer, for most of us at least, than in pediatrics. These little babies got so sick so fast and all they did was scream, and even if they weren't screaming, their little hearts were going so fast that you couldn't make out which sound was systole and which sound was diastole. Besides that, you couldn't get anything but a second-hand history, often from very emotional parents; and the poor tyke couldn't even tell you where it hurt or why he was screaming. Occasionally the parents were so distraught that they could be verbally abusive or physical. Sometimes it seemed more difficult than a veterinarian examining a sick pit bull. The best solution was usually to remove the parents from the treatment room in order to be able to focus on the child.

When I arrived on my pediatric ward, I quickly found out that of the four interns who were supposed to be on the service, two were sick. The senior intern, Dr. Peter Dent, whom I knew personally and would have been a super guy to hold my hand on this service, had just been admitted to an intensive care unit with chicken pox pneumonia.

My comrade, the other junior, had been taken out of service because he had developed a tuberculous cavity the size of a lemon in his lung. He was an "open case," meaning he had live tuberculous bacteria in his sputum, and he was admitted to the local sanatorium. It ended up that a four-man service was suddenly a two-man service. This development made me too busy to realize how really intimidated I was.

Fortunately, the head nurse on my side of the ward, Miss Fran Swain, was highly experienced and saved me from potential disasters. She would say, "We usually call Doctor So and So when this happens," or "We usually do it this way here," and then she would demonstrate expertly. We usually rotated a one-in-two system (meaning we worked every day but had to stay in the hospital on call every other night) when there were four residents on the service. Because our number had been reduced from four to two, I only had two nights off during that four-week period, and the rest of the time I spent entirely at the hospital. In fact, it was only because of a special arrangement that I had any time off at all. Most of us were chronically fatigued anyway, but this type of rotation was even worse than usual.

During all of this, there was a sweet nearly five-year-old girl on the ward. Someone on the "renal service" was looking after her, and hence she was not my direct responsibility. She had apparently become a fixture on the ward. I was told that her parents lived somewhere in northern Ontario and were able to come to visit only on occasional weekends. I never saw them, however. The little girl's face was very puffy, because of the large amount of steroids she was forced to take to keep her alive. She was apparently deteriorating slowly, but she was exceptionally bright and mature for her age.

Within a day or so of my arrival, she started to follow me around. The nursing staff would jokingly call her my mascot. She was plainly bored and wanted company, and soon we became friends.

The nurses allowed her into the treatment rooms when we were starting IVs on patients or even when we were doing spinal taps. In some of these procedures, even the parents were not allowed in. Because she was always there, and so pleasant, it was difficult not to consider her just part of the staff. She was quite helpful in the treatment room, helping to settle the young patients down, as they were often her age.

Amazingly, this little girl would come into the consulting room when I would be interviewing parents trying to get more history, or telling them about our next plan of action for their little boy or girl. Initially, I thought I had better tell her that she should stay in the hall and that I would be out in a few minutes. However, everybody seemed to appreciate her, and I think it made the parents actually more comfortable seeing this sweet, but very obviously sick, little girl sitting there on a little stool beside me with a paper and pencil, pretending to take notes. Even during my short four weeks on the service, however, I noticed that my friend was deteriorating; she was weaker, and her little face seemed fatter. But she never complained and she was always cheerful. Sometime during the third week I had to carry her little stool for her, but she wouldn't let go of her "history paper" and the pencil that the nursing staff had given her.

When I came near the end of my stint on this service I dread-

Taking a history with help from my cherished friend.

ed saying goodbye to her. I told her I would come back to visit often, and I returned a week later. (It was quite easy for me, as the Toronto General was just across the street from the Sick Kids; I would have felt terrible if I hadn't kept my promise). When I came back on the ward, she burst into tears and then settled down and we had a very nice visit, or so I thought. My little friend, however, looked worse. When I had seen her every day, her deterioration had not been so obvious. While I was visiting, Miss Swain arrived back on the ward and asked to see me in private. She told me it would be better if I did not come back to visit, because when I left the first time, they had a very difficult time for the first couple of days trying to settle her down.

I was subsequently informed that it was even worse the second time I left. I had never met the parents; in fact they seemed to have virtually abandoned their child, probably because of financial constraints in traveling, and the other pressures of looking after the rest of the family. Certainly in the 1960s there were no hospices or organizations that provided for transportation and housing for patients and families who lived far away from the city. My little friend lasted for another three months and then died of renal failure. During the last two months she couldn't walk, and I never went back to see her.

Several years later our oldest son, Michael, who was three years old at the time, was admitted to Sick Kids with a severe form of gastroenteritis, and needed IV fluids. When he was admitted he was pretty sick and he wasn't that aware of his surroundings. However once he started to get better, he started to pay attention, and after my wife and I had been to visit him the next day, he apparently kicked up quite a storm. One of the nurses phoned us and said that as he would probably be out in two days, perhaps it would be better if we did not come to visit the next day. Remembering what the head nurse on my pediatric ward had told me a few years earlier made the decision to not visit our little boy easier.

Sick Kids had, and still deservedly enjoys, a reputation as a world-renowned centre for sick children. Hopefully, the staff gets a lot of well-deserved satisfaction from all the kids they help in a major way; however, they need a lot of kudos to make up for the sadness of caring for those patients who just go on suffering and suffering.

During our medical school years, and certainly as interns, we saw many tragedies. I just could not believe the appalling heartbreak that is associated with diseases such as Duchenne muscular dystrophy. For example, to see these young boys literally crawling up on their own legs to get into an erect position, and knowing that they and their family were facing death was incredibly sad. These little kids had to push on their knees and then their thighs to get into the erect position, as their torso muscles had become so weak. These boys often looked well and were energetic, and except for their strangely and characteristically muscular-looking calves, looked the picture of good health.

In 2006 I met a young mother who had two little boys, and after the second child was born, the first-born started to show the characteristic signs of this disease. Although there is only a

Duchenne muscular dystrophy (DMD) is an inherited sex-linked recessive disease. The carrier, the mother, has two X chromosomes and because the non-affected X cancels out the bad X, she will not show signs of the disease. However, if she passes on the bad X to her son it will pair with the Y chromosome from the father and, hence, not be neutralized and her son will acquire the disease. The course is quite variable, but the child often succumbs before he finishes public school. There is also a very high mutation rate with this disease, meaning that families who never had trouble before are now producing affected children. Currently, it's an exciting field of research and perhaps with such concepts as gene transfer these children may in the future lead normal lives.

50 percent chance of the second son developing the disease, just after his second birthday, he started to show the same unmistakable signs as his older brother. There was absolutely no family history of this disease in either parent. It was, presumably, an unfortunate mutation. Almost predictably, the parents split up and the mother is now a single parent with two sick and dying children.

I think you have to be a very extraordinary person to specialize in the care and treatment of children with this type of disorder. Hopefully, now in the era of gene transplant, some of these diseases will vanish.

Although cardiology has usually a much "cheerier" outlook, we have plenty of disasters on our service too. It would be inappropriate and too depressing to relate a litany of bad cases here. However, one very interesting and tragic case that occurred on our service will give the reader an idea of how varied our practice can be.

In the early 1980s I saw a very hard-working man, with a lovely family, but who unfortunately had premature coronary heart disease. He had never smoked, was fairly thin, and had normal blood pressure; his only risk factor, apart from being a type-A personality, was a fairly strong family history with a high cholesterol level. Since we don't get to choose our parents, he could hardly be blamed for having a "heart attack" in his forties.

He did well initially, but following his attack he had pretty severe angina on the slightest exertion. We put him through the usual treadmill test, which he failed miserably, and a subsequent coronary angiogram, which showed coronary arteries with severe obstructions, but were very suitable for bypass surgery.

He underwent a very successful three-vessel bypass, and on a subsequent treadmill test, he showed no abnormality. Except for a red line down his chest, some bad memories, and the need to take some cardiac medications, he was essentially back to normal. I saw him annually, basically to have him do a treadmill test and to reassure him. He had no symptoms, and with medication his bad cholesterol (LDL) was now well below the North American average.

About five years later, I got a phone call from the Canadian Red Cross to tell me that his family doctor was away on holidays and asking if it would be all right if they could get me to call the patient back for some additional blood work. Apparently our patient had received two units of blood during his bypass surgery, and one of the donors had come back to donate blood again and been found to be HIV positive. It was possible that he had been positive when he had donated blood five years previously, as the Red Cross had not begun testing until about two months after the bypass patient had received blood.

I thought it was likely that the donor had become contaminated sometime between the two donations. However, as the patient's family doctor was going to be away another two weeks, and there was a risk that the patient's wife could become contaminated, I phoned our patient and described the whole problem to him. Predictably, he was very mature about this unsettling news and hoped for the best. The Red Cross made all the arrangements and the blood was sent off. Amazingly, it took about two weeks before the Red Cross got back to us, although I phoned them repeatedly. Indeed, the family doctor, Dr. Steve Barron, came back just before the news that this poor man was in fact positive. By coincidence, this family doctor had a strong interest in HIV–AIDS and had a number of patients in his practice who were HIV positive. He was one of my favourite family doctors, and a very compassionate man.

Our patient continued to feel well and his wife was negative for HIV. After another two years, however, the patient's lymphocyte count began to drop and the signs and symptoms of AIDS began. He carried on and, at least on the surface, had a very good outlook. I saw him for his annual treadmill test for several years after that, but then it became obvious that his heart was the least of his worries. I stopped seeing him professionally, but would see him "socially" in the Emerg fairly often. By now he had to make many trips there for complications related to his AIDS, in particular PCP pneumonia. (PCP, or pneumocystitis pneumonia, is one of the opportunist types of pneumonias seen in AIDS patients.)

For some reason, people who receive a contaminated blood donation usually have a shortened incubation period and a more lethal course, possibly a consequence of the massive viral dose that they may receive from a whole unit of blood. Every time our patient was in the Emerg, the staff would call me, and although I would not see him "professionally," I would come to visit whenever I possibly could. It was absolutely shocking to see his deterioration over the next few months. Despite his condition, he always greeted me like a long-lost friend. I just hope that if and when I ever get to a like stage with some awful illness, I will be able to have even a fraction of his courage.

I last saw him sitting in the cab of his vehicle while his wife was shopping. He had, of course, long since stopped driving. He looked like a skeleton by this time, and appeared to be sleeping. I decided not to awaken him. He died a few weeks later. It was probably seven or eight years from the time he had first been diagnosed HIV positive.

I have often marvelled at the tremendous courage of patients who face the reality of death, and how supportive their families and friends come to be at a time of crisis. It surely helps to encourage us to have faith in the human race. Despite all the hardships of looking after seriously ill and dying patients, seeing this strong bond of love mitigates some of the feelings of sorrow and helplessness.

Do doctors cry? You bet they do.

CHAPTER 14

The *Wrong* Side
of the Bed Sheets

When doctors first walk into a patient's room in hospital, there is usually a barrier between them and the patient. That is the bed covering, usually consisting of the top sheet, a thin blanket and a thin, cotton bedspread. These hospital rooms are quite warm, and the patient usually doesn't feel cold. The point is to make certain that the patient is on the bed, under these covers, and that we don't reverse positions; doctors must not be in bed as patients and have others standing looking down at us under these same covers.

Doctors don't get sick, just patients do. We must keep that straight. Besides, how are we going to look after patients if we are in bed? We tell patients what to do; nobody should have the temerity to tell us how to look after ourselves! So goes our illogical thinking.

For some reason, when a doctor gets sick, it often seems that the disease is really unusual or even strange. It may not be ordinary pneumonia or a broken bone.

Well, for me, not getting sick was all about to change and I was going to have a very weird disease. It started with a bang. My head hit the floor, scaring my poor patient out of her wits.

I slowly recovered consciousness, and thought I was waking up in my bed at home. I looked up and saw bedsprings over my head. Just as I was trying to orientate myself, sitting up now on one elbow, the crash cart came reeling into the room. I remember thinking, "Who arrested?" Then I realized that the team was coming for me! My head hurt; I had sustained a cut as I fell backwards, striking the floor beside the next bed. I immediately tried to get up, but just as soon as I was almost upright, my legs started to give out and I sat down hard on my butt. How embarrassing!

It was a Sunday afternoon in 1974, and I had gone in to see my patients who had just been admitted for heart catheterization planned for the next morning. At that time, heart catheterization was considered relatively risky and it was customary to admit these patients the evening before. The whole medical procedure was usually re-explained to the patient, who was given a sedative, a light supper, and then a sleeping pill, and advised to take nothing by mouth after eleven o'clock at night. An IV would be started early the next morning.

MALARIA?

I had been plagued by recurring high fevers for the previous two years, and, of course, they always seemed to occur at the least opportune time. They were "proper" fevers: my temperature would go up to 40°C (104°F) and profound chills would accompany the fever. My wife and I would joke and say it was probably malaria, but I had never been to any place that was exciting enough to give me malaria.

A typical bout would start with chills and last about half an hour or so. Then I would sweat profusely, and after a couple of hours, I would be able to carry on. These episodes would occur perhaps once every two months, but just before this fainting episode in the hospital, they had been happening every two weeks or so, though never regularly enough that I could predict when the next one was going to occur.

My family doctor, Fred Harder, and my old classmate, Dr. Harry Lewis, were both well aware of my problem, and innumerable tests had been done. I'd had multiple blood cultures, even during times of fever, and tons of other blood tests; and just about everything that I owned had been x-rayed. All these tests were reported to be negative.

On this particular day, I had been standing talking to an older lady who was booked for heart catheterization the next day. She was lying in bed while I was talking to her, and she said later that my eyes just "glazed over" and I fell over backwards, whacking my head quite hard on the floor. My poor patient, absolutely convinced that I had just died, yelled for the nurse. When the nurse arrived, she could not find my pulse and called a cardiac arrest. As I was partially under the next bed, and she was the only nurse on the ward at the time, she ran off to the telephone to alert the cardiac arrest team.

(My patient had seen her husband die while standing on his feet. He didn't even say goodbye; he just keeled over backwards and that was it. She was really surprised when I got myself up on one elbow. She had thought initially that I had replicated her husband's performance. This nice lady was so upset that, with apologies, she signed herself out of hospital. It was almost a year later, when my problems had been at least partially sorted out, that she came back for her heart catheterization; and this time I stayed on my feet!)

I was duly admitted to the emergency department, had the usual battery of tests and, after several hours, was discharged.

When one of my colleagues heard about my escapades in the hospital, he was most scornful.

"Fainted? Fainted! Only hysterical schoolgirls faint. What's wrong with you? You have let down all us macho males!"

It was the kind of black humour that I might have expected from Harry. But now he was one of my doctors, and although he might have thought it, he was kind enough not to say anything.

However, the fevers were coming on with shorter free periods between episodes, and eventually the fever came every day, usually in the late afternoon. They were less dramatic, never rising over much more than 39°C now, but I didn't seem to recover in-between either. I completely lost my appetite, and over the next two months lost thirty pounds in weight. Harry was very conscientious, and as they still had no idea what the hell was wrong, they decided to send me down to the University Hospital of Washington in Seattle, not too far from Vancouver. This hospital has a very specialized unit for infectious diseases. My doctors arranged my visit there because they thought that I had some sort of mysterious bacterial infection. Dr. Peter Richardson drove me down.

This hospital was a real eye-opener for me. It seemed so efficient; I had barely arrived when I was being re x-rayed and subjected to more of these interminable blood tests. Although I had not arrived until the early afternoon, they had determined in the time remaining that day that I had a bilateral bronchopneumonia and a very bad case of sinusitis and, in fact, had an abscess in my right maxillary sinus.

Harry had made sure that all my reports and my actual x-rays had been sent with me. I was informed that the sinus x-rays done almost two years earlier at the Royal Columbian, had shown severe disease, but had been read as "normal." For some reason, I had never experienced sinus pains or even headaches to tip anyone off about where my infection might be residing. I had always joked that I never get headaches — I just give them! Harry was probably thinking, "Where there's no sense, there is no feeling!"

(Skull x-rays, and sinus x-rays in particular, are difficult to read by the less experienced radiologists, and the generalist usually takes the radiologist's word at face value for this area.)

The very next morning, an ENT (Ear, Nose and Throat) specialist visited me in hospital, and took me downstairs, and very expertly broke the thin bone that connects the inside of the nose to the fairly large maxillary sinus. (This was in the days before fiberoptic scopes.) He was able to extract a large amount of pus for culture, and with the appropriate antibiotics I was well on the road to recovery. The cause of my pneumonia was undoubtedly my sinus problems.

Several months later I underwent what was, at that time, considered radical sinus surgery — a Caldwell Luke procedure — and my "malaria" never recurred. Irwin Stewart, my local ENT specialist, wondered if my long boxing career had contributed to my sinus problems, blocking the normal drainage pattern because of a "pulverized" nasal septum.

However, in the course of all this investigation, it was noticed that one of the proteins in my blood was elevated. At that time, the significance of this was not known, and as I felt well again, had completely regained my weight, and was back full speed on my exercise program, it was just put down as an interesting problem, an "elevated blood protein with unknown significance." It was actually a "macroglobulin," and it came to haunt me years later.

It is thought that the abnormal protein is manufactured by a clone of lymphocytes (a type of white blood cell) that are no longer under complete control of the body's overall system. This protein may attack the myelin (the covering or insulation) on the longer nerve fibres, by a process somewhat akin to taking the insulation off an electric wire. The muscles supplied by these "short circuited" nerves can no longer be stimulated and the affected muscles gradually disappear. In many individuals, these particular lymphocytes may become malignant, and hence this particular disease is often classified in the lymphoma group. Appropriate chemotherapy, although a double-edged sword, may delay this occurrence and reduce the production of this abnormal macroglobulin, which has caused the nerve damage, and hence muscle loss.

I was lucky though. I'd had a long "latent period" from the discovery of this abnormal protein during the investigation of my sinus abscess before the damage to my nerves became obvious, and I had enjoyed good health for a prolonged period. Any problems that did arise I ignored, or more likely rationalized. I basically ignored this protein problem, or, more likely, chose to forget about it. However, twenty years later, in 1994, after a very busy life in medical practice, that stupid macroglobulin of "unknown significance" was starting to cause big problems. I just wanted to be a cardiologist, on the right side of the bed sheets. Being a patient is humiliating. As one of the nurses told me, "When you are a patient and are admitted to hospital, you park your clothes and your dignity at the door."

A MONSTER PROTEIN

"I have to tell you, Tom, that you might have Lou Gehrig's disease."

Lou Gehrig's disease was always one of the horror stories of medicine — or one of a number of horror stories — that every medical student prays that he never gets. As medical students, we always fantasized that we would live to a ripe old age and "flame out," hopefully in less than twenty-four hours, preferably in our own beds. Or, failing that, we would die "with our boots on" hopefully doing something that we liked, again of course, at a "ripe old age". (Perhaps shot by a jealous husband at the age of ninety-five, climbing down a ladder from some young lady's bedroom window!)

During my training to become an internist, I had taken about a year of neurology and of course had seen several cases of Lou Gehrig's, which the books call amyotrophic lateral sclerosis or

ALS for short. It's such a diabolic disease that nobody ever forgets it.

This "monster disease" usually gets you at age forty and beyond, so when you are a young medical student you think you can relax as far this disease is concerned; but nobody can ever convince you just how fast time flies. (I should have known that I was getting old, because just before I realized that I had a muscle-wasting problem, one of our sons, then in his late twenties, had said that he just couldn't take the hangovers the way he used to. If he thought he was getting old, then what about me?) I had suddenly become fifty-seven, the perfect age for something like Lou Gehrig's. Perhaps the only good thing about it is that it usually polishes you off in two to five years. However, getting there is the horrible part.

For some reason, the core muscles gradually waste away. The patient often notices fasciculations, a sort of shivering or vibration of some muscle groups, and progressive weakness. He may experience difficulty getting up from a chair and eventually have difficulty doing the essential things in life — such as breathing and swallowing! The patient often dies choking on his own secretions. The onset is insidious at first, but within a two-year period or so, the patient is virtuously helpless and in constant fear of choking to death.

"I don't think I have Lou Gehrig's. I've had these symptoms too long, don't you think?" I asked, hopefully.

"Well, I suspect that you may be right, but I have to tell you that it is still a possibility."

The world was suddenly no longer real. Mercifully, I was just going to wake up and find out that this was all just a bad dream, wasn't I? I'd had dreams before where I had believed that I had a bad heart attack, and then awakened and found out it was all just a nightmare. This time, I could not just awaken and put it all behind me. This time it was all for real, and there was no waking up. I already was awake. Something inside of me kept yelling, "This is not for real!" I knew this time it was not a bad dream. It was far worse.

Dr. Grosch was always my buddy, and I could always count on him supporting the best interests of the hospital. I really liked him and, of course, trusted him completely. He was the long-standing Chief of the Neurosciences Service at our hospital, and

Dr. Eisen was well respected in the medical community, but also became known to the general public because of a very celebrated right-to-die case across Canada in the early nineties. Sue Rodriguez was a courageous woman who had developed ALS and wanted to be able to legally end her own life. She took her fight for a patient's right for physician-assisted suicide to the Supreme Court of Canada and lost. She eventually took her own life in the presence of two others: an unnamed doctor and Svend Robinson, a friend and federal politician who had supported her cause. Dr. Eisen had been her neurologist, had made the diagnosis, and was involved in her care as much as possible, but not in her assisted suicide.

sat on the executive. I know he liked me and, of course, it was for these reasons I had come to see him as a patient.

I heard him speaking, almost in a fog now, telling me that he was going to send me to Dr. Andy Eisen, a specialist in degenerative neuromuscular disorders.

Dr. Grosch was, of course, very kind and tried to comfort me as best he could, but I was still in a daze. I kept willing to just awaken from this bad dream. The good thing was that I was going to have an early appointment to see Dr. Eisen, so that I wouldn't be waiting too long "on the edge of my seat." When Dr. Grosch left the room, I just stared at the wall. I had difficulty putting my clothes back on. I was just not thinking clearly.

I certainly had the fasciculations, weakness and muscle wasting; but the symptoms had come on so slowly that I was initially oblivious to my gradual deterioration. The sterile gloves that I had to put on in the hospital prior to heart catheterization hadn't become stiffer, and hence harder to put on, as I had initially thought. The difficulty I was experiencing in spreading my fingers had nothing to do with stiffer gloves, but was due to my weakness. And again, contrary to my initial belief, it wasn't that my pants were shrinking, making my pockets tighter, and therefore more difficult to get my wallet out; and certainly I hadn't gained any weight. The problem was that I couldn't spread my fingers forcibly enough to get them around an object in my pocket. As for my stupid toes, they were always getting stuck in my pant legs when I tried to get dressed in the morning, and I had, almost as a reflex, put on my socks first to stop my toes getting bent backwards in my pant legs.

When Dr. Grosch pointed out these obvious weaknesses in my muscle groups, I was shocked that I could have been so unobservant. Had I possibly been in a state of denial? And what about my brachio-radialis? (The forearm muscle that, in the first chapter, the anatomy demonstrator had said was pretty big for such a skinny kid.) It was practically gone, and that wasn't due to the fact that because I had been married for such a long time now that I had not been using it! My right brachio-brachialis muscle was still of normal size, because the disease had not yet affected it.

He showed me my fasciculations, which were now quite obvious, and yet I had only been vaguely aware of them. Although my wife had pointed out my wasted calf muscles — and it was for this reason that I had finally sought a medical opinion — I had been totally unaware of the obvious wasting of my left forearm. I was embarrassed at how stupid I had been, and shocked to see the amount of damage that had already occurred without my even observing it. How fast had this progressed, and what was my future going to be like?

When my visit to Dr. Grosch was over, I had to go back to my own office, as I had a full office booked, and on every office day there were always "add-ons." Being a cardiologist, it was difficult to just keep up to the demand. Still, having a full office after this very depressing interview was perhaps a good thing; learning about other people's problems took my mind off my own. In a way, I was also fortunate to be called to the emergency department that same afternoon for two very interesting cases that required a lot of further investigations.

When there was a moment, however, between cases, my mind would quickly return to my own problems. I started rationalizing. My disease seemed to be "peripheral," that is to say that the weakness was largely below my knees and elbows, although my left biceps had also been affected. Dr. Grosch had told me that was a good thing as ALS favoured destroying the core muscles as well as the more peripheral muscles. My core muscles seemed to be mostly intact.

Also, when I started to think, I recalled that a few odd things had occurred years ago that I thought were strange, but had ignored or put down to old age. Fifteen years previously, I had trouble getting a canoe up on my shoulders, a task that a year or two earlier had been a piece of cake. I had also had trouble lifting a scuba tank with my left hand, even though I am left-handed.

I thought this was good news, because if I'd had Lou Gehrig's back then, I should be dead by now. Dr. Grosch thought this was good news too. Between patients, I had fully convinced myself that at least I didn't have that dreaded disease, and started to feel better. We hadn't paid any attention to my macroglobulin problem because it had been there so long and at that time was poorly understood.

That night I had thoroughly persuaded myself that I didn't have Lou Gehrig's. My core group of muscles was virtually intact, I had a mild but definite sensory loss in my feet, not seen with Lou Gehrig's, and the length of time that the symptoms had been present made the disease also less likely. Was I in denial, or was I rationalizing, or both? I know the old saying "He who has himself for a doctor has a fool for a physician."

Two weeks later, I was in Dr. Andy Eisen's office. I must say I certainly received a very complete examination, including all those strange nerve transmissions tests. His technician was very good, and absolutely beautiful. That helped take my mind off my own problems. When the results of all these tests were in, Dr. Eisen said, "You are lucky I didn't see you five or six years earlier."

"Why is that?"

"Well, if I had seen you several years ago, presenting with these symptoms, I would have told you that you had ALS, but you don't. What you do have is a very uncommon disease process that we only see occasionally in our office, and is about one tenth as common as ALS. Unlike ALS, it doesn't affect your breathing or swallowing muscles and stays mainly below your knees and elbows. In the old days, we used to think that people presenting like you had ALS, but when they didn't go on and die and the disease didn't affect their core muscles, we realized it was a different disease process. Moreover, this particular malady is partially treatable."

Well that was a big relief, but now what? During the continuing investigations, I was sent to one of the downtown hospitals for an MRI (magnetic resonance imaging). Unbelievably, I was told that I also had another rare disease — syringomyelia! This is a cavitation of the spinal cord, which is usually progressive and very debilitating. There is no known treatment.

With this condition, a cavity develops in the spinal cord, and I was told that this cavity extended from my neck all the way down to the very end of my spinal cord. I had heard of this disease, but I did not remember seeing a case in my neurology training in Toronto. This was depressing news, of course, especially because "syringo" is usually progressive. I guessed if the "macro" didn't get me, the syringo would!

Fortunately, another one of my classmates, Dr. Nick Bruchovsky, came to my rescue. He had become quite famous for his work on cancer of the prostate. He also, fortunately, had been given a healthy dose of Harry's shit-disturber chip. He felt it was virtually impossible to have two very rare diseases of this magnitude in the same patient.

Unbeknownst to me, Nick, with the permission of my wife, made arrangements for me to be sent to the Mayo Clinic in Rochester, Minnesota. Nick apparently knew some of the doctors there, and when I came home from work that night it was announced that I was going to have to cancel my office for a few days. At this point, I wasn't really sick. I just had this stupid weakness, and the fasciculations. Actually, Nick had a point. If the incidence of a rare disease occurring during someone's lifetime is approximately one in a thousand, the chances of two rare diseases of this frequency occurring in the same individual would be one thousand times a thousand, or one in a million. These numbers are probably not too far off the real incidence of these two rare diseases.

This was my second experience of being shipped off to the States. I knew better than to argue with my wife. Ten days later, I was down in the hallowed halls of the Mayo Clinic. All my reports, including my MRI from Vancouver, had been bundled up and accompanied me to Rochester.

The Mayo Clinic was an even bigger eye-opener than the University of Washington Hospital. It was also a little more frightening. When I had been shipped to Seattle, I was really too sick to really care what happened. This time, I was not feeling unwell, and whatever they found would likely have long-term consequences.

When I checked in, they took all my reports — and, of course, my credit card numbers — and I was assigned to a hotel just across the street from the hospital. It was one of several hotels all connected to the main hospital by underground tunnels. My room was simple and clean. The toilet and shower were just down the hall, and the cost was just twenty-eight US dollars a day.

I was told to meet my doctors at eight o'clock the next morning at a certain room number. And, surprise, surprise, they were both there, and on time, and had already completely gone over all my reports! They seemed to know more about me than I did.

I was then subjected to a very complete physical and neurological examination. They didn't miss any of my orifices, either. That same day, I had an MRI with contrast (injection with a special dye to enhance the MRI images and define abnormalities), and had the usual innumerable blood tests, and a spinal fluid examination. I was there for four days, and every day was like this; I had some tests whose purpose I never really did understand. Each morning I was greeted by the same two doctors, and all the tests done the day before had already been read and then reviewed, and I was told the results.

The staff was just as kind as their Canadian counterparts, but the Americans were much more efficient! Imagine having a same-day MRI and a spinal tap. This would take weeks, or more likely months, to have been booked in Canada. The Mayo apparently had a five-tesla MRI; the one in Vancouver was a three-tesla unit. The tesla unit measures the power of the unit and gives the concentration of a magnetic field, the number of field lines per square metre. From a consumer standpoint, the five-tesla unit was much faster and could give more information. The most important point was that their machine was reliable. I didn't, in fact, have syringomyelia. I had myelomalacia of a small segment of my cord, likely caused by a previous injury. The important point was that myelomalacia was non-progressive and likely asymptomatic.

Nick was right, and because of the faulty diagnosis from Vancouver, you, the taxpayer, had to reimburse me to the tune of about 6,000 US dollars. Of course, I had to pay my transportation costs and the hotel bill for the five nights that I had to stay there. However, I'm sure that the total costs that I had already run up in Canada over this "macro" thing were higher than that, and had resulted in a partially faulty diagnosis.

I am only just one "lousy patient" and my experience with

my two visits to the American system is purely anecdotal. However, it is a little embarrassing to see how far we are behind other jurisdictions, in some ways; and it's particularly sad when I can see how inefficient our system is. The bureaucracy and waiting lists in Canada are simply stifling.

You don't even have to be a good doctor in our system to survive and to be busy. We have no competition; we are the only choice. This is particularly true in some specialties that are really short-handed. In cardiology, I had a long waiting list, but that could not reassure me that I must be doing a good job. I knew of another cardiologist who, in my opinion, had a poor knowledge base and absolutely no common sense, and this individual also had a waiting list.

I guess what really annoyed me the most about all of this was that when I went back to the radiology department that had done my first MRI, and explained that the Mayo had repeated my study and disagreed with their diagnosis, and that I didn't, in fact, have "syringo," they didn't seem all that interested. I guess they just get used to making mistakes because of outdated equipment.

Despite all this, I rarely ran into a doctor or a nurse who didn't try to do the best possible job with the equipment available to them. It's the system that's screwed up.

After a number of very different opinions from various doctors, and again from some of my classmates, it was eventually decided to put me on "chemo." I was sent off to the BC Cancer Agency and saw Dr. Joe Connors, a lymphoma specialist and quite well known in the world literature for the work he has done on this collection of problems. With the chemo, I started to lose weight and developed a lot of spontaneous bruising. To say that I felt like shit was probably an understatement.

My colleagues in cardiology, always stretched to the limit, kindly agreed to take me off the call schedule. I felt guilty about this because now I was basically doing "business hours" practice, and they were having to field my night calls and come into the Emerg at times when I used to be on call.

My general condition worsened and I developed a general body rash. One day, when I was wearing a scrub suit one of my nursing friends, always the joker, said, "Dr. Godwin, look at all your bruises. Is your wife beating you again?"

Another one of my doctor colleagues, again when I was wearing my scrub suit, said, "Look at that rash! I bet you just have AIDS!"

I didn't know whether to laugh or cry. Actually, for me it was probably a good thing. Even dark humour has its place; anything that lightens the atmosphere can be helpful. I had noticed previously that the comments medical people make to each other may seem to be cruel, and a layperson might get the wrong idea, but the target of the harsh remarks understands, and the tension is often relieved.

Unfortunately, my weight loss and weakness continued, and I lost about 30 pounds in total, for the second time. I was never overweight in the first place, and I guess I began to look like someone who had just been released from Auschwitz.

On one of my visits to the cancer agency, it was suggested that I should take time off work, something I just dreaded. Would I ever be able to come back? However, at this point, I really had little choice. I told myself that it was only going to be temporary. Once the chemo had flattened my bad lymphocytes, I would be able to go back to work. It was 1996.

It was probably on the next visit that I was told that my platelets were really low, and because of the risk of serious bleeding, I was put on a large dose of prednisone. *(One hundred and twenty five mgs of prednisone a day!)* I had never realized that such huge doses of this stuff were used. (Prednisone is a cortisone-like hormone that may have many profound side effects. Maintenance dosage varies from 2.5mg to 10mg a day; 30mg is considered a large dose, and very occasionally 60mg are given for very brief periods.)

I think my mind was already playing tricks on me even before I started this treatment with prednisone. I became really depressed. Medicine was not only my vocation, it was a serious hobby, and in some ways it was almost my identity. Besides, I was in love with about five hundred nurses and technical staff at the Royal Columbian, and I was going to miss all their affection and camaraderie. I hate to admit this, but I think that I actually missed my medical friends more than I missed the patients.

Depression is a "black hole" and doesn't do anybody any good. My body was a wreck by now. One of my more serious hobbies had been trying to stay in excellent shape with a fairly scientific program of endurance and pretty heavy weight training. Despite my busy schedule at work and on the farm, I always went to the gym three times a week for an hour and a half workout. I also jogged four miles at least once a week. Now, because of my frightful weakness, just climbing a flight of stairs was about all I could manage.

The big dose of prednisone just put me over the top. Although I never mentioned it to anyone, including my wife, because it was just too embarrassing, I certainly started to think of ways to end all this horror. People say, "but suicide is so selfish." On the other hand, when you start thinking in an irrational way, all bets are off. You can rationalize almost anything. In my own case it was, "You are just going to be a nuisance to your family, and if you are going to die anyway, why wait until the bitter end and go through all that suffering?"

Fortunately, I knew that even moderate doses of prednisone could aggravate depression, and I still had enough insight to realize — a little — what was going on. Without telling anyone, I rapidly tapered and stopped this drug after eight days of treatment. This was the only time that I didn't follow my doctor's advice.

The next week, when I was back at the cancer agency, I told Dr. Connors that I had just stopped the prednisone. I fully expected him to express his disappointment in me, but he merely stated that some people just couldn't take that drug. He then told me that there had been a slight rise in my platelet count that was not due to the prednisone, because this drug doesn't cause a slight rise. It is a dramatic rise or none at all.

Over the next few weeks, my platelet count gradually rose further, but it stayed below normal for several years. I continued to have a bruising problem, and any cut would bleed for an inordinately long time. However, by this time I had started to feel a little better, and the devastating weakness was no longer so pronounced. Depression is no joke, and I think that as time goes on much more of the chemistry of depression will be better understood, and more effective treatment will result.

Three years later, when I had been off the chemo for a while, I asked Dr. Connors about going back to work again. He said, right in front of my wife, "Don't even think about it." I was initially upset, but I think in the long run it was a good thing. I had just turned 62, and I guess, in retrospect, there would have been little point in returning. I still was in love with my five hundred girlfriends at the hospital, but I had to accept that that was over.

Unfortunately, my blood work suggested that the process was still going on, and my worsening left arm weakness was making life difficult with my activities at home. I couldn't even hold a glass of beer in my left hand without the risk of dropping it, a serious problem for a confirmed left-handed beer drinker like me!

Then, Dr. Connors suggested, on the encouragement of Dr. Jim Goldie, a medical researcher and former head of the BC Cancer Agency, (another classmate and close friend, now retired) that I be tried on a newly engineered mouse protein called Rituximab. It's a strange drug. Apparently a mouse that has had some human genes transferred into it is injected with an antigen from some human lymphocytes, and the poor mouse makes antibodies to this human lymphocyte. Then the antibodies manufactured by the mouse are "harvested" and injected into the human patient. Probably President Bush would not approve of making a mouse into a partial human, but for me, and many patients, it was a great step forward. The side effects in my case were minimal, my platelet count was not adversely affected, and my left arm showed a dramatic increase in strength. My new blood work suggested that the disease process was slowing down. Now, five years later, I can safely hold a beer glass in my left hand, and can even hammer in fence staples with my left hand without giving it a thought.

Being a "medical type" and a patient has its tradeoffs. Certainly we have, perhaps, a better understanding of our illness, but sometimes we tend to think of the worst scenarios of the particular disease. We may also tend to shop around for advice from a number of our colleagues, and doing that certainly can "muddy the waters." During my medical practice, I had seen perhaps more than my share of physicians and nurses as patients. It sometimes was a battle to get these people to even take their medications, or follow advice on important decisions such as whether they should undergo open-heart surgery.

A fellow cardiologist might get "sucked in" when the medical type asks a general and seemingly innocent question, such as, "Is this particular cholesterol-lowering drug any good?" The patient doesn't let the cardiologist know that he is asking the question on his own behalf until late in the discussion. By this time it's a little late to backpedal sufficiently. Later the patient says to his own doctor, "Dr. So and So says that drug isn't as good as another drug," when Dr. So and So, of course, doesn't know even know the level of the patient's LDL cholesterol, the clinical findings, or the family setting. I, too, have been innocently sucked in by these so-called innocent questions in the doctors' coffee shop. These conversations can leave lingering doubts in the patient's mind. This questioning might not always be a bad thing, but on the whole, I don't think it usually helps the patient. The Internet has added a whole new dimension to this problem. It may start the patient worrying needlessly, and even stoke his tendencies to be a hypochondriac. However, the Internet can certainly increase the patient's knowledge about his disease and a well-informed patient is usually a pleasure to deal with. It is also a device that keeps doctors on their toes!

FATHERLY ADVICE ON YOUR PERSONAL MEDICAL HEALTH

From a very personal standpoint, my wife and family helped me tremendously in getting through this series of weird and frightening health problems. My friends too, particularly my medical friends, were very helpful, not only professionally, but also emotionally. From a selfish standpoint, times spent with your family are times well spent, for a person who might feel strong and perhaps invulnerable at the moment, might not always continue that way. During my practice, I saw lots of really sick patients who had very little family support. It must just be that much more difficult for them to get through whatever Mother Nature has dished up.

When someone gets sick, it is always necessary to ask why. If you smoke, don't exercise on regular basis, eat too many calories or the wrong kind of calories, and don't even get your blood pressure or your blood lipids checked occasionally, most of us would assume that your risks are greatly increased of experiencing a serious "cardiovascular event." In some ways, it might even be considered your own fault when it happens.

By the time you are on Harry's conveyor belt, you have already been conceived, and hence, it's a little late to choose your parents carefully. There isn't a whole lot that we can do at the

337

present about our personal heredity. (This may change with gene transfers, per the mouse protein discussed earlier.) However, we certainly can do something about our subsequent lifestyle.

In my own case, it was remarkable that my dear older brother, who had bailed me out of so many scrapes in my childhood, came down with multiple myeloma. Myeloma is caused by plasma cells, a constituent of bone marrow, that turn malignant. Lymphoma is caused by lymphocytes that turn malignant. We both had abnormal proteins in our blood, and the lymphoma group and the myelomas are considered related in some way. Could we have inherited an abnormal gene? Nobody in our ancestry, so far as we knew, had died of any kind of cancer. Certainly, in earlier generations we had our share of other problems, such as alcoholism, accidents, senility, and general degenerative diseases of old age, but no cancers.

The environment is always considered, and as far as I remember we ate what I think most people, even today, would consider a very healthy diet. At the end of World War II, my father, impressed with the merits of the "route march," encouraged my older brother and me to jog for long distances in the bush. I think it was all part of a scheme to make us so thoroughly tired that, even if we did have an idle mind, we would be just too tired to carry out any of our fiendish plans. However, there were other aftermaths from the Second World War.

My father told us that there were only two good things left over from this terrible war, and these were plywood and DDT! He was right about the plywood; DDT turned out to be a different story. It had many uses, and was sold under many different brand names. The brand we used was made by Shell and called "Fly-Tox." It was used everywhere.

We had pigs on our farm and houseflies made a moving carpet on their backs during the summer. The DDT was wonderful. We could walk through the barn spraying this stuff, and in a few minutes, all the flies would be lying on their backs, buzzing around in small circles. In that part of Ontario, during the months of September and October, we had literally plagues of cluster flies. They were so numerous that on the south side of our white farmhouse (clad in *asbestos* shingles, I might add!) the entire wall would be turned from white to grey! To get rid of these flies that crept in everywhere, DDT seemed the answer. After we had duly

338

sprayed them and they were on their backs, we just vacuumed them up.

We also discovered that DDT had other novel and exciting uses. Because it was in an oil base, we found, quite by accident, that it afforded a marvellous recreational function. For after we had "Fly-Tox-ed" the house, and once the oil base had settled on the linoleum floor, we found it made a great slide area.

My brother and I had great fun stripping down to our underwear and sliding down the whole length of our house on this linoleum. We found that with the barest minimum of clothing we had less friction, and would slide on our stomachs, arching our back as much as possible so that our underwear would not drag and slow down our speed. We also tried it on our back, arching our backs the other way, so that just the soles of our feet and the centre parts of our backs were touching the linoleum.

Nobody has a clear idea yet if this stuff, or any other common pollutants in my day, has contributed to some of our modern maladies, but it seems likely. It's obviously better, in any case, to err on the side of caution with many of these chemicals.

I can't stress enough the role of having numerous interests outside of one's profession. The person who has a physical job, and develops even a minor problem in the scheme of things, for example bad knees, can no longer do his job. He may have nothing to fall back on that he could enjoy.

My problem, I think, was not that I didn't have any interests outside my occupation. Rather, my problem was that most of my hobbies were pretty physical. Thus, when my affliction settled in, I had to radically change my lifestyle and habits in the direction of more gentle pursuits; it would be an understatement to say that I found it a little difficult to make the transition.

The reality was that my situation hit me like a sledgehammer. All kinds of feelings converged at once: anger, frustration, bitterness and, at first, denial that I needed to change at all. It took a while, and a lot of internal self-counselling, along with the sympathy and guidance of long-suffering family and friends, until I finally saw the need to get a grip on the new realities confronting me, and started to accept the changes and adaptations I needed to make.

We just see so many elderly patients who, once their job is over and they are retired, really have nothing to do that is mean-

DDT kills flies — dead flies everywhere! — in an oil base that made a good sliding surface on linoleum for human kids.

ingful to them. We can only watch so much television and do so much reading. Most of us feel better when we are doing something that might be useful. What are you supposed to do when, because of poor health or money problems, you can't play golf or travel? What are the backup activity options you have?

I remember that when I was a kid I greatly enjoyed most of my grandparents (except that Presbyterian one). Returning the favour to our kids and grandchildren is also nurturing to my wife and me. In my opinion, we should all make a conscious effort to socialize, particularly with younger people.

It is always sad to see people in an old-age home sitting constantly alone, making no effort to talk even to their immediate neighbours. There are many sedentary hobbies they might enjoy, but it is perhaps better to get a little understanding while we are still young of which ones might be appealing, and start doing some of them.

For some reason, I came by my hobbies naturally. I didn't engage in them to protect myself from poor health or old age in the future. But had I known in my youth what I know now, and wasn't already involved in a hobby, I would have at least thought of getting involved in some more sedentary activities totally unrelated to my profession.

On the other hand, I also think that striving to be as physically fit as possible really pays off, as it may give us more reserve to draw on should the untoward happen. It has been shown, for a long time now, that being physically active helps our brain to function better and it makes us a little more resistant to depression. Those "endorphins" that all the joggers speak about likely play a serious role in our mental health.

I have been very fortunate during my entire life. Who you end up marrying is largely luck, but it doesn't hurt to be a little pragmatic or "clinical" about it as well in making the decision. The best-looking women may not have the long-term brain that will be compatible to our own, and, of course, vice versa. One of my old battleaxe head nurses asked me one day, "Do you know why you men always give your penises a name, such as 'Little Willie' or 'Oscar'?"

I, of course, said I had no idea, and she said in her loud laughing voice, "It's because you guys always like to be on a first-name basis with something that is making all the important decisions!" Those old head nurses are pretty smart, and have seen it all.

Our four little boys have grown up to become admirable young men who are now supplying us with grandchildren. My professional life has been very rewarding, and looking back, I can't think of anything that I would have preferred to do.

I didn't get the music, language, or directional chips inserted into my brain as I went by on that conveyor belt that Harry described. At some point, however, according to Harry, I must have been in the "knee–chest position" on this conveyor belt, because it is clear that Lady Luck must have shoved a horseshoe up my ass, and when I responded so well to that Rituximab stuff, I must have had a second horseshoe put in at the same time!

Actually, I don't know if horseshoes have anything to do with it. Perhaps I owe my good fortune to my former and dear secretary who prays for me every night, or maybe it's all that cheap red wine that I drink. Perhaps it's all that good food that my loving wife stuffs down my throat every day, or even someone or something that is looking out for me. Who knows? The important thing is to carry on, try to be somewhat productive, and enjoy life to the best of your ability.

CHAPTER 15

The Business of Medicine

Financially, medicine in the western world is in a bit of a mess. Certainly this is particularly true in Canada, and it's only going to get a lot worse. We have an aging population, and we also have new and expanding technology that is becoming increasingly expensive. Also, because of these advances the population is living longer, and those that survive one crisis will now live long enough to have another crisis, and then perhaps a third problem.

When I started practice, there were no joint replacements, no bypass surgeries, only a very limited number of antibiotics, and no antiviral agents. Moreover, the cost of pharmaceuticals has now surpassed the cost of physician care. Taxes can only be raised to a certain point, after which the amount of tax revenues generated starts to decline. Most western nations are just about at that level. In Canada and elsewhere, we have reached the point of rationing our medical care, as these long waiting lists allow only a certain number of cases or procedures to be performed each year.

If there are many complaints in one particular area, the government will step in and "put the fire out" by injecting more cash into something like joint replacement to shorten the waiting list in that area. Obviously difficult choices have to be made, but our politicians avoid even discussing the fundamental problems. The public — you and I — have to start these discussions before our entire medical system collapses.

Perhaps, as a start, we can "cherry pick" some things that worked well in the past, but got steamrolled over by our new-age, ivory-tower medical bureaucrats, and discuss some changes that might improve our medical system and at the same time reduce costs.

DOCTOR TRAINING

Originally the various governments, federal and provincial, thought that by reducing the number of positions in medical school, the reduction in the numbers of doctors would lessen the strain on the medical system as a whole. We are now in a position that has resulted in a critical shortage in doctor manpower. To fill this gap, the training of new doctor manpower has to be streamlined, without compromising the training in essential areas. Also, the cost of this training has to be reduced, where practically possible.

In premed, I think we should stress the essential things that would give students the background necessary before entering medical school. They would need the academic subjects, such as basic biology, and need to be able to work with a microscope. They should have enough math and physics skills to understand the principles of radiation, and collection of statistics, and enough inorganic chemistry to act as a stepping-stone to organic chemistry. Good computer skills are now a must, and students should be familiar with the various programs available. The humanities should be added to make students more rounded, but the emphasis should be on the scientific subjects.

With bright, dedicated students, I believe that these premed requirements could be accomplished within two years after grade twelve, instead of taking four years to obtain a bachelor's degree. This would shave two years off the usual requirement before entering medical school. In Great Britain, they don't insist on having a BS before entering medical school, and some doctors graduate with an MD at age twenty-one!

However, I would increase medical school itself to at least five years, but add a large service component, similar to the experience that I found so useful during my externship at Soldiers Memorial Hospital in Orillia, Ontario, described in part in chapter two. I know that my work in Orillia saved the hospital money — I was paid only one hundred dollars a month plus board, but had a great many duties to perform.

I would also go back to that junior rotating internship; it would not be the slave-driving stuff that we experienced, but it would still have a very large service component. And students should not be forced to decide what type of physician they want to become until near the end of this rotating internship, when they would have a better idea of where their interests and abilities would be best accommodated.

How do we get these "educators," most of whom haven't seen a sick patient in years (if ever), on side? How do they possibly know what is needed in our training? The people making these disastrous decisions in both medicine and nursing should be practicing professionals, and the ivory-tower types should have a very small input.

It always annoyed me to hear someone pontificating about how much our training in hospital cost the taxpayer. After we left university and started our internship and residency programs, our service to the hospital was far larger than any training costs. Nowadays we hear that hospitals don't have enough training positions because of the costs. With the old system they made money! Where else could you get people to dictate the histories, write the orders, start the IVs, draw the bloods, and do much of the routine lab work for a pittance? At this point in our training, as we climbed the ladder of the residency program, supervision became lessened, although it was always available if we asked for advice when we needed it.

Even after the various types of universal health insurance came in, it was pretty obvious to most of us that those patients with intern and resident coverage — previously called public patients — actually got better doctor care than those exclusively private patients that were hived off into their private or semi-private rooms, often in a more posh, but remote, wing of the hospital. It's difficult for the public to believe this. Having twenty-four-hour intern coverage was just not available in many private units. These units were covered by the private physicians who had to be called from home. Moreover, the interns and residents were constantly reading around their cases and arguing what was the best management for a particular patient, the staff man in charge was constantly challenging the resident staff, and of course, the resident staff was asking important questions to challenge the staff man. This "hands on" apprenticeship also gave us a real understanding of how hospitals worked and how the various services intermeshed.

It is to be hoped that, with some radical "surgery," we eventually will have enough nurses and doctors for all these aging baby boomers. Bringing back an apprenticeship program to un-

345

dergraduate medical school training, and increasing it after graduating in an expanded internship program, would cause some changes and perhaps more work for our educators, many of whom have a vested interest in preserving the status quo. Those professors who want to teach humanities to premedical students would have fewer students to teach if this discipline was de-emphasized. In effect, an apprenticeship program would act as that education. An expanded internship program would mean that the staff person would have to take on an expanded supervisory role, but the trade-off would be positive, because they would be freed up from doing a great many of the routine tasks of medical care. Medical doctors who have worked their way up to become university professors have often lost touch with the day-to-day workings of medical practice and the problems that their front line medical colleagues face. I suspect that some specialties may even limit the number of practitioners in their particular field, simply to reduce the competition.

Expanding the role of the internship program would actually save the taxpayer money, and would provide more doctors in training for our aging population.

NURSING TRAINING

In the mid 1980s I was finally given a room in the nursing residence at Royal Columbian, the Sherbrooke Medical Centre. My timing, as usual, was way off, because student nurses hadn't been living and training there for at least three years. The really sad thing, however, was not only that the nursing school had been closed at the Royal Columbian, but that the whole training program of this type was closed across Canada.

The first floor of this building had now been made into administration offices that dealt, more or less, with the public, the second and third floors were turned into a psychiatric unit, the next two floors contained more administration offices, and the top floors were empty. It was on one of these upper floors that I was given an on-call room. I had been bugging the administration for a bed at the hospital for some time, because when I was on call, if I went home at two or three in the morning I still would have to be back no later than seven-thirty or even earlier in the morning to do rounds or work in the heart catheterization lab.

The bridge traffic was becoming so intolerable by this late hour in the morning that I would have to leave my house at five forty-five. (I suspect the administration probably thought that one of the psychiatric floors would have been more appropriate for me! But I would have been glad to give up my on-call room and gone back to sleeping on a stretcher in the back of the Emerg, if the nursing school would only reopen.)

My contemporary physicians have seen the transition go from resident nursing school nurses to university-trained nurses. I am sure the majority of us much preferred the former. I have noticed that a few of these new types seem to resent getting their hands dirty, and don't even want to carry a bed pan.

I have been told countless times by some of these nursing educators that medicine has become far too complicated to train nurses the "old-fashioned way." It's not a valid point, because we specialize now. And so do the nurses. I would not be very competent if I had to do most branches of internal medicine now, having done straight cardiology for so many years, and how would I handle pediatrics? (My obstetrical shenanigans have already been described in chapter eleven.)

It is true that the number of drugs we use is much larger, and the complications seem to be ever increasing, but that's why we now rely so heavily on the hospital pharmacists and their ever-present computers. It's the doctors who still write the orders and it is the doctors who get blamed if something goes wrong, but we would be crazy not to listen to our colleagues from the pharmacy. The same principle applies to so much of what we do. I don't know how to slice up tissue down to a millionth of an inch thick in order to see it under the electron microscope; I rely on these very well trained technicians. Equally, I have no idea how to even run an x-ray machine; I rely on the x-ray techs. And so it goes.

I would love to see nursing go back to what was basically an apprenticeship program. We all can learn on the job, and I think we often learn more effectively that way. Medicine should not be raised on some sort of a pedestal. If an apprentice steel worker doesn't put his rivets in correctly, a whole bridge can come down, with catastrophic consequences. The airline pilots we rely upon so heavily learn basically on an apprenticeship program. Why is nursing so special that they have to have a university degree? I

347

believe the reason is nothing more than "elitism," and it costs the taxpayer a bundle.

Nursing is also in a straitjacket in that unions don't want specializing if it results in a pay differential. They believe that all nurses should be treated equally regardless of the type of problems that they are forced to deal with. But, in my view, the work in some branches of nursing is more demanding, and requires more expertise than in others. For example, an intensive care nurse has a much tougher time, if we consider the number of night shifts required, the emotional drain, and the urgency of the problems, than a nurse working in an outpatient department, strictly eight to four, five days a week.

Why can't we go back to the old system? When a student finished high school and had reasonable marks and aptitude, one option used to be going into residence and in three years becoming an RN. The first year was basically all classroom work; the second year was half classroom and half on the wards, with a clinical supervisor keeping an eye on the nursing students. The third year was mostly clinical, again with a supervisor keeping track of things, and there was a three-month option. The student could pick a specialty for this period. If the student liked, for example, orthopedics, this option might be chosen, and if there was a vacancy on the orthopedic ward in that particular hospital, the student might become a junior staff nurse on this floor the following year. There is no doubt that these nurses in training provided a service to the hospital in the second and third years of their course and, in my view, the quality of these hospital-trained nurses was excellent and better than that of those nurses with their degrees who were parachuted into our hospital.

Much greater use should be made of nurses' aides, nurse practitioners, operating room technicians, and other paramedic services, freeing up the nurses and doctors who seem to be in such short supply.

A PONDEROUS MONOPOLY

Our present health care system in Canada is a huge monopoly. Because there is no competition, it just moves ponderously along, top-heavy with bureaucracy, and is very expensive. In Canada we have the constant battle for beds between the emergent and elective admissions. Many days each year a hospital may be virtually shut down because it is full and overflowing. At this point, all elective procedures are stopped until the hospital can "sort itself out." We spend an inordinate amount of time trying to transfer patients from one facility to another to deal with this problem.

When the hospital is "jammed up" like this it is actually saving money, because it's cheaper to keep some of the long-term-care patients blocking the beds than to have a high turnover requiring expensive procedures to be carried out in hospital.

Inevitably, as the bed-blocking situation becomes chronic, the emergent patients win out over the elective patients. This results in longer waiting lists for all these elective procedures, everything from hernia repairs to joint replacements, and on the medical side, complicated elective investigations requiring hospitalization.

As a result, the surgical specialist requiring elective admissions sees his OR time being cut back, or in the case of the medical specialist, his medical elective beds being continuously cut back. Not only does he see his income being cut back, but also at some point he will not be able to do enough cases even to maintain his skills. At what point does the frustrated doctor decide to cut and run? These policies will undoubtedly contribute to our increasing shortage of manpower in some specialties.

During my time as a cardiologist, I was less affected by these problems than many of my specialist colleagues, because it always looked bad when someone died on the waiting list for angioplasty or open heart surgery, or for that matter someone on the list for urgent heart catheterization. The politicians were always sensitive to this problem and a write-up in the local newspapers of someone dying on our waiting list was always bad press. Hence, we got more of our share of the beds; we were more part of the emergent than the elective battle for beds. But is this fair to the patient who has been waiting for a hip replacement for eighteen months and can no longer get a comfortable night's sleep because of his chronic pain?

When I was training in Toronto as a resident in the 1960s, a patient could come to the "The Big House" (the Toronto General Hospital) to have a hernia repair, or he could go to the Shouldice Clinic nearby to have the same procedure. As residents, we all knew that the better choice would be to go to this clinic. At the Big

House in those days, the patient was admitted the night before the procedure, was sedated and taken to the OR the next morning, and then stayed in hospital for three or more days after the surgery.

At the Shouldice Clinic, the patient came in the day of his surgery having had nothing by mouth from the evening before. He walked to the operating room, and after his surgery, got off the table himself and walked back to an outpatient short-stay area, and was home the same day. The Shouldice Clinic became very efficient and streamlined, and because of their special expertise, their results were better than in the public system. This was in the early 60s! It took a long time for the Big House to catch up to this more modern method.

Our "leaders" kept telling us that the clinic was doing only the easy cases, but that was simply not true. This clinic, being private, was paid by the number of procedures it did. If, for example, it did only one procedure a day, it would lose money because it could not even pay its overhead for doing next to nothing. If the clinic was doing fifty or more cases a day, it not only paid its overhead, but also made a profit. On the other hand, in the publicly run system, the hospital uses less of its "global budget" if it does less. It's the patients and the procedures that eat into the budget, and the only way not to run a deficit is to do less. I believe that the public system has got the funding backwards — it has, in effect, the cart before the horse. In the public system you do better by doing less. A hospital should only be paid for the service that it renders to the patients.

The Shouldice Clinic, to be able to do more cases, had to be innovative and it pioneered the use of various synthetic materials for the larger hernias. In short, the clinic's methods were better, and saved a lot of money for the amount of work done.

The Shouldice Clinic was initially a private hospital, but when universal health insurance came in, it was forced to join the public system. Fortunately, the public hospitals started adopting some of the Shouldice ways. But the need to be continuously more innovative and efficient now largely vanished.

I CAN'T FIND A FAMILY DOCTOR!

The general practitioner used to be in charge of his patients, whether those patients were in or out of hospital. Today in the larger hospitals, the GP rarely shows up, and often has been replaced by a "hospitalist" who does the day-to-day management of the inpatient population not being carried out by the appropriate in-hospital specialist. Very unfortunately, in my view, the GP's outpatient office practice in many communities has also been largely replaced by impersonal walk-in clinics.

There is no longer any continuity in patient care. Each doctor only sees the patient for a short time and usually has no idea of the home environment or any detailed knowledge of the patient's past history. A lot of duplication takes place; it's expensive and simply not good medicine.

Every effort should be taken to put the family doctor back in charge — whatever it takes. A much greater effort should be made to enhance the training and prestige of the family doctor. Their remuneration should be greatly improved and they should no longer be relegated to the bottom of the financial pile. Two of my close and old-fashioned GP friends work approximately fifty hours a week. They are very conscientious in the way they practice medicine, but after deducting office expenses, they make slightly less than a head nurse. Some GPs who face this problem run their offices like assembly lines just to improve their remuneration; again, this is not good medicine.

PRIVATE MEDICAL CARE?

I firmly believe that we have to have some forms of competition in the healthcare business in this country. To me it seems draconian that if I want a hernia repair and am willing to pay the cost to have it done, I cannot have it done in Canada and will have to go to the United States, or elsewhere, to have this relatively simple procedure performed. Detractors of private medical care tell us that all the doctors will move to private care, and the public service will suffer. I believe the opposite may be true. At present, we lose specialists to other countries because in Canadian hospitals their OR time is often eroded by emergent care taking up their precious beds and OR time. The result is that they have so few hours of operating time per week that they cannot even maintain their skills.

We all complained about our poor telephone service in Canada under Bell Canada. Once competition was allowed in, look what happened to our phone rates and service. What an improvement! Why is medicine deemed to be so different? Strict standards would have to be maintained in both the government-run hospitals and the private hospitals, of course, but competition would allow new ideas to be tried to improve the efficiencies of the system, and would ultimately shorten the waiting times for hospital admissions.

OUTCOMES

In my view, medicine in general has not been as diligent as it should have been in deciding if a particular procedure or medication is, in fact, useful or better than other procedures or medications. A number of procedures are in a "grey area." Back surgery, just for an example, should perhaps be examined much more closely. There is no question that a disc that has not settled down after a trial of good conservative treatment may have a spectacular improvement following surgery. But what about multiple low back fusions, particularly if it is the third time that the procedure has been carried out? (We went for years and years carrying out radical mastectomies with little gain over much less mutilating procedures. Is radical surgery for prostate cancer better than less mutilating procedures?) We should be keeping "score" very closely and change our policies accordingly, instead of listening to people with a purely vested interest.

We also need to know what the record is not only for that particular procedure, but also for the individual hospital and doctor. Follow-up is the key, and a knowledgeable, but disinterested, party should assess the patient's outcome. This is where competition comes in. If a doctor or hospital has a significantly better outcome than another doctor or hospital, shouldn't the patient know about it? And what about the taxpayer who is funding all this?

DEATH AND DYING

Another huge problem that we face is when to decide not to do any more "heroic" medical procedures on a given patient. Should a patient who is basically being "warehoused" in a nursing home have a full cardiac arrest procedure? Should this patient be given

352

antibiotics if he or she contracts pneumonia? After all, Sir William Osler, perhaps Canada's greatest physician of all time, once said, "Pneumonia is the old man's friend." (Of course he said that in the days before antibiotics.)

What happens to our grandfather or father aged eighty, who has advanced chronic heart failure, or metastatic cancer and is in a lot of pain, or has a severe and limiting stroke, or is in an advanced state of dementia? Do we treat him with antibiotics merely because we can, and thereby delay his death? Is pneumonia no longer the old man's friend?

Sir William Osler (1849–1919) was the best-known physician in the English-speaking world at the turn of the twentieth century. He was born in Canada, trained at the University of Toronto, and then McGill University in Montreal. He taught and practiced in Canada, the USA, and then England, and in 1892 wrote the "bible" of medicine, The Principles and Practice of Medicine.

My own family, like many families, has faced the kinds of situations that required these hard decisions. My mother, discussed in chapter two, was in an advanced state of dementia and developed pneumonia. She was residing in a very nice nursing home, called the Royal City Manor, in New Westminster, BC. When she developed the characteristic signs of pneumonia, I took the liberty of writing on her chart "No IV and no antibiotics." She died peacefully over a period of about three days. I know my mother would have heartily approved, and the nursing staff and my mother's family doctor, Isabel Rimmer, were fully onside.

My paternal grandfather, age ninety-six, was one of the kindest and most gentle of men that I ever met. Unfortunately, he became demented during the last year of his life. By this time he was also blind and almost stone deaf. The year before, he had told me he didn't want to go on any longer. But then he developed a urinary tract infection and was, unfortunately, admitted to a Toronto hospital. The attending physician, Dr. John Taylor, was a classmate of mine, and he agreed to "only keep him comfortable." However, when the weekend came, another doctor who was on duty started my poor grandfather on a heavy regime of IV antibiotics. I was ready to do combat with this "doctor" who hadn't even taken the trouble to read the chart or contact the family. He soon saw the error of his ways, and the regime was stopped. My grandfather slipped into unconsciousness and passed away two days later.

Hopefully, if Harry can get some brash biomechanical engineer off his butt, he might finally get a reliable "self-destruct button" built, and then I won't have to worry about being a long-term nuisance (translation: "pain in the ass") to my wife and kids.

Over my career, particularly in my earlier career, I spent a lot of time in the intensive care unit. With the advent of respirologists, anesthetists, and intensivists spending more time in the intensive care area, the need to have a cardiologist there became less important, unless, of course, the patient had some really weird cardiac arrhythmia or needed a pacemaker. I got so I didn't like working in this area, because it so often seemed apparent to me that the patient I was asked to see didn't have any hope of a useful outcome. I just hoped that if I, or any of my relatives or friends, ended up in one of these units, the doctors would show some appropriate compassion and common sense.

Sometimes, I felt that I was actually called to see patients in these intensive care units not because of any particular expertise I might have from a cardiology point of view, but to talk to the relatives. I would explain to the family in a very detailed way what the patient's outcome was going to be, and ask them if it was worthwhile to employ all this high tech-stuff just to postpone the inevitable. (You see, looking old, bald, and wise can have some advantages because I usually got the family onside.)

A huge amount of hospital resources is spent on the last thirty days of a patient's life. Of course we don't know that it will be the last thirty days, but we often have a pretty good idea. We should use a little more common sense and compassion, and not treat everything just because we can.

I, of course, don't know the answers to any of these questions of life and death, but we certainly should start thinking about them and discussing them, and formulating some policies. Sooner rather than later we are going to have to make decisions about them, because of the financial crunch if for no other reason. At the present time, the politicians are just burying their heads in the sand over these questions, while the patient's and his or her family's agony is prolonged and the cost keeps escalating. It's time that the general public got involved.

THE FUTURE OF MEDICINE

The last forty-five years have seen sensational changes in medicine, and the horizon looks very bright for new advances in the future. Unfortunately, the business of medicine isn't going to dry up soon and the reason, at least in part, is the western world's atrocious lifestyle. It has been estimated, for example, that 40 percent of cancers in general are preventable.

Obesity is galloping along at a furious rate. Type 2 diabetes is occurring more frequently in young kids now; it used to be a rarity. These problems will only increase the frequency of premature cardiovascular disease and all the other issues of diabetes as our children grow up. We must find ways to reduce the huge amount of animal fat, animal protein, and refined carbohydrates (cakes, cookies, soda pop, candies, and "munchies"—all the tasty stuff).

Our society needs a big wakeup call if we are to tackle these problems of diet and the lack of exercise in a more meaningful way. We might even be able to save the taxpayer money.

In my own area of cardiology, I think the future is particularly bright. With the introduction of useful cholesterol-lowering drugs, much better blood-pressure-control drugs, and perhaps islet cell transplant to produce insulin, some of these problems will be mitigated. Islet cells are located in the pancreas and produce insulin. Attempts are being made to transfer these cells from cadavers into patients with diabetes, much like other transplants. Experiments are being undertaken to put these cells into special containers that are implanted into the patient to reduce the problems of rejection.

With the advent of angioplasty, and particularly with the advent of emergency angioplasty (24/7), we are already seeing the salvaging of heart muscle, which has resulted in fewer problems of chronic heart failure.

Coronary care units have changed dramatically; the unstable angina patients and recent heart attack patients are being effectively treated and discharged in one or two days. We anticipate further development of surgical management of troublesome cardiac arrhythmias.

Mechanical hearts, although very primitive now, may be a big bonus for long-term life-saving care in the future.

Cardiac imaging has made great strides with improved definition of cardiac structures and three-dimensional views are now coming on stream. Ultrasonic probes are not only giving a better view of the lumen of coronary arteries, but also showing us abnormalities in the wall of these small vessels.

The role of inflammation and even infection in the formation of atherosclerosis (hardening of the arteries) is an expanding area of exploration.

Stem cell and gene therapy in various forms may prove to be a big bonus for those patients who have lost a larger portion of their heart muscle.

With the Democrats back in power in the USA in 2009, it is hoped that stem cell research will receive a big boost. With greater knowledge of growth factors and switches to activate certain strips of genes, and perhaps some as-yet-undesigned scaffolding structures, whole organs, even from patients' own cells (which will eliminate rejection problems), may be manufactured for those people in the greatest need.

Telomeres, which are, simply put, small "caps" situated at the end of each of our chromosomes, have come under intense study, and stopping their age-related disintegration may increase man's useful lifespan.

The field of antiviral agents is just exploding, particularly in the treatment of AIDS. Hopefully, in the near future, we will have suitable vaccines for malaria, and better vaccines for cholera and some of the E coli infestations.

Fiberscopic surgery has made big inroads into general surgery, with improved benefits and shorter rehabilitation times for the patient. Nanomachines (ultra-tiny machines measured in billionths of a meter) may, in the more distant future, revolutionize some aspects of surgery and cancer therapy.

The ongoing research into effective treatment for solid cancers (breast, lung, colon, prostate, etc.) has seen advances and gives hope of bigger results in the future.

There have been recent improvements in the treatment of autoimmune diseases, and more are on the horizon.

With all of these positive breakthroughs in medical management, we can say that the golden age of medicine is only in its infancy.

Acknowledgements

This book would not have been possible without a lot of help from my teachers in cardiology, my professional colleagues, family, friends, and my editors and publisher.

A close school friend who was present when I broke my neck in a football game and subsequently became a successful author, Michael Vickers, helped me with major surgery on my book, suggested rearranging several chapters, and corrected a number of glaring grammatical mistakes. He also gave me a lot of encouragement and made many useful suggestions to get this book published.

Joan Parolin, a longtime family friend who just happened to be a retired high school English teacher, helped me immensely with my diction and sentence structure, and was very encouraging.

My family, particularly our second son David who is mentioned prominently in this book, was also a great help, reading through the manuscript several times and making a number of useful suggestions. My wife, Elaine, has been a pillar of strength and support over the years, running the farm and the kids, which allowed me to pursue my medical career and activities outside of medicine. She is convinced I have used up several of my nine lives.

Florence Carlsen, who spent a lot of time with our growing family and had firsthand experience in some of the escapades on our farm, read the manuscript and did the sketches.

By a total fluke, I ran into Mary Scott and David Hancock of Hancock House Publishers who agreed to publish my manuscript. Their staff, including in-house editor Theresa Laviolette and production editor Ingrid Luters, have been helpful in making my English clearer and have made many useful suggestions that have been incorporated into this book.

Many other people also read the manuscript and made many useful suggestions that were incorporated into this book, and were very generous in their positive feedback. This list includes:

my two former and dear teachers in cardiology, Dr. Ramsay Gunton, and Dr. Doug Wigle, both well known in their field across Canada and the wider world of cardiology; Mr. Jim Fair, the former CEO of the Royal Columbian Hospital, who was a major player in getting open heart surgery into this hospital and was a very strong advocate for the cardiac program during his tenure there; the former head cardiac nurse, Fran Kuhn, and the former chief cardiac technician, Marjorie McKnight; my esteemed colleague in cardiology, Dr. Bob Brown, son of the famous K.W.G. Brown described in these pages; two of the very supportive general practitioners, Dr. Don Hutchins and Dr. Bernie Toews; Belle Puri, chair of the Royal Columbian Hospital Foundation and an anchor person for CBC-TV; my old rugby colleague, Dr. Bob McMurtry, who subsequently became well known in the field of orthopedics and medical education; and my dear neighbour, Mr. Tom Smith.

Without all this help my "little book" would still just be a pile of notes gathering dust.

Index

Afloat in Time
Jim Sirois
ISBN 0-88839-455-1
5.5 x 8.5 • sc • 288 pages

**Alaska in the Wake
of the North Star**
Loel Shuler
ISBN 0-88839-587-6
5.5 x 8.5 • sc • 224 pages

Beyond the Northern Lights
W. H. Bell
ISBN 0-88839-432-2
5.5 x 8.5 • sc • 288 pages

Bootlegger's Lady
Edward Sager
ISBN 0-88839-976-6
5.5 x 8.5 • sc • 286 pages

Broken Arrow #1
John M. Clearwater
ISBN 978-0-88839-596-2
5.5 x 8.5 • sc • 160 pages

**Captain McNeill and His Wife
the Nishga Chief**
Robin Percival Smith
ISBN 0-88839-472-1
5.5 x 8.5 • sc • 256 pages

Cold Lead
Mark Dugan
ISBN 0-88839-559-0
5.5 x 8.5 • sc • 176 pages

Crazy Cooks & Gold Miners
Joyce Yardley
ISBN 0-88839-294-X
5.5 x 8.5 • sc • 224 pages

Curse of Gold
Elizabeth Hawkins, Jack Mould
ISBN 0-88839-281-8
5.5 x 8.5 • sc • 288 pages

Deadman's Clothes
Dale Davidson
ISBN 0-88839-608-2
5.5 x 8.5 • sc • 144 pages

Descent Into Madness
Vern Frolick
ISBN 0-88839-321-0
5.5 x 8.5 • sc • 361 pages

Discovery at Prudhoe Bay: Oil
John M. Sweet
ISBN 978-0-88839-630-3
5.5 x 8.5 • sc • 304 pages

End of Custer
Dale Schoenberger
ISBN 0-88839-288-5
5.5 x 8.5 • sc • 336 pages

Fogswamp
Trudy Turner, Ruth McVeigh
ISBN 0-88839-104-8
5.5 x 8.5 • sc • 255 pages

Fraser Canyon
Lorraine Harris
ISBN 978-0-88839-182-7
5.5 x 8.5 • sc • 64 pages

**Frontier Forts & Posts of the
Hudson's Bay Company**
Kenneth E. Perry
ISBN 0-88839-598-1
8.5 x 11 • sc • 96 pages

**Gold Creeks and
Ghost Towns (BC)**
N. L. Barlee
ISBN 0-88839-988-X
8.5 x 11 • sc • 192 pages

**Gold Creeks and
Ghost Towns (WA)**
N. L. Barlee
ISBN 0-88839-452-7
8.5 x 11 • sc • 224 pages

www.hancockhouse.com

Good Lawyer Bad Lawyer
David Nuttall
ISBN 0-88839-315-6
5.5 x 8.5 • sc • 256 pages

Incredible Gang Ranch
Dale Alsager
ISBN 0-88839-211-7
5.5 x 8.5 • sc • 448 pages

Into the Savage Land
Ernest Sipes
ISBN 0-88839-562-0
5.5 x 8.5 • sc • 160 pages

Jailbirds & Stool Pigeons
Norman Davis
ISBN 0-88839-431-4
5.5 x 8.5 • sc • 144 pages

Journal of a Country Lawyer
E. C. Burton
ISBN 0-88839-364-4
5.5 x 8.5 • sc • 240 pages

Klondike Paradise
C.R. Porter
ISBN 0-88839-402-0
8.5 x 11 • sc • 176 pages

Lady Rancher
Gertrude Minor Roger
ISBN 0-88839-099-8
5.5 x 8.5 • sc • 184 pages

Lewis & Clark Across the Northwest
Cheryll Halsey
ISBN 0-88839-560-4
5.5 x 8.5 • sc • 112 pages

Loggers of the BC Coast
Hans Knapp
ISBN 0-88839-588-4
5.5 x 8.5 • sc • 200 pages

Nahanni Trailhead
Joanne Ronan Moore
ISBN 0-88839-464-0
5.5 x 8.5 • sc • 256 pages

New Exploration of the Canadian Arctic
Ronald E. Seavoy
ISBN 0-88839-522-1
5.5 x 8.5 • sc • 192 pages

Out of the Rain
Paul Jones
ISBN 0-88839-541-8
5.5 x 8.5 • sc • 272 pages

Outposts & Bushplanes
Bruce Lamb
ISBN 0-88839-556-6
5.5 x 8.5 • sc • 208 pages

Puffin Cove
Neil Carey
ISBN 0-88839-216-8
5.5 x 8.5 • sc • 178 pages

Quest for Empire
Kyra Wayne
ISBN 0-88839-191-9
5.5 x 8.5 • sc • 415 pages

Raven and the Mountaineer
Monty Alford
ISBN 0-88839-542-6
5.5 x 8.5 • sc • 152 pages

Rivers of Gold
Gwen & Don Lee
ISBN 0-88839-555-8
5.5 x 8.5 • sc • 204 pages

Ruffles on my Longjohns
Isabel Edwards
ISBN 0-88839-102-1
5.5 x 8.5 • sc • 297 pages

More HANCOCK HOUSE biography and history titles

Songs of the Pacific Northwest
Philip J. Thomas
ISBN 978-0-88839-610-5
8.5 x 11 • sc • 208 pages

Stagecoaches Across the American West 1850-1920
John A. Sells
ISBN 978-0-88839-605-1
8.5 x 11 • sc • 336 pages

Timeless Trails of the Yukon
Dolores Cline Brown
ISBN 0-88839-584-5
5.5 x 8.5 • sc • 184 pages

Tomekichi Homma
K.T. Homma, C.G. Isaksson
ISBN 978-0-88839-660-0
5.5 x 8.5 • sc • 72 pages

Vancouver's Bravest
Alex Matches
ISBN 978-0-88839-615-0
8.5 x 11 • sc • 352 pages

Walter Moberly and the Northwest Passage by Rail
Daphne Sleigh
ISBN 0-88839-510-8
5.5 x 8.5 • sc • 272 pages

White Water Skippers of the North
Nancy Warren Ferrell
ISBN 978-0-88839-616-7
5.5 x 8.5 • sc • 216 pages

Wild Roses
dutchie Rutledge-Mathison
ISBN 0-88839-625-2
8.5 x 11 • hc • 72 pages

Wild Trails, Wild Tales
Bernard McKay
ISBN 0-88839-395-4
5.5 x 8.5 • sc • 176 pages

Wings Over the Wilderness
Blake W. Smith
ISBN 978-0-88839-595-7
8.5 x 11 • sc • 296 pages

Wild Canadian West
E. C. (Ted) Meyers
ISBN 0-88839-469-1
5.5 x 8.5 • sc • 208 pages

Yukon Gold
James/Susan Preyde
ISBN 0-88839-362-8
5.5 x 8.5 • sc • 96 pages

Yukon Riverboat Days
Joyce Yardley
ISBN 0-88839-386-5
5.5 x 8.5 • sc • 176 pages

Yukon Tears and Laughter
Joyce Yardley
ISBN 0-88839-594-9
5.5 x 8.5 • sc • 176 pages

Yukoners: True Tales
H. Gordon-Cooper
ISBN 0-88839-232-X
5.5 x 8.5 • sc • 144 pages